Mike Holt's

NEC® EXAM
PRACTICE QUESTIONS

Contains 2,300 NEC® Practice Exam Questions

10 Practice Quizzes in Code Order · 10 Practice Quizzes in Random Order
5 Practice Exams

Suitable for all electrical exams based on the NEC®, such as:
AMP, ICC, Local/State Examining Boards, Pearson VUE, Prometric, Prov, PSI

Based on the 2014 NEC®

Mike Holt Enterprises, Inc.
888.NEC.CODE (632.2633) • www.MikeHolt.com

NOTICE TO THE READER

Mike Holt's NEC® Exam Practice Questions, based on the 2014 NEC®

First Printing: May 2014

Author: Mike Holt
Technical Illustrator: Mike Culbreath
Cover Design: Madalina Iordache-Levay
Layout Design and Typesetting: Cathleen Kwas

COPYRIGHT © 2014 Charles Michael Holt
ISBN 978-1-932685-65-7

Produced and Printed in the USA

For more information, call 888.NEC.CODE (632.2633), or e-mail Info@MikeHolt.com.

NEC®, NFPA 70®, NFPA 70E® and National Electrical Code® are registered trademarks of the National Fire Protection Association.

 This logo is a registered trademark of Mike Holt Enterprises, Inc.

If you are an instructor and would like to request an examination copy of this or other Mike Holt Publications:

Call: 888.NEC.CODE (632.2633) • Fax: 352.360.0983
E-mail: Info@MikeHolt.com • Visit: www.MikeHolt.com

You can download a sample PDF of all our publications by visiting www.MikeHolt.com

I dedicate this book to the
Lord Jesus Christ, my mentor and teacher

Our Commitment

We are committed to serving the electrical industry with integrity and respect by always searching for the most accurate interpretation of the *NEC*® and creating the highest quality instructional material that makes learning easy.

We are invested in the idea of changing lives, and build our products with the goal of not only helping you meet your licensing requirements, but also with the goal that this knowledge will improve your expertise in the field and help you throughout your career.

We are committed to building a life-long relationship with you, and to helping you in each stage of your electrical career. Whether you are an apprentice just getting started in the industry, or an electrician preparing to take an exam, we are here to help you. When you need Continuing Education credits to renew your license, we will do everything we can to get our online courses and seminars approved in your state. Or if you are a contractor looking to train your team, we have a solution for you. And if you have advanced to the point where you are now teaching others, we are here to help you build your program and provide tools to make that task easier.

We genuinely care about providing quality electrical training that will help you take your skills to the next level.

Thanks for choosing Mike Holt Enterprises for your electrical training needs. We are here to help you every step of the way and encourage you to contact us so we can be a part of your success.

God bless,

TABLE OF CONTENTS

ABOUT THIS TEXTBOOK

Mike Holt's NEC® Exam Practice Questions, based on the 2014 NEC®

This workbook is designed to give you practice in answering *Code* questions and is intended to be used with the 2014 *National Electrical Code®*. As you progress you will become more familiar with your *Code* book so that you know where to go to quickly find the answer, and you will gain the confidence you need to sit for your *NEC* exam. In working through the questions, a good rule-of-thumb to use is that it should take you about one hour for every 25 questions that you answer. This is a great way to chart your progress.

Most licensing exams are open book, but check with the testing authority in your region what books you are allowed to take in, and what you need to know for your exam.

If you have difficulty with a question or section in the textbook, skip it for the moment and get back to it later. Don't frustrate yourself! The answer key is very clear, so be sure you use it to refer back to review those questions that you miss.

This workbook has three types of questions:

Practice Quizzes in Straight Order. There are ten practice quizzes, each with 100 questions, in the same order as found in the Code book.

Practice Quizzes in Random Order. There are ten practice quizzes in random order. The first four consist of 50 questions each, and the other six have 100 questions each. As they progress, these quizzes include progressively more articles, to give you extra practice in finding answers in the *Code* book.

Practice Exams. The five practice exams will help evaluate your exam-taking skills. The questions in the Practice Exams don't follow the chapters of the *Code* book; they're organized in a random manner, and include Articles 90 through Chapter 9.

If you find after working through these question banks and reviewing the answer key that you don't understand the material, *Mike Holt's Understanding the National Electrical Code* series provides you with detailed instruction on the *Code*. For a complete study, Mike's Detailed *Code* Library, that includes DVDs, provides a comprehensive overview.

The Scope of this Textbook

This workbook presumes the following stipulations:

- **Power Systems and Voltage.** All power-supply systems are assumed to be solidly grounded and any of the following voltages: 120V single-phase, 120/240V single-phase, 120/208V three-phase, 120/240V three-phase, or 277/480V three-phase, unless identified otherwise.

- **Electrical Calculations.** Unless the question or example specifies three-phase, the questions and examples are based on a single-phase power supply.

- **Rounding.** All calculations are rounded to the nearest ampere in accordance with 220.5(B).

- **Conductor Material.** Conductors are considered copper, unless aluminum is identified or specified.

- **Conductor Sizing.** Conductors are sized based on a THHN copper conductor terminating on a 75°C terminal in accordance with 110.14(C), unless the question or example identifies otherwise.

- **Overcurrent Device.** The term "overcurrent device" in this textbook refers to a molded case circuit breaker, unless identified otherwise. Where a fuse is identified, it's to be of the single-element type, also known as a "one-time fuse," unless identified otherwise.

Author's Comment:

- Because the neutral conductor of a solidly grounded system is always grounded to the earth, it's both a "grounded conductor" and a "neutral" conductor. To make it easier for the reader of this textbook, we'll refer to the "grounded" conductor of a solidly grounded system as the "neutral" conductor.

Corrections

We take great care to ensure our textbooks are correct, but we're realistic and know that there may be errors found after the book is printed. If you find an error that isn't already listed on the website page www.MikeHolt.com/bookcorrections, e-mail Corrections@MikeHolt.com. Be sure to include the textbook title, page number, and any other pertinent information.

ABOUT THE AUTHOR

Mike Holt—Author

Founder and President
Mike Holt Enterprises
Groveland, FL
www.MikeHolt.com

Mike Holt worked his way up through the electrical trade. He began as an apprentice electrician and became one of the most recognized experts in the world as it relates to electrical power installations. He's worked as a journeyman electrician, master electrician, and electrical contractor. Mike's experience in the real world gives him a unique understanding of how the *NEC* relates to electrical installations from a practical standpoint. You'll find his writing style to be direct, nontechnical, and powerful.

Did you know Mike didn't finish high school? So if you struggled in high school or didn't finish at all, don't let it get you down. However, realizing that success depends on one's continuing pursuit of education, Mike immediately attained his GED, and ultimately attended the University of Miami's Graduate School for a Master's degree in Business Administration.

Mike resides in Central Florida, is the father of seven children, has five grandchildren, and enjoys many outside interests and activities. He's a nine-time National Barefoot Water-Ski Champion (1988, 1999, 2005–2009, 2012–2013). He's set many national records and continues to train year-round at a World competition level (www.barefootwaterskier.com).

What sets him apart from some is his commitment to living a balanced lifestyle; placing God first, family, career, then self.

Special Acknowledgments—First, I want to thank God for my godly wife who's always by my side and my children, Belynda, Melissa, Autumn, Steven, Michael, Meghan, and Brittney.

A special thank you must be sent to the staff at the National Fire Protection Association (NFPA), publishers of the *NEC*—in particular Jeff Sargent for his assistance in answering my many *Code* questions over the years. Jeff, you're a "first class" guy, and I admire your dedication and commitment to helping others understand the *NEC*. Other former NFPA staff members I would like to thank include John Caloggero, Joe Ross, and Dick Murray for their help in the past.

A personal thank you goes to Sarina, my long-time friend and office manager. It's been wonderful working side-by-side with you for over 25 years nurturing this company's growth from its small beginnings.

PASSING YOUR EXAM

If you are using this textbook to help you prepare for your electrical exam, these tips can help you succeed in the process.

How to Achieve Your Best Grade

In order to pass an exam, a few things need to happen. You need to:

- Prepare yourself mentally, emotionally, and physically.
- Create a proper study program so that you have the time to learn the technical material to answer all the questions.
- Prepare for the exam by knowing what to expect with the exam taking process.
- Understand how to take an exam, how to approach questions, and how to manage your time during the test.
- Have the confidence that you can pass.

Prepare Mentally, Emotionally and Physically

Studies have concluded that for students to achieve their best grades, they must learn to obtain the most from their natural abilities. It's not how long you study or how high your IQ is, it's how you study that counts the most. To get your best grade, you must make a decision to do your best and follow as many of the following techniques and suggestions as possible.

Reality. These instructions are a basic guide to help you achieve your maximum grade. It's unreasonable to think that all of the instructions can be followed to the letter all of the time. Day-to-day events and unexpected situations must be taken into consideration.

Support. You need encouragement in your studies and you need support from your loved ones and colleagues. To properly prepare for your exam, you need to study a few hours per week for several months, depending on your existing knowledge.

Communication With Your Family. Good communication with your family is very important because studying every night and on weekends can cause much tension and stress. Try to win their support, cooperation, and encouragement during this difficult time. Let them

know the long-term benefits to the family and what passing the exam means. Be sure to plan some special time with them during this preparation period; don't go overboard and neglect them.

Stress. Stress can really take the wind out of you. It takes practice, but develop the habit of relaxing before you begin your studies. Stretch, do a few sit-ups and push-ups, take a 20-minute walk, or a few slow, deep breaths. Close your eyes for a couple of minutes, and deliberately relax the muscle groups that are associated with tension, such as the shoulders, back, neck, and jaw.

Attitude. Maintaining a positive attitude is important. It helps keep you going and helps keep you from becoming discouraged.

Eye Care. It's very important to have your eyes checked! Human eyes weren't designed to constantly focus on something less than an arm's length away. Our eyes were designed for survival, spotting food and enemies at a distance. Your eyes will be under tremendous stress because of prolonged reading, which can result in headaches, fatigue, nausea, squinting, or eyes that burn, ache, water, or tire easily. Be sure to tell your eye doctor that you are studying to pass an exam (bring this textbook and the *Code* book with you) and that you expect to do a tremendous amount of reading and writing. Reading glasses can reduce eye discomfort.

Reducing Eye Strain. Be sure to look up occasionally, away from near tasks to distant objects. Your work area should be three times brighter than the rest of the room. Don't read under a single lamp in a dark room. Try to eliminate glare. Mixing of fluorescent and incandescent lighting can be helpful.

Posture. Sit up straight, with your chest up and your shoulders back, so both eyes are an equal distance from what you're viewing.

Training. Preparing for the exam is the same as training for any other event. Get plenty of rest and avoid intoxicating drugs, including alcohol. Stretching or exercising each day for at least 10 minutes helps you get in a better mood. Eat light meals such as pasta, chicken, fish, vegetables, fruit, and so forth. Try to avoid red meat, butter, sugar, salt, and high-fat content foods. They slow you down and make you tired and sleepy.

Mike Holt's NEC Exam Practice Questions, based on the 2014 NEC

Set Your Study Program

Make Sure You Start to Prepare Early Enough. Many people fail an exam because they haven't given themselves enough time to properly prepare and study. Determine the date of your exam, and then work backwards to be sure that you give yourself the time that you need to thoroughly cover the material you know you will be tested on.

Getting Organized. Our lives are so busy that simply making time for homework and exam preparation is almost impossible. You can't waste time looking for a pencil or missing paper. Keep everything you need together. Maintain folders, one for notes, one for exams and answer keys, and one for miscellaneous items.

Study Location. It's very important that you have a private study area available at all times. Keep your materials there.

Time Management. Time management and planning are very important. There simply aren't enough hours in the day to complete everything, but having a calendar is a great way to make sure the highest priority items get done. Make a schedule that allows time for work, rest, study, meals, family, and recreation. Establish one that's consistent from day to day. Have a calendar and immediately plan your exam preparation schedule. Try to follow the same routine each week and try not to become overtired. Learn to pace yourself to accomplish as much as you can without the need for cramming.

Speak Up in Class. If you're in a classroom setting, the most important part of the learning process is participation. If you don't understand the instructor's point, ask for clarification. Don't seek to get attention by asking questions to which you already know the answers.

Study With a Friend. Studying with a friend can make learning more enjoyable. You can push and encourage each other. You're more likely to study if someone else is depending on you. Students who study together perform above average because they try different approaches and explain their solutions to each other. This kind of interaction is a significant aid to learning retention. Those who study alone may spend much of their time reading and rereading the text and trying the same approach time after time with less success.

Study Anywhere/Anytime. To make the most of your limited time, always keep a copy of the book(s) with you. Any time you find a free minute, study! Continue to study any chance you have. You can study at the

supply house when waiting for your material; you can study during your coffee break, or even while you're at the doctor's office. Become creative!

You Need to Find Your Best Study Time. For some, it's late at night when the house is quiet. For others, it's the first thing in the morning before things get going.

Set Priorities. Once you begin your study, stop all phone calls, TV shows, radio, snacks, and other interruptions. You can always take care of it later.

Prepare for the Exam

Get Advance Information. Check with your Local/State Examining Boards well in advance so that you understand what's expected of you. Most states require you to first register with the State Electrical Licensing Board, and once you have been approved, you would contact the agency that administers their exams, if it's not the State Board itself. The Candidate Bulletin will provide you with information about the examination and the application process. You can visit the website www.mikeholt.com/statelicense for state contact information, licensing requirements, and where available, the Candidate Bulletin. Always verify with your State office to be sure this information is the most up-to-date.

Some of the things you'll want to clarify:

- Which edition of the *NEC* you will be tested on, and if the exam is open book or not.
- What reference books you are allowed to bring in (loose-leaf, hard bound, spiral, etc.) and if and how you are allowed to mark them up.
- If you will be doing a paper-and-pencil test, or a computerized one; take any sample online test(s) on the testing company's website so you're familiar with the testing process.
- What personal items are permitted in the testing room: If they allow you to bring in a watch, or a calculator [and if so, what kind is allowed]. Consider bringing a jacket in case the room is cold.
- Meals. It's a good idea to pack a lunch rather than going out if a lunch break is allowed—it can give you a little extra time to review the material for the afternoon portion of the exam, and it reduces the chance of coming back late. However, many testing companies will not allow you to bring food into the exam room but might provide a locker in which you can store it.

- Know where the exam is going to take place and how long it takes to get there. Arrive at least 30 minutes early.

Learn How to Use Your Books. One of the best ways to be prepared is to know how to use your *Code* book. Check whether or not you can take your own *Code* book into the exam, if you are allowed to mark it up, and which kind of notes are allowed, if you can highlight information in different colors, and if you are allowed to tab it. Become really efficient at using your *Code* book so you can be ready in a timed test environment. Review the table of contents and graphics in all your study books. This will help you to develop a sense of the material. As you read the text, continually ask yourself questions. This should help you to develop a better understanding of the text's message.

Taking the Exam

Being prepared for an exam means more than just knowing electrical concepts, the *Code*, and the calculations. Have you felt prepared for an exam, and then choked when actually taking it? Many good and knowledgeable people didn't pass their exam because they didn't know "how to take an exam."

Taking exams is a learned process that takes practice and involves strategies. The following suggestions are designed to help you develop your strategies:

Relax. This is easier said than done, but it's one of the most important factors in passing your exam. Stress and tension cause us to choke or forget. Everyone has had experiences where they became tense and couldn't think straight. The first step is becoming aware of the tension, and the second is to make a deliberate effort to relax. Make sure you're comfortable; wear layers so you can remove clothing if you're hot, or put on a jacket if you're cold.

There are many ways to relax and you have to find a method that works for you. Two of the easiest methods that work very well for many people follow:

Breathing Technique: Take a few slow deep breaths every few minutes. Don't confuse this with hyperventilation, which is abnormally fast breathing.

Single-Muscle Relaxation: When we're tense or stressful, many of us do things like clench our jaw, squint our eyes, or tense our shoulders without even being aware of it. If you find a muscle group that does this, deliberately relax that one group. The rest of the muscles will automatically relax also. Try to repeat this every few minutes, and it will help you stay more relaxed during the exam.

Understand the Question. To answer a question correctly, you must first understand it. One word in a question can totally change its meaning. Carefully read every word of every question. Underlining key words in the question will help you focus.

Skip the Difficult Questions. Contrary to popular belief, you don't have to answer one question before going on to the next one. The irony is that the question you become stuck on is one that you'll probably answer wrong anyway. This will result in not having enough time to answer the easy questions. You'll become all stressed-out worrying that you won't complete the exam on time, and a chain reaction starts. More people fail their exams this way than for any other reason.

Most states are using computerized testing, and have a way for you to "mark" a question for later review and return to that question after you've answered the easier ones. Make sure you mark question number one for further review, because on some tests they limit you to returning no further than to the first question you marked.

The following strategy should be used to avoid getting into this situation:

First Pass: Answer the questions you know. Give yourself about 30 seconds for each question. If you can't find the answer in your reference book within the 30 seconds, go on to the next question. Chances are that you'll come across the answers while looking up another question. The total time for the first pass should be 25 percent of the exam time.

Second Pass: This pass is done the same as the first one except that you allow a little more time for each question, about 60 seconds. If you still can't find the answer, go on to the next one. Don't get stuck. The total time for the second pass should be about 30 percent of the exam time.

Third Pass: See how much time is left and subtract 30 minutes. Spend the remaining time equally on each question. If you still haven't answered the question, it's time to make an educated guess. Never leave a question unanswered.

Fourth Pass: Use the last 30 minutes of the exam for review. Read each question and verify that you selected the correct answer. If it's a paper and pencil test verify that you you transferred the answers carefully to the answer key. With the remaining time, see if you can find the answer to those questions for which you made an estimated guess.

Guessing. When time is running out and you still have unanswered questions, GUESS! Never leave a question unanswered. You can improve your chances of getting a question correct by the process of elimination. Many times, there are a couple of choices that can be easily eliminated as illogical or outside the range of expected answers.

How do you pick one of the remaining answers? Some people toss a coin; others count up how many of the answers were As, Bs, Cs, and Ds and use the one with the most as the basis for their guess.

Checking Your Work. The first thing to check (and you should be watching out for this during the whole exam) is to make sure you mark the answer in the correct spot, whether taking a paper- or computer-based exam. People have failed the exam by one-half of a point. When they reviewed their exam, they found they correctly answered several questions on the test booklet, but marked the wrong spot on the exam answer sheet. They knew the answer was "(b) False" but marked in "(d)" in error. Another thing to be very careful of, is marking the answer for, let's say Question 7, in the spot reserved for Question 8.

Changing Answers. When re-reading the question and checking the answers during the fourth pass, resist the urge to change an answer. In most cases, your first choice is best and, if you aren't sure, stick with that choice. Only change answers if you're positive that you made a mistake. Paper and pencil multiple choice exams are graded electronically so be sure to thoroughly erase any answer that you changed. Also erase any stray pencil marks from the answer sheet.

Rounding Off. You should always round your answers to the same number of places as the exam's answers.

Example: If an exam has multiple choice of:

    (a) 2.10   (b) 2.20   (c) 2.30   (d) none of these

And your calculation comes out to 2.16; don't choose the answer (d) none of these. The correct answer is (b) 2.20, because the answers in this case are rounded off to the nearest tenth.

Example: It can be rounded to tens, such as:

    (a) 50   (b) 60   (c) 70   (d) none of these

For this group, an answer such as 67 will be (c) 70, while an answer of 63 will be (b) 60. The general rule is to check the question's choice of answers and then round off your answer to match it.

Things To Be Careful Of

- Don't get stuck on any one question.
- Read each question carefully.
- Be sure you mark the answer in the correct spot on the screen, or answer sheet if the test is paper-based.
- Don't become flustered or extremely tense.

Summary

- Make sure everything is ready and packed the night before the exam.
- Don't try to cram the night before the exam—if you don't know it by then, it's too late!
- Have a good breakfast. Get the thermos and energy snacks ready.
- Take all your reference books. Let the proctors tell you what you can't use.
- Know where the exam is to be held and arrive early.
- Bring identification and your confirmation papers from the license board if this is required.
- Review your *NEC* while you wait for your exam to begin.
- Try to stay relaxed.
- Determine the time per question for each pass and don't forget to save time to go back to the ones you skipped over.
- Remember—in the first pass answer only the easy questions. In the second, spend a little more time with each question, but don't become stuck. In the third pass, use the remainder of the time minus 30 minutes to answer the remaining questions. In the fourth pass, check your work.

Watch Mike's video clip on How to Prepare for an Electrical Exam. Use this QR code to go directly to the video, or visit www.MikeHolt.tv to see this and other video clips.

Additional Products To Help You Learn

Understanding the 2014 National Electrical Code, Volume 1 and Volume 2

Mike's best-selling *Illustrated Guide to Understanding the National Electrical Code* has become the standard for comprehensive *NEC* training. Mike's ability to clarify the meaning of the *Code* with his clear concise writing style, along with his highly praised full-color detailed color illustrations is the reason that these books continue to grow in popularity around the industry. Volume 1 covers General Requirements, Wiring & Protection, Wiring Methods, and Equipment for General Use. Volume 2 walks you step-by-step through Special Occupancies, Special Equipment, Special Conditions, and Communications Systems.

- **Understanding the NEC Volume 1** textbook [Articles 90–480]
- **Understanding the NEC Volume 2** textbook [Articles 500–820]

To order visit www.mikeholt.com/14Code or call 888.632.2633.

Detailed *Code* Library

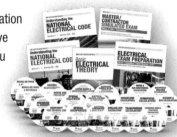

When you really need to understand the *NEC*, there's no better way to learn it than with Mike's Detailed *Code* Library. It takes you step-by-step through the *NEC*, in *Code* order with detailed illustrations, great practice questions, and in-depth DVD analysis. This library is perfect for engineers, electricians, contractors, and electrical inspectors.

- **Understanding the National Electrical Code—Volume 1**
- **Understanding the National Electrical Code—Volume 2**
- **NEC Exam Practice Questions** workbook
- General Requirements DVD
- Wiring and Protection DVD
- Grounding versus Bonding DVDs (2)
- Wiring Methods and Materials DVDs (2)
- Equipment for General Use DVD
- Special Occupancies DVD
- Special Equipment DVD
- Limited Energy and Communications Systems DVD.

We can get you a discounted price for the items you need to complete this program. Call us at 888.632.2633.

Journeyman and Master/Contractor Intermediate Library

The Journeyman Intermediate Library includes the full-color *Electrical Exam Preparation* textbook and seven DVDs, as well as Mike's 2011 *Changes to the NEC* textbook and two DVDs. The Master/Contractor Intermediate Library includes everything in the Journeyman Library, plus three additional Calculation DVDs.

To order visit www.MikeHolt.com/14ExamPrep or call 888.632.2633.

Journeyman and Master/Contractor Comprehensive Library

The Comprehensive Exam Preparation Library is based on a full term of live classes. You'll learn everything you need to know to pass your exam the first time. Mike's dynamic style and detailed graphics easily explain the most difficult subjects.

The Comprehensive Library includes the following:

- **Understanding the NEC,** Volume 1 textbook, plus 7 DVDs
- **Understanding the NEC,** Volume 2 textbook, plus 3 DVDs
- **Basic Electrical Theory** textbook/workbook, plus 3 DVDs
- **Electrical Exam Preparation** textbook/workbook, plus 5 DVDs for Journeyman, 8 DVDs for Master Simulated Exam
- **Journeyman or Master/Contractor Simulated Exam**

To order visit www.MikeHolt.com/14ExamPrep or call 888.632.2633.

ABOUT THE
NATIONAL ELECTRICAL CODE

The *National Electrical Code* is written for persons who understand electrical terms, theory, safety procedures, and electrical trade practices. These individuals include electricians, electrical contractors, electrical inspectors, electrical engineers, designers, and other qualified persons. The *Code* isn't written to serve as an instructional or teaching manual for untrained individuals [90.1(A)].

Learning to use the *NEC* can be likened to learning the strategy needed to play the game of chess well; it's a great game if you enjoy mental warfare. When learning to play chess, you must first learn the names of the game pieces, how they're placed on the board, and how each one is moved.

Once you understand the fundamentals, you're ready to start playing the game. Unfortunately, at this point all you can do is make crude moves, because you really don't understand how all the information works together. To play chess well, you'll need to learn how to use your knowledge by working on subtle strategies before you can work your way up to the more intriguing and complicated moves.

The *Code* is updated every three years to accommodate new electrical products and materials, changing technologies, improved installation techniques, and to make editorial refinements to improve readability and application. While the uniform adoption of each new edition of the *NEC* is the best approach for all involved in the electrical industry, many inspection jurisdictions modify the *Code* when it's adopted. To further complicate this situation, the *NEC* allows the authority having jurisdiction, typically the "Electrical Inspector," the flexibility to waive specific *Code* requirements, and to permit alternative methods. This is only allowed when he or she is assured the completed electrical installation is equivalent in establishing and maintaining effective safety [90.4].

Keeping up with requirements of the *Code* should be the goal of everyone involved in the safety of electrical installations. This includes electrical installers, contractors, owners, inspectors, engineers, instructors, and others concerned with electrical installations.

About the 2014 *NEC*

The actual process of changing the *Code* takes about two years, and it involves hundreds of individuals making an effort to have the *NEC* as current and accurate as possible. Let's review how this process worked for the 2014 *NEC*:

Step 1. Proposals—November, 2011. Anybody can submit a proposal to change the *Code* before the proposal closing date. Thousands of proposals were submitted to modify the 2011 *NEC* and create the 2014 *Code*. Of these proposals, several hundred rules were revised that significantly affect the electrical industry. Some changes were editorial revisions, while others were more significant, such as new articles, sections, exceptions, and Informational Notes.

Step 2. *Code*-Making Panel(s) Review Proposals—January, 2012. All *Code* change proposals were reviewed by *Code*-Making Panels. There were 19 panels in the 2014 revision process who voted to accept, reject, or modify proposals.

Step 3. Report on Proposals (ROP)—July, 2012. The voting of the *Code*-Making Panels on the proposals was published for public review in a document called the "Report on Proposals," frequently referred to as the "ROP."

Step 4. Public Comments—October, 2012. Once the ROP was available, public comments were submitted asking the *Code*-Making Panel members to revise their earlier actions on change proposals, based on new information. The closing date for "Comments" was October, 2012.

Step 5. Comments Reviewed by *Code* Panels—December, 2012. The *Code*-Making Panels met again to review, discuss, and vote on public comments.

Step 6. Report on Comments (ROC)—March, 2013. The voting on the "Comments" was published for public review in a document called the "Report on Comments," frequently referred to as the "ROC."

Step 7. Electrical Section—June, 2013. The NFPA Electrical Section discussed and reviewed the work of the *Code*-Making Panels. The Electrical Section developed recommendations on last-minute motions to revise the proposed *NEC* draft that would be presented at the NFPA's annual meeting.

Step 8. NFPA Annual Meeting—June, 2013. The 2014 *NEC* was voted by the NFPA members to approve the action of the *Code*-Making Panels at the annual meeting, after a number of motions (often called "floor actions" or "NITMAMs") were voted on.

Step 9. Standards Council Review Appeals and Approves the 2014 *NEC*—July, 2013. The NFPA Standards Council reviewed the record of the *Code*-making process and approved publication of the 2014 *NEC*.

Step 10. 2014 *NEC* Published—September, 2013. The 2014 *National Electrical Code* was published, following the NFPA Board of Directors review of appeals.

Author's Comment:

- Proposals and comments can be submitted online at the NFPA website (www.nfpa.org). From the homepage, click on "Codes and Standards", then find NFPA 70 (*National Electrical Code*). From there, follow the on screen instructions to download the proposal form. The deadline for proposals to create the 2017 *National Electrical Code* will be around November of 2014. If you would like to see something changed in the *Code*, you're encouraged to participate in the process.

Not a Game

Electrical work isn't a game, and it must be taken very seriously. Learning the basics of electricity, important terms and concepts, as well as the basic layout of the *NEC* gives you just enough knowledge to be dangerous. There are thousands of specific and unique applications of electrical installations, and the *Code* doesn't cover every one of them. To safely apply the *NEC*, you must understand the purpose of a rule and how it affects the safety aspects of the installation.

NEC Terms and Concepts

The *NEC* contains many technical terms, so it's crucial for *Code* users to understand their meanings and their applications. If you don't understand a term used in a *Code* rule, it will be impossible to properly apply the *NEC* requirement. Be sure you understand that Article 100 defines the terms that apply to two or more *Code* articles. For example, the term "Dwelling Unit" is found in many articles; if you don't know what a dwelling unit is, how can you apply the requirements for it?

In addition, many articles have terms unique for that specific article and definitions of those terms are only applicable for that given article. For example, Section 250.2 contains the definitions of terms that only apply to Article 250—Grounding and Bonding.

Small Words, Grammar, and Punctuation

It's not only the technical words that require close attention, because even the simplest of words can make a big difference to the application of a rule. The word "or" can imply alternate choices for wiring methods, while "and" can mean an additional requirement. Let's not forget about grammar and punctuation. The location of a comma can dramatically change the requirement of a rule.

Slang Terms or Technical Jargon

Electricians, engineers, and other trade-related professionals use slang terms or technical jargon that isn't shared by all. This makes it very difficult to communicate because not everybody understands the intent or application of those slang terms. So where possible, be sure you use the proper word, and don't use a word if you don't understand its definition and application. For example, lots of electricians use the term "pigtail" when describing the short conductor for the connection of a receptacle, switch, luminaire, or equipment. Although they may understand it, not everyone does.

NEC Style and Layout

Before we get into the details of the *NEC*, we need to take a few moments to understand its style and layout. Understanding the structure and writing style of the *Code* is very important before it can be used and applied effectively. The *National Electrical Code* is organized into ten major components.

1. Table of Contents
2. Article 90 (Introduction to the *Code*)
3. Chapters 1–9 (major categories)
4. Articles 90–840 (individual subjects)
5. Parts (divisions of an article)
6. Sections and Tables (*NEC* requirements)
7. Exceptions (*Code* permissions)
8. Informational Notes (explanatory material)
9. Annexes (information)
10. Index

1. Table of Contents. The Table of Contents displays the layout of the chapters, articles, and parts as well as the page numbers. It's an excellent resource and should be referred to periodically to observe the interrelationship of the various *NEC* components. When attempting to locate the rules for a particular situation, knowledgeable *Code* users often go first to the Table of Contents to quickly find the specific *NEC* Part that applies.

2. Introduction. The *NEC* begins with Article 90, the introduction to the *Code*. It contains the purpose of the *NEC*, what's covered and what isn't covered along with how the *Code* is arranged. It also gives information on enforcement and how mandatory and permissive rules are written as well as how explanatory material is included. Article 90 also includes information on formal interpretations, examination of equipment for safety, wiring planning, and information about formatting units of measurement.

3. Chapters. There are nine chapters, each of which is divided into articles. The articles fall into one of four groupings: General Requirements (Chapters 1–4), Specific Requirements (Chapters 5–7), Communications Systems (Chapter 8), and Tables (Chapter 9).

Chapter 1—General
Chapter 2—Wiring and Protection
Chapter 3—Wiring Methods and Materials
Chapter 4—Equipment for General Use
Chapter 5—Special Occupancies
Chapter 6—Special Equipment
Chapter 7—Special Conditions
Chapter 8—Communications Systems (Telephone, Data, Satellite, Cable TV and Broadband)
Chapter 9—Tables–Conductor and Raceway Specifications

4. Articles. The *NEC* contains approximately 140 articles, each of which covers a specific subject. For example:

Article 110—General Requirements
Article 250—Grounding and Bonding
Article 300—General Requirements for Wiring Methods and Materials
Article 430—Motors and Motor Controllers
Article 500—Hazardous (Classified) Locations
Article 680—Swimming Pools, Fountains, and Similar Installations
Article 725—Remote-Control, Signaling, and Power-Limited Circuits
Article 800—Communications Circuits

5. Parts. Larger articles are subdivided into parts. Because the parts of a *Code* article aren't included in the section numbers, we have a tendency to forget what "part" the *NEC* rule is relating to. For example, Table 110.34(A) contains working space clearances for electrical equipment. If we aren't careful, we might think this table applies to all electrical installations, but Table 110.34(A) is located in Part III, which only contains requirements for "Over 600 Volts, Nominal" installations. The rules for working clearances for electrical equipment for systems 600V, nominal, or less are contained in Table 110.26(A)(1), which is located in Part II—600 Volts, Nominal, or Less.

6. Sections and Tables.

Sections. Each *NEC* rule is called a "*Code* Section." A *Code* section may be broken down into subsections by letters in parentheses (A), (B), and so on. Numbers in parentheses (1), (2), and so forth, may further break down a subsection, and lowercase letters (a), (b), and so on, further break the rule down to the third level. For example, the rule requiring all receptacles in a dwelling unit bathroom to be GFCI protected is contained in Section 210.8(A)(1). Section 210.8(A)(1) is located in Chapter 2, Article 210, Section 8, Subsection (A), Sub-subsection (1).

Many in the industry incorrectly use the term "Article" when referring to a *Code* section. For example, they say "Article 210.8," when they should say "Section 210.8." Section numbers in this textbook are shown without the word "Section," unless they begin a sentence. For example, Section 210.8(A) is shown as simply 210.8(A).

Tables. Many *NEC* requirements are contained within tables, which are lists of *Code* rules placed in a systematic arrangement. The titles of the tables are extremely important; you must read them carefully in order to understand the contents, applications, limitations, and so forth, of each table in the *NEC*. Many times notes are provided in or below a table; be sure to read them as well since they're also part of the requirement. For example, Note 1 for Table 300.5 explains how to measure the cover when burying cables and raceways, and Note 5 explains what to do if solid rock is encountered.

7. Exceptions. Exceptions are *Code* requirements or permissions that provide an alternative method to a specific rule. There are two types of exceptions—mandatory and permissive. When a rule has several exceptions, those exceptions with mandatory requirements are listed before the permissive exceptions.

Mandatory Exceptions. A mandatory exception uses the words "shall" or "shall not." The word "shall" in an exception means that if you're using the exception, you're required to do it in a particular way. The phrase "shall not" means it isn't permitted.

Permissive Exceptions. A permissive exception uses words such as "shall be permitted," which means it's acceptable (but not mandatory) to do it in this way.

8. Informational Notes. An Informational Note contains explanatory material intended to clarify a rule or give assistance, but it isn't a *Code* requirement.

9. Annexes. Annexes aren't a part of the *NEC* requirements, and are included in the *Code* for informational purposes only.

> Annex A. Product Safety Standards
>
> Annex B. Application Information for Ampacity Calculation
>
> Annex C. Raceway Fill Tables for Conductors and Fixture Wires of the Same Size
>
> Annex D. Examples
>
> Annex E. Types of Construction
>
> Annex F. Critical Operations Power Systems (COPS)
>
> Annex G. Supervisory Control and Data Acquisition (SCADA)
>
> Annex H. Administration and Enforcement
>
> Annex I. Recommended Tightening Torques
>
> Annex J. ADA Standards for Accessible Design

10. Index. The Index at the back of the *Code* book is helpful in locating a specific rule.

Changes to the *NEC* since the previous edition(s), are identified by shading, but rules that have been relocated aren't identified as a change. A bullet symbol "•" is located on the margin to indicate the location of a rule that was deleted from a previous edition. New articles contain a vertical line in the margin of the page.

Different Interpretations

Some electricians, contractors, instructors, inspectors, engineers, and others enjoy the challenge of discussing the *NEC* requirements, hopefully in a positive and productive manner. This give-and-take is important to the process of better understanding the *Code* requirements and application(s). However, if you're going to participate in an *NEC* discussion, please don't spout out what you think without having the actual *Code* book in your hand. The professional way of discussing an *NEC* requirement is by referring to a specific section, rather than talking in vague generalities.

How to Locate a Specific Requirement

How to go about finding what you're looking for in the *Code* book depends, to some degree, on your experience with the *NEC*. *Code* experts typically know the requirements so well they just go to the correct rule without any outside assistance. The Table of Contents might be the only thing very experienced *NEC* users need to locate the requirement they're looking for. On the other hand, average *Code* users should use all of the tools at their disposal, including the Table of Contents and the Index.

Table of Contents. Let's work out a simple example: What *NEC* rule specifies the maximum number of disconnects permitted for a service? If you're an experienced *Code* user, you'll know Article 230 applies to "Services," and because this article is so large, it's divided up into multiple parts (actually eight parts). With this knowledge, you can quickly go to the Table of Contents and see it lists the Service Equipment Disconnecting Means requirements in Part VI.

Author's Comment:

■ The number 70 precedes all page numbers because the *NEC* is NFPA Standard Number 70.

Index. If you use the Index, which lists subjects in alphabetical order, to look up the term "service disconnect," you'll see there's no listing. If you try "disconnecting means," then "services," you'll find that the Index indicates that the rule is located in Article 230, Part VI. Because the *NEC* doesn't give a page number in the Index, you'll need to use the Table of Contents to find it, or flip through the *Code* book to Article 230, then continue to flip through pages until you find Part VI.

Many people complain that the *NEC* only confuses them by taking them in circles. As you gain experience in using the *Code* and deepen your understanding of words, terms, principles, and practices, you'll find the *NEC* much easier to understand and use than you originally thought.

Customizing Your *Code* Book

One way to increase your comfort level with the *Code* book is to customize it to meet your needs. **Be aware that if you're using it to take an exam, you should check to see which kind of markings, if any, are permitted.**

Highlighting. Highlight those requirements in the *Code* that are the most important or relevant to you. Use one color for general interest and a different one for important requirements you want to find quickly, including the Index and the Table of Contents.

Underlining. Underline or circle key words and phrases with a red pen (not a lead pencil) and use a short ruler or other straightedge to keep lines straight and neat. This is a very handy way to make important requirements stand out. A short ruler or other straightedge also comes in handy for locating specific information in the many *Code* tables.

Tabbing the *NEC*. By placing tabs on *Code* articles, sections and tables, it will make it easier for you to use the *NEC*. Too many tabs defeat the purpose. Order a set designed by Mike Holt, online at www. MikeHolt.com/14tabs, or by calling 888.632.2633

NEC PRACTICE QUIZZES

- *NEC* Practice Quizzes (Straight Order)

- *NEC* Practice Quizzes (Random Order)

There are ten Practice Quizzes, each with 100 questions in straight order, which is the same order as found in the *Code* book. There are also ten Practice Quizzes in random order. The first four random order quizzes consist of 50 questions each, and the rest contain 100 questions each. As they progress, the random order quizzes include progressively more articles to give you extra practice finding answers in the *Code* book. Most licensing exams are open book, but check with the testing authority in your region.

Notes

_____

_____

_____

_____

_____

_____

_____

_____

_____

_____

_____

_____

_____

_____

_____

_____

_____

_____

_____

_____

_____

_____

_____

STRAIGHT ORDER [ARTICLES 90–110]

Please use the 2014 *Code* book to answer the following questions.

1. The *NEC* is _____.

   (a) intended to be a design manual
   (b) meant to be used as an instruction guide for untrained persons
   (c) for the practical safeguarding of persons and property
   (d) published by the Bureau of Standards

2. Hazards often occur because of _____.

   (a) overloading of wiring systems by methods or usage not in conformity with the *NEC*
   (b) initial wiring not providing for increases in the use of electricity
   (c) a and b
   (d) none of these

3. The *NEC* applies to the installation of _____.

   (a) electrical conductors and equipment within or on public and private buildings
   (b) outside conductors and equipment on the premises
   (c) optical fiber cables and raceways
   (d) all of these

4. This *Code* covers the installation of _____ for public and private premises, including buildings, structures, mobile homes, recreational vehicles, and floating buildings.

   (a) optical fiber cables
   (b) electrical equipment
   (c) raceways
   (d) all of these

5. Utilities may be subject to compliance with codes and standards covering their regulated activities as adopted under governmental law or regulation.

   (a) True
   (b) False

6. The _____ has the responsibility for deciding on the approval of equipment and materials.

   (a) manufacturer
   (b) authority having jurisdiction
   (c) testing agency
   (d) none of these

7. The authority having jurisdiction has the responsibility for _____.

    (a) making interpretations of rules
    (b) deciding upon the approval of equipment and materials
    (c) waiving specific requirements in the *Code* and permitting alternate methods and material if safety is maintained
    (d) all of these

8. In the *NEC*, the words "_____" indicate a mandatory requirement.

    (a) shall
    (b) shall not
    (c) shall be permitted
    (d) a or b

9. When the *Code* uses "_____," it means the identified actions are allowed but not required, and they may be options or alternative methods.

    (a) shall
    (b) shall not
    (c) shall be permitted
    (d) a or b

10. Nonmandatory Informative Annexes contained in the back of the *Code* book _____.

    (a) are for information only
    (b) aren't enforceable as a requirement of the *Code*
    (c) are enforceable as a requirement of the *Code*
    (d) a and b

11. Factory-installed _____ wiring of listed equipment need not be inspected at the time of installation of the equipment, except to detect alterations or damage.

    (a) external
    (b) associated
    (c) internal
    (d) all of these

12. Capable of being removed or exposed without damaging the building structure or finish, or not permanently closed in by the structure or finish of the building is known as _____.

    (a) accessible (as applied to equipment)
    (b) accessible (as applied to wiring methods)
    (c) accessible, readily
    (d) all of these

13. Capable of being reached quickly for operation, renewal, or inspections without resorting to portable ladders or the use of tools is known as _____.

    (a) accessible (as applied to equipment)
    (b) accessible (as applied to wiring methods)
    (c) accessible, readily
    (d) all of these

14. "_____" means acceptable to the authority having jurisdiction.

    (a) Identified
    (b) Listed
    (c) Approved
    (d) Labeled

15. According to the *Code*, "automatic" is performing a function without the necessity of _____.

    (a) protection from damage
    (b) human intervention
    (c) mechanical linkage
    (d) all of these

16. The connection between the grounded circuit conductor and the equipment grounding conductor at the service is accomplished by installing a(n) _____ bonding jumper.

    (a) main
    (b) system
    (c) equipment
    (d) circuit

17. The connection between the grounded circuit conductor and the supply-side bonding jumper or equipment grounding conductor, or both, at a _____ is called a "system bonding jumper."

    (a) service disconnect
    (b) separately derived system
    (c) motor control center
    (d) separate building or structure disconnect

18. A(n) _____ branch circuit supplies energy to one or more outlets to which appliances are to be connected.

    (a) general purpose
    (b) multiwire
    (c) individual
    (d) appliance

19. A cable routing assembly is composed of single or connected multiple channels as well as associated fittings, forming a structural system to _____ high densities of wires and cables, typically communications wires and cables, optical fiber and data (Class 2 and Class 3) cables.

    (a) support
    (b) route
    (c) protect
    (d) a and b

20. A circuit breaker is a device designed to _____ the circuit automatically on a predetermined overcurrent without damage to itself when properly applied within its rating.

    (a) energize
    (b) reset
    (c) connect
    (d) open

21. _____ is a term indicating that there is an intentional delay in the tripping action of the circuit breaker, which decreases as the magnitude of the current increases.

    (a) Adverse time
    (b) Inverse time
    (c) Time delay
    (d) Timed unit

22. A clothes closet is defined as a _____ room or space intended primarily for storage of garments and apparel.

    (a) habitable
    (b) non-habitable
    (c) conditioned
    (d) finished

23. Communications equipment includes equipment and conductors used for the transmission of _____.

    (a) audio
    (b) video
    (c) data
    (d) any of these

24. Wires are considered _____ if rendered inaccessible by the structure or finish of the building.

    (a) inaccessible
    (b) concealed
    (c) hidden
    (d) enclosed

25. A solderless pressure connector is a device that _____ between two or more conductors or between one or more conductors and a terminal by means of mechanical pressure and without the use of solder.

    (a) provides access
    (b) protects the wiring
    (c) is never needed
    (d) establishes a connection

26. A load is considered to be continuous if the maximum current is expected to continue for _____ or more.

    (a) one-half hour
    (b) 1 hour
    (c) 2 hours
    (d) 3 hours

27. A unit of an electrical system, other than a conductor, that carries or controls electric energy as its principal function is a(n) "_____."

(a) raceway
(b) fitting
(c) device
(d) enclosure

28. An enclosure or piece of equipment constructed so that dust will not enter the enclosure under specified test conditions is known as "_____."

(a) dusttight
(b) dustproof
(c) dust rated
(d) all of these

29. A _____ is a single unit that provides independent living facilities for one or more persons, including permanent provisions for living, sleeping, cooking, and sanitation.

(a) one-family dwelling
(b) two-family dwelling
(c) dwelling unit
(d) multifamily dwelling

30. A fixed, stationary, or portable self-contained, electrically illuminated equipment with words or symbols designed to convey information or attract attention describes _____.

(a) an electric sign
(b) equipment
(c) appliances
(d) none of these

31. Surrounded by a case, housing, fence, or wall(s) that prevents persons from accidentally contacting energized parts is called "_____."

(a) guarded
(b) covered
(c) protection
(d) enclosed

32. As used in the *NEC*, equipment includes _____.

(a) fittings
(b) appliances
(c) machinery
(d) all of these

33. Equipment enclosed in a case that is capable of withstanding an explosion of a specified gas or vapor that may occur within it, and of preventing the ignition of a specified gas or vapor surrounding the enclosure by sparks, flashes, or explosion of the gas or vapor within, and that operates at such an external temperature that a surrounding flammable atmosphere will not be ignited thereby defines the phrase "_____."

(a) overcurrent device
(b) thermal apparatus
(c) explosionproof equipment
(d) bomb casing

34. When the term "exposed," as it applies to live parts, is used in the *Code*, it refers to _____.

(a) being capable of being inadvertently touched or approached nearer than a safe distance by a person
(b) parts that are not suitably guarded, isolated, or insulated
(c) wiring on, or attached to, the surface or behind panels designed to allow access
(d) a and b

35. For wiring methods, "on or attached to the surface, or behind access panels designed to allow access" is known as _____.

(a) open
(b) uncovered
(c) exposed
(d) bare

36. Connected to ground or to a conductive body that extends the ground connection is called "_____."

(a) equipment grounding
(b) bonded
(c) grounded
(d) all of these

37. A device intended for the protection of personnel that functions to de-energize a circuit or portion thereof within an established period of time when a current to ground exceeds the values established for a Class A device, is a(n) "_____."

    (a) dual-element fuse
    (b) inverse time breaker
    (c) ground-fault circuit interrupter
    (d) safety switch

38. A Class A GFCI protection device is designed to trip when the current to ground is _____ or higher.

    (a) 4 mA
    (b) 5 mA
    (c) 6 mA
    (d) none of these

39. A ground-fault current path is an electrically conductive path from the point of a ground fault through normally noncurrent-carrying conductors, equipment, or the earth to the _____.

    (a) ground
    (b) earth
    (c) electrical supply source
    (d) none of these

40. Examples of ground-fault current paths include any combination of conductive materials including _____.

    (a) equipment grounding conductors
    (b) metallic raceways
    (c) metal water and gas piping
    (d) all of these

41. The installed conductive path(s) that provide(s) a ground-fault current path and connects normally noncurrent-carrying metal parts of equipment together and to the system grounded conductor or to the grounding electrode conductor, or both, is known as a(n) _____.

    (a) grounding electrode conductor
    (b) grounding conductor
    (c) equipment grounding conductor
    (d) none of these

42. A "_____" is an accommodation that combines living, sleeping, sanitary, and storage facilities within a compartment.

    (a) guest room
    (b) guest suite
    (c) dwelling unit
    (d) single-family dwelling

43. A handhole enclosure is an enclosure for use in underground systems, provided with an open or closed bottom, and sized to allow personnel to _____.

    (a) enter and exit freely
    (b) reach into but not enter
    (c) have full working space
    (d) examine it visually

44. A hybrid system is comprised of multiple power sources, such as _____, but not the utility power system.

    (a) photovoltaic
    (b) wind
    (c) micro-hydro generators
    (d) all of these

45. A hybrid system includes the utility power system.

    (a) True
    (b) False

46. A device that provides a means to connect intersystem bonding conductors for _____ systems to the building grounding electrode system is an intersystem bonding termination.

    (a) limited energy
    (b) low-voltage
    (c) communications
    (d) power and lighting

47. A kitchen is defined as an area with a sink and _____ provisions for food preparation and cooking.

    (a) listed
    (b) labeled
    (c) temporary
    (d) permanent

48. Lighting track is a manufactured assembly designed to support and _____ luminaires that are capable of being readily repositioned on the track.

    (a) connect
    (b) protect
    (c) energize
    (d) all of these

49. Equipment or materials included in a list published by a testing laboratory acceptable to the authority having jurisdiction is said to be "_____."

    (a) book
    (b) digest
    (c) manifest
    (d) listed

50. A _____ location is protected from weather and not subject to saturation with water or other liquids.

    (a) dry
    (b) damp
    (c) wet
    (d) moist

51. A _____ location may be temporarily subject to dampness and wetness.

    (a) dry
    (b) damp
    (c) moist
    (d) wet

52. Conduit installed underground or encased in concrete slabs that are in direct contact with the earth is considered a _____ location.

    (a) dry
    (b) damp
    (c) wet
    (d) moist

53. A(n) _____ is intended to provide limited overcurrent protection for specific applications and utilization equipment such as luminaires and appliances. This limited protection is in addition to the protection provided by the required branch-circuit overcurrent protective device.

    (a) supplementary overcurrent device
    (b) surge protection device
    (c) arc-fault circuit interrupter
    (d) Class A GFCI

54. An overload is the same as a short circuit or ground fault.

    (a) True
    (b) False

55. A panel, including buses and automatic overcurrent devices, designed to be placed in a cabinet or cutout box and accessible only from the front is known as a "_____."

    (a) switchboard
    (b) disconnect
    (c) panelboard
    (d) switch

56. A _____ is a chamber to which one or more ducts are connected and form part of the air distribution system.

    (a) riser
    (b) plenum
    (c) a or b
    (d) none of these

57. Constructed, protected, or treated so as to prevent rain from interfering with the successful operation of the apparatus under specified test conditions defines the term "_____."

    (a) raintight
    (b) waterproof
    (c) weathertight
    (d) rainproof

58. A contact device installed at an outlet for the connection of an attachment plug is known as a(n) "_____."

    (a) attachment point
    (b) tap
    (c) receptacle
    (d) wall plug

59. A single receptacle is a single contact device with no other contact device on the same _____.

(a) circuit
(b) yoke
(c) run
(d) equipment

60. When one electrical circuit controls another circuit through a relay, the first circuit is called a "_____."

(a) primary circuit
(b) remote-control circuit
(c) signal circuit
(d) controller

61. Equipment enclosed in a case or cabinet with a means of sealing or locking so that live parts cannot be made accessible without opening the enclosure is said to be "_____."

(a) guarded
(b) protected
(c) sealable
(d) lockable

62. A(n) _____ system is an electrical source, other than a service, having no direct connection(s) to circuit conductors of any other electrical source other than those established by grounding and bonding connections.

(a) separately derived
(b) classified
(c) direct
(d) emergency

63. The conductors and equipment from the electric utility that deliver electric energy to the wiring system of the premises is called a "_____."

(a) branch circuit
(b) feeder
(c) service
(d) none of these

64. Service conductors originate at the service point and terminate at the service disconnecting means.

(a) True
(b) False

65. The overhead system service-entrance conductors are the service conductors between the terminals of _____ and a point where they are joined by a tap or splice to the service drop or overhead service conductors.

(a) service equipment
(b) service point
(c) grounding electrode
(d) equipment grounding conductor

66. The underground system service-entrance conductors are the service conductors between the terminals of _____ and the point of connection to the service lateral or underground service conductors.

(a) service equipment
(b) service point
(c) grounding electrode
(d) equipment grounding conductor

67. The prospective symmetrical fault current at a nominal voltage to which an apparatus or system is able to be connected without sustaining damage exceeding defined acceptance criteria is known as the "_____."

(a) short-circuit current rating
(b) arc flash rating
(c) overcurrent rating
(d) available fault current

68. A structure is that which is built or constructed.

(a) True
(b) False

69. A thermal protector may consist of one or more sensing elements integral with the motor or motor-compressor and an external control device.

(a) True
(b) False

70. "Ungrounded" means not connected to ground or to a conductive body that extends the ground connection.

(a) True
(b) False

71. A power supply used to provide alternating current power to a load for some period of time in the event of a power failure is known as a(n) "_____."

    (a) uninterruptible power supply
    (b) power management system
    (c) surge protective device
    (d) arc fault interrupter

72. A value assigned to a circuit or system for the purpose of conveniently designating its voltage class, such as 120/240V, is called "_____ voltage."

    (a) root-mean-square
    (b) circuit
    (c) nominal
    (d) source

73. An enclosure constructed so that moisture will not enter the enclosure under specific test conditions is called "_____."

    (a) watertight
    (b) moistureproof
    (c) waterproof
    (d) rainproof

74. A(n) _____ enclosure is constructed or protected so that exposure to the weather will not interfere with successful operation.

    (a) weatherproof
    (b) weathertight
    (c) weather-resistant
    (d) all weather

75. Listed or labeled equipment shall be installed and used in accordance with any instructions included in the listing or labeling.

    (a) True
    (b) False

76. Conductor sizes are expressed in American Wire Gage (AWG) or in _____.

    (a) inches
    (b) circular mils
    (c) square inches
    (d) cubic inches

77. Equipment intended to interrupt current at fault levels shall have an interrupting rating at nominal circuit voltage sufficient for the current that is available at the line terminals of the equipment.

    (a) True
    (b) False

78. Some cleaning and lubricating compounds can cause severe deterioration of many plastic materials used for insulating and structural applications in equipment.

    (a) True
    (b) False

79. The *NEC* requires that electrical equipment be _____.

    (a) installed in a neat and workmanlike manner
    (b) installed under the supervision of a licensed person
    (c) completed before being inspected
    (d) all of these

80. Accepted industry workmanship practices are described in ANSI/NECA 1-2010, *Standard Practice of Good Workmanship in Electrical Construction*, and other ANSI-approved installation standards.

    (a) True
    (b) False

81. Conductor terminal and splicing devices must be _____ for the conductor material and they must be properly installed and used.

    (a) listed
    (b) approved
    (c) identified
    (d) all of these

82. Connectors and terminals for conductors more finely stranded than Class B and Class C, as shown in Table 10 of Chapter 9, must be _____ for the specific conductor class or classes.

    (a) listed
    (b) approved
    (c) identified
    (d) all of these

83. Connection by means of wire-binding screws, studs, or nuts having upturned lugs or the equivalent shall be permitted for _____ or smaller conductors.

    (a) 12 AWG
    (b) 10 AWG
    (c) 8 AWG
    (d) 6 AWG

84. Conductor ampacity shall be determined using the _____ column of Table 310.15(B)(16) for circuits rated 100A or less or marked for 14 AWG through 1 AWG conductors, unless the equipment terminals are listed for use with conductors that have higher temperature ratings.

    (a) 30°C
    (b) 60°C
    (c) 75°C
    (d) 90°C

85. Conductors shall have their ampacity determined using the _____ column of Table 310.15(B)(16) for circuits rated over 100A, or marked for conductors larger than 1 AWG, unless the equipment terminals are listed for use with higher temperature-rated conductors.

    (a) 30°C
    (b) 60°C
    (c) 75°C
    (d) 90°C

86. On a 4-wire, delta-connected system where the midpoint of one phase winding is grounded, the conductor having the higher phase voltage-to-ground shall be durably and permanently marked by an outer finish that is _____ in color.

    (a) black
    (b) red
    (c) blue
    (d) orange

87. Where required by the *Code*, markings or labels on all electrical equipment shall contain voltage, current, wattage, or other ratings with sufficient durability to withstand _____.

    (a) the voltages encountered
    (b) painting and other finishes applied
    (c) the environment involved
    (d) any lack of planning by the installer

88. The *NEC* requires tested series-rated installations of circuit breakers or fuses to be legibly marked in the field to indicate the equipment has been applied with a series combination rating.

    (a) True
    (b) False

89. _____ in other than dwelling units must be legibly field marked with the maximum available fault current, including the date the fault-current calculation was performed and be of sufficient durability to withstand the environment involved.

    (a) Service equipment
    (b) Sub panels
    (c) Motor control centers
    (d) all of these

90. When modifications to the electrical installation affect the maximum available fault current at the service, the maximum available fault current shall be verified or _____ as necessary to ensure the service equipment ratings are sufficient for the maximum available fault current at the line terminals of the equipment.

    (a) recalculated
    (b) increased
    (c) decreased
    (d) adjusted

91. Field markings of maximum available fault current at a service are not required in industrial installations where conditions of maintenance and supervision ensure that only qualified persons service the equipment.

    (a) True
    (b) False

92. A minimum working space depth of _____ to live parts operating at 277 volts-to-ground is required where there are exposed live parts on one side and no live or grounded parts on the other side.

    (a) 2 ft
    (b) 3 ft
    (c) 4 ft
    (d) 6 ft

93. The minimum working space on a circuit that is 120 volts-to-ground, with exposed live parts on one side and no live or grounded parts on the other side of the working space, is _____.

    (a) 1 ft
    (b) 3 ft
    (c) 4 ft
    (d) 6 ft

94. The required working space for access to live parts operating at 300 volts-to-ground, where there are exposed live parts on one side and grounded parts on the other side, is _____.

    (a) 3 ft
    (b) 3½ ft
    (c) 4 ft
    (d) 4½ ft

95. When normally enclosed live parts are exposed for inspection or servicing, the working space, if in a passageway or general open space, shall be suitably _____.

    (a) accessible
    (b) guarded
    (c) open
    (d) enclosed

96. Illumination shall be provided for all working spaces about service equipment, switchboards, switchgear, panelboards, and motor control centers _____.

    (a) over 600V
    (b) located indoors
    (c) rated 1,200A or more
    (d) using automatic means of control

97. All switchboards, panelboards, and motor control centers shall be _____.

    (a) located in dedicated spaces
    (b) protected from damage
    (c) in weatherproof enclosures
    (d) a and b

98. The dedicated equipment space for electrical equipment that is required for panelboards installed indoors is measured from the floor to a height of _____ above the equipment, or to the structural ceiling, whichever is lower.

    (a) 3 ft
    (b) 6 ft
    (c) 12 ft
    (d) 30 ft

99. The dedicated space above a panelboard extends to a dropped or suspended ceiling, which is considered a structural ceiling.

    (a) True
    (b) False

100. Electrical equipment rooms or enclosures housing electrical apparatus that are controlled by a lock(s) shall be considered _____ to qualified persons.

    (a) readily accessible
    (b) accessible
    (c) available
    (d) none of these

Please use the 2014 *Code* book to answer the following questions.

1. Conductors normally used to carry current shall be _____ unless otherwise provided in this *Code*.

   (a) bare
   (b) stranded
   (c) of copper
   (d) of aluminum

2. Unless identified for use in the operating environment, no conductors or equipment shall be _____ having a deteriorating effect on the conductors or equipment.

   (a) located in damp or wet locations
   (b) exposed to fumes, vapors, liquids, or gases
   (c) exposed to excessive temperatures
   (d) all of these

3. A battery system includes storage batteries and battery chargers, and can include inverters, converters, and associated electrical equipment.

   (a) True
   (b) False

4. For equipment rated 1,200A or more and over 6 ft wide that contains overcurrent devices, switching devices, or control devices, there shall be one entrance to and egress from the required working space not less than 24 in. wide and _____ high at each end of the working space.

   (a) 5½ ft
   (b) 6 ft
   (c) 6½ ft
   (d) any of these

5. The material located in the *NEC* Annexes are part of the requirements of the *Code* and shall be complied with.

   (a) True
   (b) False

6. The highest current at rated voltage that a device is identified to interrupt under standard test conditions is the _____.

   (a) interrupting rating
   (b) manufacturer's rating
   (c) interrupting capacity
   (d) withstand rating

7. An outlet intended for the direct connection of a lampholder or a luminaire is a(n) "_____."

    (a) outlet
    (b) receptacle outlet
    (c) lighting outlet
    (d) general-purpose outlet

8. Utilities may include entities that are designated or recognized by governmental law or regulation by public service/utility commissions.

    (a) True
    (b) False

9. Installations of communications equipment that are under the exclusive control of communications utilities, and located outdoors or in building spaces used exclusively for such installations _____ covered by the *NEC*.

    (a) are
    (b) are sometimes
    (c) are not
    (d) may be

10. Soldered splices shall first be spliced or joined so as to be mechanically and electrically secure without solder and then be soldered.

    (a) True
    (b) False

11. The voltage of a circuit is defined by the *Code* as the _____ root-mean-square (effective) difference of potential between any two conductors of the circuit concerned.

    (a) lowest
    (b) greatest
    (c) average
    (d) nominal

12. "Varying duty" is defined as _____.

    (a) intermittent operation in which the load conditions are regularly recurrent
    (b) operation at a substantially constant load for an indefinite length of time
    (c) operation for alternate intervals of load and rest, or load, no load, and rest
    (d) operation at loads, and for intervals of time, both of which may be subject to wide variation

13. Compliance with either the metric (SI) or the inch-pound unit of measurement system shall be permitted.

    (a) True
    (b) False

14. Separately installed pressure connectors shall be used with conductors at the _____ not exceeding the ampacity at the listed and identified temperature rating of the connector.

    (a) voltages
    (b) temperatures
    (c) listings
    (d) ampacities

15. Unused openings other than those intended for the operation of equipment, intended for mounting purposes, or permitted as part of the design for listed equipment shall be _____.

    (a) filled with cable clamps or connectors only
    (b) taped over with electrical tape
    (c) repaired only by welding or brazing in a metal slug
    (d) closed to afford protection substantially equivalent to the wall of the equipment

16. A signaling circuit is any electrical circuit that energizes signaling equipment.

    (a) True
    (b) False

17. A device that establishes a connection between the conductors of the attached flexible cord and the conductors connected to the receptacle is called a(n) "_____."

    (a) attachment plug
    (b) plug cap
    (c) plug
    (d) any of these

18. Equipment associated with the electrical installation can be located above or below other electrical equipment within their working space when the associated equipment does not extend more than _____ from the front of the electrical equipment.

    (a) 3 in.
    (b) 6 in.
    (c) 12 in.
    (d) 30 in.

19. In judging equipment for approval, considerations such as the following shall be evaluated:

    (a) mechanical strength
    (b) wire-bending space
    (c) arcing effects
    (d) all of these

20. A raintight enclosure is constructed or protected so that exposure to a beating rain will not result in the entrance of water under specified test conditions.

    (a) True
    (b) False

21. Entrances to rooms and other guarded locations containing exposed live parts shall be marked with conspicuous _____ forbidding unqualified persons to enter.

    (a) warning signs
    (b) alarms
    (c) a and b
    (d) neither a nor b

22. Lighting track is a manufactured assembly and its length may not be altered by the addition or subtraction of sections of track.

    (a) True
    (b) False

23. Compliance with the provisions of the *NEC* will result in _____.

    (a) good electrical service
    (b) an efficient electrical system
    (c) an electrical system essentially free from hazard
    (d) all of these

24. The required working space for access to live parts operating at 300 volts-to-ground, where there are exposed live parts on both sides of the workspace is _____.

    (a) 3 ft
    (b) 3½ ft
    (c) 4 ft
    (d) 4½ ft

25. "Nonautomatic" is defined as requiring _____ to perform a function.

    (a) protection from damage
    (b) human intervention
    (c) mechanical linkage
    (d) all of these

26. The maximum current, in amperes, that a conductor can carry continuously, where the temperature will not be raised in excess of the conductor's insulation temperature rating is called its "_____."

    (a) short-circuit rating
    (b) ground-fault rating
    (c) ampacity
    (d) all of these

27. In locations where electrical equipment is likely to be exposed to _____, enclosures or guards shall be so arranged and of such strength as to prevent such damage.

    (a) corrosion
    (b) physical damage
    (c) magnetic fields
    (d) weather

28. A switch constructed so that it can be installed in device boxes or on box covers, or otherwise used in conjunction with wiring systems recognized by the *NEC* is called a "_____ switch."

    (a) transfer
    (b) motor-circuit
    (c) general-use snap
    (d) bypass isolation

29. Many terminations and equipment are either marked with _____, or have that information included in the product's installation instructions.

    (a) an etching tool
    (b) a removable label
    (c) a tightening torque
    (d) the manufacturer's initials

30. The *Code* isn't intended as a design specification standard or instruction manual for untrained persons.

    (a) True
    (b) False

31. A _____ is an area that includes a basin with a toilet, urinal, tub, shower, bidet, or similar plumbing fixtures.

    (a) bath area
    (b) bathroom
    (c) rest area
    (d) none of these

32. Working space shall not be used for _____.

    (a) storage
    (b) raceways
    (c) lighting
    (d) accessibility

33. The common point on a wye-connection in a polyphase system describes a neutral point.

    (a) True
    (b) False

34. The *NEC* does not cover electrical installations in ships, watercraft, railway rolling stock, aircraft, or automotive vehicles.

    (a) True
    (b) False

35. A(n) _____ is a point on the wiring system at which current is taken to supply utilization equipment.

    (a) box
    (b) receptacle
    (c) outlet
    (d) device

36. Internal parts of electrical equipment, including _____, shall not be damaged or contaminated by foreign materials such as paint, plaster, cleaners, abrasives, or corrosive residues.

    (a) busbars
    (b) wiring terminals
    (c) insulators
    (d) all of these

37. A surge-protective device (SPD) intended for installation on the load side of the service disconnect overcurrent device, including SPDs located at the branch panel, is a _____ SPD.

    (a) Type 1
    (b) Type 2
    (c) Type 3
    (d) Type 4

38. An accessory, such as a locknut, intended to perform a mechanical function best describes _____.

    (a) a part
    (b) equipment
    (c) a device
    (d) a fitting

39. _____ are designed for surface mounting that have swinging doors or covers.

    (a) Outlet boxes
    (b) Cabinets
    (c) Cutout boxes
    (d) none of these

40. Within sight means visible and not more than _____ ft distant from the equipment.

    (a) 10
    (b) 20
    (c) 25
    (d) 50

41. Only wiring methods recognized as _____ are included in this *Code*.

    (a) expensive
    (b) efficient
    (c) suitable
    (d) cost-effective

42. The _____ is the point of connection between the facilities of the serving utility and the premises wiring.

    (a) service entrance
    (b) service point
    (c) overcurrent protection
    (d) beginning of the wiring system

43. A _____ is a device or group of devices that govern, in some predetermined manner, the electric power delivered to the apparatus to which it is connected.

    (a) relay
    (b) breaker
    (c) transformer
    (d) controller

44. NFPA 70E—Standard for Electrical Safety in the Workplace, provides information to help determine the electrical safety training requirements expected of a qualified person.

    (a) True
    (b) False

45. Special permission is the written consent from the _____.

    (a) testing laboratory
    (b) manufacturer
    (c) owner
    (d) authority having jurisdiction

46. The _____ is the necessary equipment, usually consisting of a circuit breaker(s) or switch(es) and fuse(s) and their accessories, connected to the load end of service conductors, and intended to constitute the main control and cutoff of the supply.

    (a) service equipment
    (b) service
    (c) service disconnect
    (d) service overcurrent device

47. Connected to ground without the insertion of any resistor or impedance device is referred to as "_____."

    (a) grounded
    (b) solidly grounded
    (c) effectively grounded
    (d) grounding conductor

48. A(n) _____ is an unintentional, electrically conductive connection between an ungrounded conductor of an electrical circuit, and the normally noncurrent-carrying conductors, metallic enclosures, metallic raceways, metallic equipment, or earth.

    (a) grounded conductor
    (b) ground fault
    (c) equipment ground
    (d) bonding jumper

49. For equipment rated 800A or more that contains overcurrent devices, switching devices, or control devices; and where the entrance to the working space has a personnel door less than 25 ft from the working space, the door shall _____.

    (a) open either in or out with simple pressure and shall not have any lock
    (b) open in the direction of egress and be equipped with listed panic hardware
    (c) be equipped with a locking means
    (d) be equipped with an electronic opener

50. The term "rainproof" is typically used in conjunction with Enclosure-Type Number _____.

    (a) 3
    (b) 3R
    (c) 3RX
    (d) b and c

STRAIGHT ORDER
[ARTICLES 200–230]

Please use the 2014 *Code* book to answer the following questions.

1. Article 200 contains the requirements for _____.

   (a) identification of terminals
   (b) grounded conductors in premises wiring systems
   (c) identification of grounded conductors
   (d) all of these

2. Grounded conductors _____ and larger can be identified by distinctive white or gray markings at their terminations.

   (a) 10 AWG
   (b) 8 AWG
   (c) 6 AWG
   (d) 4 AWG

3. If grounded conductors of different voltage systems are installed in the same raceway, cable, or enclosure, each neutral conductor must be identified to distinguish the systems by _____.

   (a) a continuous white or gray outer finish for one system
   (b) a neutral conductor with a different continuous white or gray outer finish or white or gray with a stripe for one system
   (c) other identification allowed by 200.6(a) or (b) that distinguishes each system from other systems
   (d) any of these

4. If used for single-pole, 3-way or 4-way switch loops, the reidentified conductor with white or gray insulation or three continuous white or gray stripes can be used for the supply to the switch but not as a return conductor from the switch to the outlet.

   (a) True
   (b) False

5. The identification of _____ to which a grounded conductor is to be connected shall be substantially white in color.

   (a) wire connectors
   (b) circuit breakers
   (c) terminals
   (d) ground rods

6. No _____ shall be attached to any terminal or lead so as to reverse the designated polarity.

   (a) grounded conductor
   (b) grounding conductor
   (c) ungrounded conductor
   (d) grounding connector

7. A three-phase, 4-wire, _____ power system used to supply power to nonlinear loads may necessitate that the power system design allow for the possibility of high harmonic currents on the neutral conductor.

   (a) wye-connected
   (b) delta-connected
   (c) wye/delta-connected
   (d) none of these

8. In dwelling units, the voltage between conductors that supply the terminals of _____ shall not exceed 120V, nominal.

   (a) luminaires
   (b) cord-and-plug-connected loads of 1,440 VA or less
   (c) cord-and-plug-connected loads of more than ¼ hp
   (d) a and b

9. The GFCI protection required by 210.8(A), (B), (C), and (d) must be _____.

   (a) the circuit breaker type only
   (b) accessible
   (c) readily accessible
   (d) concealed

10. GFCI protection shall be provided for all 15A and 20A, 125V receptacles installed in a dwelling unit _____.

    (a) attic
    (b) garage
    (c) laundry room
    (d) all of these

11. GFCI protection shall be provided for all 15A and 20A, 125V receptacles in dwelling unit accessory buildings that have a floor located at or below grade level not intended as _____ and limited to storage areas, work areas, or similar use.

    (a) habitable rooms
    (b) finished space
    (c) a or b
    (d) none of these

12. All 15A and 20A, 125V receptacles installed in crawl spaces at or below grade level of dwelling units shall have GFCI protection.

    (a) True
    (b) False

13. All 15A and 20A, 125V receptacles installed in _____ of dwelling units shall have GFCI protection.

    (a) unfinished attics
    (b) finished attics
    (c) unfinished basements and crawl spaces
    (d) finished basements

14. GFCI protection shall be provided for all 15A and 20A, 125V receptacles installed within 6 ft of all dwelling unit sinks located in _____.

    (a) laundry rooms
    (b) bathrooms
    (c) dens
    (d) all of these

15. All 15A and 20A, 125V receptacles installed in dwelling unit boathouses shall have GFCI protection.

    (a) True
    (b) False

16. In other than dwelling units, GFCI protection shall be provided for all outdoor 15A and 20A, 125V receptacles.

    (a) True
    (b) False

17. All 15A and 20A, 125V receptacles installed in locker rooms with associated showering facilities must be GFCI protected.

    (a) True
    (b) False

18. There shall be a minimum of one _____ branch circuit for the laundry outlet(s) required by 210.52(F).

    (a) 15A
    (b) 20A
    (c) 30A
    (d) b and c

19. The recommended maximum total voltage drop on branch-circuit conductors is _____ percent.

    (a) 2
    (b) 3
    (c) 4
    (d) 6

20. A single receptacle installed on an individual branch circuit shall have an ampere rating not less than that of the branch circuit.

    (a) True
    (b) False

21. When connected to a branch circuit supplying two or more 15A receptacles, each receptacle shall not supply a total cord-and-plug-connected load in excess of _____.

    (a) 12A
    (b) 16A
    (c) 20A
    (d) 24A

22. The total rating of utilization equipment fastened in place shall not exceed _____ percent of the branch-circuit ampere rating where lighting units and cord-and-plug-connected utilization equipment are supplied.

    (a) 50
    (b) 75
    (c) 100
    (d) 125

23. In multi-occupancy buildings, branch circuits for _____ shall not be supplied from equipment that supplies an individual dwelling unit or tenant space.

    (a) a central alarm
    (b) parking lot lighting
    (c) common area purposes
    (d) all of these

24. When applying the general provisions for receptacle spacing to the rooms of a dwelling unit which require receptacles in the wall space, no point along the floor line in any wall space of a dwelling unit may be more than _____ from an outlet.

    (a) 6 ft
    (b) 8 ft
    (c) 10 ft
    (d) 12 ft

25. In dwelling units, when determining the spacing of receptacle outlets, _____ on exterior walls shall not be considered wall space.

    (a) fixed panels
    (b) fixed glass
    (c) sliding panels
    (d) all of these

26. A receptacle connected to a dwelling unit small-appliance circuit can supply gas-fired ranges, ovens, or counter-mounted cooking units.

    (a) True
    (b) False

27. Receptacles installed in a dwelling unit kitchen to serve countertop surfaces shall be supplied by not fewer than _____ small-appliance branch circuits.

    (a) one
    (b) two
    (c) three
    (d) four

28. A receptacle outlet shall be installed at each dwelling unit kitchen wall countertop space that is 12 in. or wider and receptacle outlets shall be installed so that no point along the wall line is more than _____ in., measured horizontally from a receptacle outlet in that space.

    (a) 10
    (b) 12
    (c) 16
    (d) 24

29. In dwelling units, at least one receptacle outlet shall be installed at each peninsular countertop having a long dimension of _____ in. or greater, and a short dimension of _____ in. or greater.

    (a) 12, 24
    (b) 24, 12
    (c) 24, 48
    (d) 48, 24

30. Receptacle outlets can be installed below the countertop surface in dwelling units when necessary for the physically impaired, or if there is no means available to mount a receptacle above an island or peninsular countertop.

    (a) True
    (b) False

31. The receptacle outlet for a dwelling unit bathroom must be located on a _____ adjacent to the basin or basin counter surface, or on the side or face of the basin cabinet, and never more than 12 in. below the top of the basin.

    (a) wall
    (b) partition
    (c) light fixture
    (d) a or b

32. At least one receptacle outlet not more than _____ above a balcony, deck, or porch shall be installed at each balcony, deck, or porch that is attached to and accessible from a dwelling unit.

    (a) 3 ft
    (b) 6½ ft
    (c) 8 ft
    (d) 24 in.

33. For a one-family dwelling, at least one receptacle outlet shall be installed in each _____.

    (a) basement
    (b) attached garage
    (c) detached garage or accessory building with electric power
    (d) all of these

34. Where a portion of the dwelling unit basement is finished into one or more habitable rooms, each separate unfinished portion shall have a receptacle outlet installed.

    (a) True
    (b) False

35. Hallways in dwelling units that are _____ long or longer require a receptacle outlet.

    (a) 6 ft
    (b) 8 ft
    (c) 10 ft
    (d) 12 ft

36. The number of receptacle outlets for guest rooms in hotels and motels shall not be less than that required for a dwelling unit. These receptacles can be located to be convenient for permanent furniture layout, but at least _____ receptacle outlet(s) shall be readily accessible.

    (a) one
    (b) two
    (c) three
    (d) four

37. At least one 125V, 15A or 20A receptacle outlet shall be installed within 18 in. of the top of a show window for each _____ linear ft, or major fraction thereof, of show-window area measured horizontally at its maximum width.

    (a) 10
    (b) 12
    (c) 18
    (d) 24

38. In a dwelling unit, at least one lighting outlet _____ shall be located at the point of entry to the attic, underfloor space, utility room, or basement where these spaces are used for storage or contain equipment requiring servicing.

    (a) that is unswitched
    (b) containing a switch
    (c) controlled by a wall switch
    (d) b or c

39. For attics and underfloor spaces in other than dwelling units that contain heating, air-conditioning, and refrigeration equipment requiring servicing, at least one lighting outlet containing a switch or controlled by a wall switch shall be installed _____ the equipment requiring servicing.

    (a) at
    (b) near
    (c) a or b
    (d) none of these

40. When a feeder supplies _____ in which equipment grounding conductors are required, the feeder shall include or provide an equipment grounding conductor.

    (a) an equipment disconnecting means
    (b) electrical systems
    (c) branch circuits
    (d) electric-discharge lighting equipment

41. Ground-fault protection of equipment shall be required for a feeder disconnect if the disconnect is rated _____.

    (a) 800A, 208V
    (b) 800A, 480V
    (c) 1,000A, 208V
    (d) 1,000A, 480V

42. The 3 VA per-square-foot general lighting load for dwelling units does not include _____.

    (a) open porches
    (b) garages
    (c) unused or unfinished spaces not adaptable for future use
    (d) all of these

43. Where fixed multioutlet assemblies are used in other than dwelling units or the guest rooms of hotels or motels, each _____ or fraction thereof of each separate and continuous length shall be considered as one outlet of not less than 180 VA where appliances are unlikely to be used simultaneously.

    (a) 5 ft
    (b) 5½ ft
    (c) 6 ft
    (d) 6½ ft

44. For other than dwelling occupancies, banks, or office buildings, each receptacle outlet shall be calculated at not less than _____ VA.

    (a) 90
    (b) 180
    (c) 270
    (d) 360

45. The 3 VA per-square-foot general lighting load for dwelling units includes general-use receptacles and lighting outlets.

    (a) True
    (b) False

46. The minimum feeder load for show-window lighting is _____ per linear foot.

    (a) 180 VA
    (b) 200 VA
    (c) 300 VA
    (d) 400 VA

47. For other than dwelling units or guest rooms of hotels or motels, the feeder and service calculation for track lighting shall be calculated at 150 VA for every _____ ft of lighting track or fraction thereof unless the track is supplied through a device that limits the current to the track.

    (a) 1
    (b) 2
    (c) 3
    (d) 4

48. A dwelling unit containing two 120V laundry branch circuits has a calculated load of _____ VA for the laundry circuits.

    (a) 1,500
    (b) 3,000
    (c) 4,500
    (d) 6,000

49. The load for electric clothes dryers in a dwelling unit shall be _____ watts or the nameplate rating, whichever is larger, per dryer.

    (a) 1,500
    (b) 4,500
    (c) 5,000
    (d) 8,000

50. To determine the feeder calculated load for ten 3 kW household cooking appliances, use _____ of Table 220.55.

    (a) Column A
    (b) Column B
    (c) Column C
    (d) none of these

51. The feeder/service calculated load for a multifamily dwelling containing nine 12 kW ranges is _____.

    (a) 13,000W
    (b) 14,700W
    (c) 16,000W
    (d) 24,000W

52. Table 220.56 may be applied to determine the load for thermostatically controlled or intermittently used _____ and other kitchen equipment in a commercial kitchen.

    (a) commercial electric cooking equipment
    (b) dishwasher booster heaters
    (c) water heaters
    (d) all of these

53. When applying the demand factors of Table 220.56, the feeder or service demand load shall not be less than the sum of the _____.

    (a) total number of receptacles at 180 VA per receptacle outlet
    (b) VA rating of all of the small-appliance branch circuits combined
    (c) largest two kitchen equipment loads
    (d) kitchen heating and air-conditioning loads

54. Overhead feeder conductors shall have a minimum _____ vertical clearance over residential property and driveways, as well as those commercial areas not subject to truck traffic, where the voltage is limited to 300 volts-to-ground.

    (a) 10 ft
    (b) 12 ft
    (c) 15 ft
    (d) 18 ft

55. The minimum clearance for overhead feeder conductors that pass over track rails of railroads is _____.

    (a) 10 ft
    (b) 12 ft
    (c) 24.50 ft
    (d) 30 ft

56. Overhead feeder conductors installed over roofs shall have a vertical clearance of _____ above the roof surface, unless permitted by an exception.

    (a) 3 ft
    (b) 8 ft
    (c) 12 ft
    (d) 15 ft

57. Vegetation such as trees shall not be used for support of _____.

    (a) overhead conductor spans
    (b) surface wiring methods
    (c) luminaires
    (d) electric equipment

58. Underground raceways entering a _____ from an underground distribution system shall be sealed or plugged at either or both ends to prevent moisture from contacting energized live parts.

    (a) building
    (b) structure
    (c) highway right-of-way
    (d) a or b

59. A building or structure shall be supplied by a maximum of _____ feeder(s) or branch circuit(s), unless specifically permitted otherwise.

    (a) one
    (b) two
    (c) three
    (d) four

60. Where documented safe switching procedures are established and maintained and the installation is monitored by _____ individuals, the disconnecting means for a building supplied by a feeder can be located elsewhere on the premises.

    (a) maintenance
    (b) management
    (c) service
    (d) qualified

61. A building disconnecting means that supplies only limited loads of a single branch circuit shall have a rating of not less than _____.

    (a) 15A
    (b) 20A
    (c) 25A
    (d) 30A

62. Additional services shall be permitted for different voltages, frequencies, or phases, or for different uses such as for _____.

    (a) gymnasiums
    (b) different rate schedules
    (c) flea markets
    (d) special entertainment events

63. Where a building or structure is supplied by more than one service, a permanent plaque or directory shall be installed at each service disconnect location denoting all other services supplying that building or structure and the area served by each.

    (a) True
    (b) False

64. Service conductors supplying a building or other structure shall not _____ of another building or other structure.

    (a) be installed on the exterior walls
    (b) pass through the interior
    (c) a and b
    (d) none of these

65. Service conductors installed in overhead masts on the outside surface of the building traveling through the eave, but not the wall, of that building are considered to be outside of the building.

    (a) True
    (b) False

66. Service conductors shall not be installed beneath openings through which materials may be moved and shall not be installed where they will obstruct entrance to these buildings' openings.

    (a) True
    (b) False

67. Overhead service conductors can be supported to hardwood trees.

    (a) True
    (b) False

68. The minimum size service-drop conductor permitted is _____ AWG copper or _____ AWG aluminum or copper-clad aluminum.

    (a) 8, 8
    (b) 8, 6
    (c) 6, 8
    (d) 6, 6

69. The requirement to maintain a 3-foot vertical clearance from the edge of a roof does not apply to the final conductor span where the service drop is attached to _____.

    (a) a service pole
    (b) the side of a building
    (c) an antenna
    (d) the base of a building

70. If the voltage between overhead service conductors does not exceed 300V and the roof area is guarded or isolated, a reduction in clearance to 3 ft is permitted.

    (a) True
    (b) False

71. Where communications cables and electric service drop conductors are supported by the same pole, communications cables must have a minimum separation of _____ in. at any point in the span, including the point of attachment to the building.

    (a) 2
    (b) 6
    (c) 12
    (d) 24

72. Where conduits are used as service masts, hubs shall be _____ for use with service entrance equipment.

    (a) identified
    (b) approved
    (c) of a heavy-duty type
    (d) listed

73. Underground copper service conductors supplying more than a single branch circuit shall not be smaller than _____ AWG copper.

    (a) 3
    (b) 4
    (c) 6
    (d) 8

74. Underground service conductors that supply power to limited loads of a single branch circuit shall not be smaller than _____.

    (a) 14 AWG copper
    (b) 14 AWG aluminum
    (c) 12 AWG copper
    (d) 12 AWG aluminum

75. Underground service conductors shall be protected from damage in accordance with _____ including minimum cover requirements.

    (a) 240.6(A)
    (b) 300.5
    (c) 310.15(B)(16)
    (d) 430.52

76. The general requirement for each service drop, set of overhead service conductors, set of underground service conductors, or service lateral is that it shall supply _____ set(s) of service-entrance conductors.

    (a) only one
    (b) only two
    (c) up to six
    (d) an unlimited number of

77. A single-family dwelling unit and its accessory structure(s) shall be permitted to have one set of service conductors run to each structure from a single service drop, set of overhead service conductors, set of underground service conductors, or service lateral.

    (a) True
    (b) False

78. Two-family dwellings, multifamily dwellings, and multiple occupancy buildings shall be permitted to have one set of service-entrance conductors to supply branch circuits for public or common areas.

    (a) True
    (b) False

79. One set of service-entrance conductors connected to the supply side of the normal service disconnecting means shall be permitted to supply standby power systems, fire pump equipment, and fire and sprinkler alarms covered by 230.82(5).

    (a) True
    (b) False

80. Service-entrance cables which are not installed underground, where subject to physical damage, shall be protected by _____.

    (a) rigid metal conduit
    (b) IMC
    (c) Schedule 80 PVC conduit
    (d) any of these

81. Individual open conductors and cables, other than service-entrance cables, shall not be installed within _____ ft of grade level or where exposed to physical damage.

    (a) 8
    (b) 10
    (c) 12
    (d) 15

82. Service raceways for overhead service drops or overhead service conductors shall have a service head listed for _____.

    (a) wet locations
    (b) damp locations
    (c) Class 2 locations
    (d) NEMA 3R

83. Overhead service-entrance cables shall be equipped with a _____.

    (a) raceway
    (b) service head
    (c) cover
    (d) all of these

84. Overhead service-entrance conductors of Type SE cable can be formed into a _____ and taped with self-sealing weather-resistant thermoplastic.

    (a) loop
    (b) circle
    (c) gooseneck
    (d) none of these

85. To prevent moisture from entering service equipment, service-entrance conductors shall _____.

    (a) be connected to service-drop conductors below the level of the service head
    (b) have drip loops formed on the individual service-entrance conductors
    (c) a or b
    (d) a and b

86. The service disconnecting means shall be marked as suitable for use as service equipment and shall be _____.

    (a) weatherproof
    (b) listed
    (c) approved
    (d) acceptable

87. A service disconnecting means shall be installed at a(n) _____ location.

    (a) dry
    (b) readily accessible
    (c) outdoor
    (d) indoor

88. A service disconnecting means shall not be installed in bathrooms.

    (a) True
    (b) False

89. Where a remote-control device actuates the service disconnecting means, the service disconnecting means must still be at a readily accessible location either outside the building or structure, or nearest the point of entry of the service conductors.

    (a) True
    (b) False

90. Each service disconnecting means shall be permanently _____ to identify it as a service disconnect.

    (a) identified
    (b) positioned
    (c) marked
    (d) none of these

91. When the service contains two to six service disconnecting means, they shall be _____.

    (a) the same size
    (b) grouped
    (c) in the same enclosure
    (d) none of these

92. In a multiple-occupancy building, each occupant shall have access to the occupant's _____.

    (a) service disconnecting means
    (b) service drops
    (c) distribution transformer
    (d) lateral conductors

93. When the service disconnecting means is a power-operated switch or circuit breaker, it shall be able to be opened by hand in the event of a _____.

    (a) ground fault
    (b) short circuit
    (c) power surge
    (d) power supply failure

94. For installations consisting of not more than two 2-wire branch circuits, the service disconnecting means shall have a rating of not less than _____.

    (a) 15A
    (b) 20A
    (c) 25A
    (d) 30A

95. Electrical equipment shall not be connected to the supply side of the service disconnecting means, except for a few specific exceptions such as _____.

    (a) Type 1 surge protective devices
    (b) taps used to supply standby power systems, fire pump equipment, fire and sprinkler alarms, and load (energy) management devices
    (c) solar photovoltaic systems
    (d) all of these

96. Each _____ service conductor shall have overload protection.

    (a) overhead
    (b) underground
    (c) ungrounded
    (d) none of these

97. Ground-fault protection of equipment shall be provided for solidly grounded wye electrical services of more than 150 volts-to-ground, but not exceeding 1,000V phase-to-phase for each service disconnecting means rated _____ or more.

    (a) 1,000A
    (b) 1,500A
    (c) 2,000A
    (d) 2,500A

98. As defined by 230.95, the rating of the service disconnect shall be considered to be the rating of the largest _____ that can be installed or the highest continuous current trip setting for which the actual overcurrent device installed in a circuit breaker is rated or can be adjusted.

    (a) fuse
    (b) circuit
    (c) conductor
    (d) all of these

99. The maximum setting for ground-fault protection in a service disconnecting means is _____.

    (a) 800A
    (b) 1,000A
    (c) 1,200A
    (d) 2,000A

100. When service equipment has ground-fault protection installed, it may be necessary to review the overall wiring system for proper selective overcurrent protection _____.

    (a) rating
    (b) coordination
    (c) devices
    (d) none of these

RANDOM ORDER
[ARTICLES 90–230]

Please use the 2014 *Code* book to answer the following questions.

1. Receptacle outlets in or on floors shall not be counted as part of the required number of receptacle outlets for dwelling unit wall spaces, unless they are located within _____ in. of the wall.

    (a) 6
    (b) 12
    (c) 18
    (d) 24

2. Wiring methods permitted for service-entrance conductors include _____.

    (a) rigid metal conduit
    (b) electrical metallic tubing
    (c) PVC conduit
    (d) all of these

3. For installations that supply only limited loads of a single branch circuit, the service disconnecting means shall have a rating not less than _____.

    (a) 15A
    (b) 20A
    (c) 25A
    (d) 30A

4. The following systems shall be installed in accordance with the *NEC* requirements:

    (a) signaling conductors, equipment, and raceways
    (b) communications conductors, equipment, and raceways
    (c) electrical conductors, equipment, and raceways
    (d) all of these

5. In a dwelling unit, illumination for outdoor entrances that have grade-level access can be controlled by _____.

    (a) remote
    (b) central
    (c) automatic control
    (d) any of these

6. The white conductor within a cable can be used for a(n) _____ conductor where permanently reidentified to indicate its use as an ungrounded conductor at each location where the conductor is visible and accessible.

    (a) grounded
    (b) ungrounded
    (c) a and b
    (d) none of these

7. Receptacle outlets installed for a specific appliance in a dwelling unit, such as laundry equipment, shall be located within _____ of the intended location of the appliance.

    (a) sight
    (b) 3 ft
    (c) 6 ft
    (d) none of these

8. A raceway is an enclosure designed for the installation of wires, cables, or busbars.

    (a) True
    (b) False

9. Each disconnecting means shall be legibly marked to indicate its purpose unless located and arranged so _____.

    (a) that it can be locked out and tagged
    (b) it is not readily accessible
    (c) the purpose is evident
    (d) that it operates at less than 300 volts-to-ground

10. Service heads shall be located _____ the point of attachment, unless impracticable.

    (a) above
    (b) below
    (c) even with
    (d) none of these

11. There shall be a minimum of _____ receptacle(s) installed outdoors at a one-family or each unit of a two-family dwelling unit.

    (a) one
    (b) two
    (c) three
    (d) four

12. Communications wiring such as telephone, antenna, and CATV wiring within a building shall not be required to comply with the installation requirements of Chapters 1 through 7, except where specifically referenced in Chapter 8.

    (a) True
    (b) False

13. Ungrounded service-entrance conductors shall be sized not less than _____ percent of the continuous load, plus 100 percent of the noncontinuous load.

    (a) 100
    (b) 115
    (c) 125
    (d) 150

14. In dwelling units, outdoor receptacles can be connected to one of the 20A small-appliance branch circuits.

    (a) True
    (b) False

15. The minimum clearance for overhead feeder conductors not exceeding 1,000V that pass over commercial areas subject to truck traffic is _____.

    (a) 10 ft
    (b) 12 ft
    (c) 15 ft
    (d) 18 ft

16. A building that contains three or more dwelling units is called a "_____."

    (a) one-family dwelling
    (b) two-family dwelling
    (c) dwelling unit
    (d) multifamily dwelling

17. The word "Earth" best describes what *NEC* term?

    (a) Bonded
    (b) Ground
    (c) Effective ground-fault current path
    (d) Guarded

18. The continuity of a grounded conductor shall not depend on a connection to a _____.

    (a) metallic enclosure
    (b) raceway
    (c) cable armor
    (d) all of these

19. Ground-fault circuit-interrupter protection shall be provided for outlets not exceeding 240V that supply boat hoists installed in dwelling unit locations.

    (a) True
    (b) False

20. When the disconnecting means for a building supplied by a feeder is a power-operable switch or circuit breaker, it shall be able to be opened by hand in the event of a _____.

    (a) ground fault
    (b) short circuit
    (c) power surge
    (d) power failure

21. Where a premises wiring system contains feeders supplied from more than one nominal voltage system, each ungrounded conductor of a feeder shall be identified by phase or line and system by _____, or other approved means.

    (a) color coding
    (b) marking tape
    (c) tagging
    (d) any of these

22. Where a branch circuit supplies continuous loads, or any combination of continuous and noncontinuous loads, the rating of the overcurrent device shall not be less than the noncontinuous load plus 125 percent of the continuous load.

    (a) True
    (b) False

23. The selection and installation of overcurrent devices so that an overcurrent condition will be localized and restrict outages to the circuit or equipment affected, is called "_____."

    (a) overcurrent protection
    (b) interrupting capacity
    (c) selective coordination
    (d) overload protection

24. Conductors other than service conductors shall not be installed in the same _____.

    (a) service raceway
    (b) service cable
    (c) enclosure
    (d) a or b

25. Guest rooms or guest suites provided with permanent provisions for _____ shall have receptacle outlets installed in accordance with all of the applicable requirements for a dwelling unit in accordance with 210.52.

    (a) whirlpool tubs
    (b) bathing
    (c) cooking
    (d) internet access

26. Receptacles installed for countertop surfaces as required by 210.52(c) shall not be used to meet the receptacle requirements for wall space as required by 210.52(A).

    (a) True
    (b) False

27. The screw shell of a luminaire or lampholder shall be connected to the _____.

    (a) grounded conductor
    (b) ungrounded conductor
    (c) equipment grounding conductor
    (d) forming shell terminal

28. The minimum height of dedicated equipment space for motor control centers installed indoors is _____ above the enclosure, or to the structural ceiling, whichever is lower.

    (a) 3 ft
    (b) 5 ft
    (c) 6 ft
    (d) 6½ ft

29. A conducting object through which a direct connection to earth is established is a "_____."

    (a) bonding conductor
    (b) grounding conductor
    (c) grounding electrode
    (d) grounded conductor

30. A laundry receptacle outlet shall not be required in each dwelling unit of a multifamily building, if laundry facilities are provided on the premises for all building occupants.

   (a) True
   (b) False

31. Live parts of electrical equipment operating at _____ or more shall be guarded against accidental contact by approved enclosures or by suitable permanent, substantial partitions or screens arranged so that only qualified persons have access to the space within reach of the live parts.

   (a) 20V
   (b) 30V
   (c) 50V
   (d) 100V

32. Each multiwire branch circuit shall be provided with a means that will simultaneously disconnect all _____ conductors at the point where the branch circuit originates.

   (a) circuit
   (b) grounded
   (c) grounding
   (d) ungrounded

33. Kitchen and dining room countertop receptacle outlets in dwelling units shall be installed above the countertop surface, and not more than _____ in. above the countertop.

   (a) 12
   (b) 18
   (c) 20
   (d) 24

34. The *Code* provides rules for the minimum number of receptacle outlets required in a dwelling unit. The minimum required receptacle outlets shall be in addition to receptacle outlets that are _____.

   (a) part of a luminaire or appliance
   (b) controlled by a wall switch for use as required illumination
   (c) located more than 5½ ft above the floor
   (d) all of these

35. In dwelling units, the required bathroom receptacle outlet can be installed on the side or face of the basin cabinet if no lower than _____ in. below the top of the basin.

   (a) 12
   (b) 18
   (c) 24
   (d) 36

36. The feeder conductor ampacity shall not be less than that of the service conductors where the feeder conductors carry the total load supplied by service conductors with an ampacity of _____ or less.

   (a) 30A
   (b) 55A
   (c) 60A
   (d) 100A

37. The underground conductors between the utility electric supply system and the service point are known as the "_____."

   (a) utility service
   (b) service lateral
   (c) service drop
   (d) main service conductors

38. Feeder neutral conductors shall be permitted to be sized at _____ percent of the continuous and noncontinuous load.

   (a) 80
   (b) 100
   (c) 125
   (d) 150

39. All 15A and 20A, 125V receptacles _____ of commercial occupancies shall have GFCI protection.

   (a) in bathrooms
   (b) on rooftops
   (c) in kitchens
   (d) all of these

40. Service conductors installed as unjacketed multiconductor cable shall have a minimum clearance of _____ ft from windows that are designed to be opened, doors, porches, stairs, fire escapes, or similar locations.

    (a) 3
    (b) 4
    (c) 6
    (d) 10

41. In a dwelling unit, illumination from a lighting outlet shall be provided on the exterior side of each outdoor entrance or exit that has grade-level access.

    (a) True
    (b) False

42. All 15A and 20A, 125V receptacles installed indoors, in other than dwelling units, in wet locations must be GFCI protected.

    (a) True
    (b) False

43. An effective ground-fault current path is an intentionally constructed, low-impedance electrically conductive path designed and intended to carry current under ground-fault conditions from the point of a ground fault on a wiring system to _____.

    (a) ground
    (b) earth
    (c) the electrical supply source
    (d) none of these

44. The term "Luminaire" includes an individual lampholder.

    (a) True
    (b) False

45. Access and _____ shall be provided and maintained about all electrical equipment to permit ready and safe operation and maintenance of such equipment.

    (a) ventilation
    (b) cleanliness
    (c) circulation
    (d) working space

46. Where a service raceway enters a building or structure from a(n) _____, it shall be sealed in accordance with 300.5(G).

    (a) transformer vault
    (b) underground distribution system
    (c) cable tray
    (d) overhead rack

47. There shall be no more than _____ disconnects installed for each service or for each set of service-entrance conductors as permitted in 230.2 and 230.40.

    (a) two
    (b) four
    (c) six
    (d) eight

48. The working space in front of the electric equipment shall not be less than _____ wide, or the width of the equipment, whichever is greater.

    (a) 15 in.
    (b) 30 in.
    (c) 40 in.
    (d) 60 in.

49. An isolating switch is one that is _____.

    (a) not readily accessible to persons unless special means for access are used
    (b) capable of interrupting the maximum operating overload current of a motor
    (c) intended for use in general distribution and branch circuits
    (d) intended for isolating an electrical circuit from the source of power

50. Explanatory material, such as references to other standards, references to related sections of the *NEC*, or information related to a *Code* rule, are included in the form of Informational Notes.

    (a) True
    (b) False

Mike Holt's NEC Exam Practice Questions, based on the 2014 NEC

STRAIGHT ORDER
[ARTICLES 240–285]

Please use the 2014 *Code* book to answer the following questions.

1. Overcurrent protection for conductors and equipment is designed to _____ the circuit if the current reaches a value that will cause an excessive or dangerous temperature in conductors or conductor insulation.

   (a) open
   (b) close
   (c) monitor
   (d) record

2. Conductor overload protection shall not be required where the interruption of the _____ would create a hazard, such as in a material-handling magnet circuit or fire pump circuit. However, short-circuit protection is required.

   (a) circuit
   (b) line
   (c) phase
   (d) system

3. If the circuit's overcurrent device exceeds _____, the conductor ampacity must have a rating not less than the rating of the overcurrent device.

   (a) 800A
   (b) 1,000A
   (c) 1,200A
   (d) 2,000A

4. Flexible cords approved for and used with a specific listed appliance or luminaire shall be considered to be protected by the branch-circuit overcurrent device when _____.

   (a) not more than 6 ft in length
   (b) 20 AWG and larger
   (c) applied within the listing requirements
   (d) 16 AWG and larger

5. The standard ampere ratings for fuses includes _____.

   (a) 1A
   (b) 6A
   (c) 601A
   (d) all of these

6. Supplementary overcurrent devices used in luminaires or appliances are not required to be readily accessible.

   (a) True
   (b) False

7. Circuit breakers shall _____ all ungrounded conductors of the circuit both manually and automatically unless specifically permitted otherwise.

   (a) open
   (b) close
   (c) isolate
   (d) inhibit

8. Conductors supplied under the tap rules are allowed to supply another conductor using the tap rules.

   (a) True
   (b) False

9. The maximum length of a feeder tap conductor in a high-bay manufacturing building over 35 ft high shall be _____.

   (a) 15 ft
   (b) 20 ft
   (c) 50 ft
   (d) 100 ft

10. Outside feeder tap conductors can be of unlimited length without overcurrent protection at the point they receive their supply if the tap conductors _____.

    (a) are suitably protected from physical damage
    (b) terminate at a single circuit breaker or a single set of fuses that limits the load to the ampacity of the conductors
    (c) a and b
    (d) none of these

11. Overcurrent devices shall be _____.

    (a) accessible (as applied to wiring methods)
    (b) accessible (as applied to equipment)
    (c) readily accessible
    (d) inaccessible to unauthorized personnel

12. Overcurrent devices shall not be located _____.

    (a) where exposed to physical damage
    (b) near easily ignitible materials, such as in clothes closets
    (c) in bathrooms of dwelling units
    (d) all of these

13. _____ shall not be located over the steps of a stairway.

    (a) Disconnect switches
    (b) Overcurrent devices
    (c) Knife switches
    (d) Transformers

14. Plug fuses of 15A or less shall be identified by a(n) _____ configuration of the window, cap, or other prominent part to distinguish them from fuses of higher ampere ratings.

    (a) octagonal
    (b) rectangular
    (c) hexagonal
    (d) triangular

15. Plug fuses of the Edison-base type shall be used _____.

    (a) where overfusing is necessary
    (b) as a replacement in existing installations
    (c) as a replacement for Type S fuses
    (d) 50A and above

16. Which of the following statements about Type S fuses are true?

    (a) Adapters shall fit Edison-base fuseholders.
    (b) Adapters are designed to be easily removed.
    (c) Type S fuses shall be classified as not over 125V and 30A.
    (d) a and c

17. Dimensions of Type S fuses, fuseholders, and adapters shall be standardized to permit interchangeability regardless of the _____.

    (a) model
    (b) manufacturer
    (c) amperage
    (d) voltage

18. Fuseholders for cartridge fuses shall be so designed that it is difficult to put a fuse of any given class into a fuseholder that is designed for a _____ lower or a _____ higher than that of the class to which the fuse belongs.

    (a) voltage, wattage
    (b) wattage, voltage
    (c) voltage, current
    (d) current, voltage

19. Fuses shall be marked with their _____.

    (a) ampere and voltage rating
    (b) interrupting rating where other than 10,000A
    (c) name or trademark of the manufacturer
    (d) all of these

20. Cartridge fuses and fuseholders shall be classified according to their _____ ranges.

    (a) voltage
    (b) amperage
    (c) a or b
    (d) a and b

21. Circuit breakers shall be capable of being closed and opened by manual operation. Operation by other means, such as electrical or pneumatic, shall be permitted if means for _____ operation is also provided.

    (a) automated
    (b) timed
    (c) manual
    (d) shunt trip

22. Where the circuit breaker handles are operated vertically, the up position of the handle shall be the _____ position.

    (a) on
    (b) off
    (c) tripped
    (d) any of these

23. Circuit breakers shall be marked with their ampere rating in a manner that is durable and visible after installation. Such marking can be made visible by removal of a _____.

    (a) trim
    (b) cover
    (c) box
    (d) a or b

24. A circuit breaker having an interrupting current rating of other than _____ shall have its interrupting rating marked on the circuit breaker.

    (a) 5,000A
    (b) 10,000A
    (c) 22,000A
    (d) 50,000A

25. A circuit breaker with a _____ voltage rating, such as 240V or 480V, can be used where the nominal voltage between any two conductors does not exceed the circuit breaker's voltage rating.

    (a) straight
    (b) slash
    (c) high
    (d) low

26. An important consideration for limiting imposed voltage on electrical systems is to remember that bonding and grounding electrode conductors shouldn't be any longer than necessary and unnecessary bends and loops should be avoided.

    (a) True
    (b) False

27. For grounded systems, normally noncurrent-carrying conductive materials enclosing electrical conductors or equipment shall be connected to earth so as to limit the voltage-to-ground on these materials.

    (a) True
    (b) False

28. For grounded systems, normally noncurrent-carrying conductive materials enclosing electrical conductors or equipment, or forming part of such equipment, shall be connected together and to the _____ to establish an effective ground-fault current path.

    (a) ground
    (b) earth
    (c) electrical supply source
    (d) none of these

29. For grounded systems, the earth is considered an effective ground-fault current path.

    (a) True
    (b) False

30. Temporary currents resulting from abnormal conditions, such as ground faults, are not considered to be objectionable currents.

    (a) True
    (b) False

31. _____ alternating-current systems operating at 480V shall have ground detectors installed on the system.

    (a) Grounded
    (b) Solidly grounded
    (c) Effectively grounded
    (d) Ungrounded

32. Alternating current systems from 50V to less than 1,000V that aren't required to be grounded in accordance with 250.20(b) must have _____.

    (a) ground detectors installed
    (b) the ground detection sensing equipment connected as close as practicable to where the system receives its supply
    (c) a and b
    (d) ground fault protection for equipment

33. The grounding electrode conductor shall be connected to the grounded service conductor at the _____.

    (a) load end of the service drop
    (b) load end of the service lateral
    (c) service disconnecting means
    (d) any of these

34. Where an alternating-current system operating at 1,000V or less is grounded at any point, the _____ conductor(s) shall be routed with the ungrounded conductors to each service disconnecting means and shall be connected to each disconnecting means grounded conductor(s) terminal or bus.

    (a) ungrounded
    (b) grounded
    (c) grounding
    (d) none of these

35. The grounded conductor of an alternating-current system operating at 1,000V or less shall be routed with the ungrounded conductors and connected to each disconnecting means grounded conductor terminal or bus, which is then connected to the service disconnecting means enclosure via a(n) _____ that's installed between the service neutral conductor and the service disconnecting means enclosure.

    (a) equipment bonding conductor
    (b) main bonding jumper
    (c) grounding electrode
    (d) intersystem bonding terminal

36. Where service-entrance phase conductors are installed in parallel in two or more raceways, the size of the grounded conductor in each raceway shall be based on the total circular mil area of the parallel ungrounded service-entrance conductors in the raceway, sized in accordance with 250.24(C)(1), but not smaller than _____.

    (a) 1/0 AWG
    (b) 2/0 AWG
    (c) 3/0 AWG
    (d) 4/0 AWG

37. A grounding electrode conductor, sized in accordance with 250.66, shall be used to connect the equipment grounding conductors, the service-equipment enclosures, and, where the system is grounded, the grounded service conductor to the grounding electrode(s).

    (a) True
    (b) False

38. A main bonding jumper shall be a _____ or similar suitable conductor.

    (a) wire
    (b) bus
    (c) screw
    (d) any of these

39. Main bonding jumpers and system bonding jumpers shall not be smaller than specified in _____.

    (a) Table 250.102(C)(1)
    (b) Table 250.122
    (c) Table 310.15(B)(16)
    (d) Chapter 9, Table 8

40. Where the supply conductors are larger than 1,100 kcmil copper or 1,750 kcmil aluminum, the main bonding jumper shall have an area that is _____ the area of the largest phase conductor when of the same material.

    (a) at least equal to
    (b) at least 50 percent of
    (c) not less than 12½ percent of
    (d) not more than 12½ percent of

41. A grounded conductor shall not be connected to normally non-current-carrying metal parts of equipment on the _____ side of the system bonding jumper of a separately derived system except as otherwise permitted in Article 250.

    (a) supply
    (b) grounded
    (c) high-voltage
    (d) load

42. An unspliced _____ that is sized based on the derived phase conductors shall be used to connect the grounded conductor and the supply-side bonding jumper, or the equipment grounding conductor, or both, at a separately derived system.

    (a) system bonding jumper
    (b) equipment grounding conductor
    (c) grounded conductor
    (d) grounding electrode conductor

43. Each tap conductor to a common grounding electrode conductor for multiple separately derived systems shall be sized in accordance with _____, based on the derived ungrounded conductors of the separately derived system it serves.

    (a) 250.66
    (b) 250.118
    (c) 250.122
    (d) 310.15

44. Tap connections to a common grounding electrode conductor for multiple separately derived systems shall be made at an accessible location by _____.

    (a) a connector listed as grounding and bonding equipment
    (b) listed connections to aluminum or copper busbars
    (c) the exothermic welding process
    (d) any of these

45. Tap connections to a common grounding electrode conductor for multiple separately derived systems may be made to a copper or aluminum busbar that is _____.

    (a) smaller than ¼ in. x 4 in.
    (b) not smaller than ¼ in. x 2 in.
    (c) not smaller than ½ in. x 2 in.
    (d) a and c

46. In an area served by a separately derived system, the _____ shall be connected to the grounded conductor of the separately derived system.

    (a) structural steel
    (b) metal piping
    (c) metal building skin
    (d) a and b

47. A grounding electrode at a separate building or structure shall be required where one multiwire branch circuit serves the building or structure.

    (a) True
    (b) False

48. When supplying a grounded system at a separate building or structure, an equipment grounding conductor shall be run with the supply conductors and connected to the building or structure disconnecting means.

    (a) True
    (b) False

49. For a separate building or structure supplied by a separately derived system when overcurrent protection is provided where the conductors originate, the supply conductors must contain a(n) _____.

    (a) equipment grounding conductor
    (b) copper conductors only
    (c) GFI protection for the feeder
    (d) all of these

50. The frame of a portable generator shall not be required to be connected to a(n) _____ if the generator only supplies equipment mounted on the generator, or cord-and-plug connected equipment using receptacles mounted on the generator, or both.

    (a) grounding electrode
    (b) grounded conductor
    (c) ungrounded conductor
    (d) equipment grounding conductor

51. When a permanently installed generator ____, the requirements of 250.30 apply.

    (a) is a separately derived system
    (b) is not a separately derived system
    (c) supplies only cord and plug connected loads
    (d) none of these

52. High-impedance grounded neutral systems shall be permitted for three-phase ac systems of 480V to 1,000V where ____.

    (a) the conditions of maintenance ensure that only qualified persons service the installation
    (b) ground detectors are installed on the system
    (c) line-to-neutral loads are not served
    (d) all of these

53. A bare 4 AWG copper conductor installed horizontally near the bottom or vertically, and within that portion of a concrete foundation or footing that is in direct contact with the earth can be used as a grounding electrode when the conductor is at least ____ ft in length.

    (a) 10
    (b) 15
    (c) 20
    (d) 25

54. An electrode encased by at least 2 in. of concrete, located horizontally near the bottom or vertically and within that portion of a concrete foundation or footing that is in direct contact with the earth, shall be permitted as a grounding electrode when it consists of ____.

    (a) at least 20 ft of ½ in. or larger steel reinforcing bars or rods
    (b) at least 20 ft of bare copper conductor of 4 AWG or larger
    (c) a or b
    (d) none of these

55. A ground ring encircling the building or structure can be used as a grounding electrode when ____.

    (a) the ring is in direct contact with the earth
    (b) the ring consists of at least 20 ft of bare copper conductor
    (c) the bare copper conductor is not smaller than 2 AWG
    (d) all of these

56. Grounding electrodes of the rod type less than ____ in. in diameter shall be listed.

    (a) ½ in.
    (b) ⅝ in.
    (c) ¾ in.
    (d) none of these

57. Local metal underground systems or structures such as ____ are permitted to serve as grounding electrodes.

    (a) piping systems
    (b) underground tanks
    (c) underground metal well casings that are not bonded to a metal water pipe
    (d) all of these

58. Where the resistance-to-ground of 25 ohms or less is not achieved for a single rod electrode, ____.

    (a) other means besides electrodes shall be used in order to provide grounding
    (b) the single rod electrode shall be supplemented by one additional electrode
    (c) no additional electrodes are required
    (d) none of these

59. Where a metal underground water pipe is used as a grounding electrode, the continuity of the grounding path or the bonding connection to interior piping shall not rely on ____ and similar equipment.

    (a) bonding jumpers
    (b) water meters or filtering devices
    (c) grounding clamps
    (d) all of these

60. Where the supplemental electrode is a rod, that portion of the bonding jumper that is the sole connection to the supplemental grounding electrode shall not be required to be larger than ____ AWG copper.

    (a) 8
    (b) 6
    (c) 4
    (d) 1

61. When a ground ring is used as a grounding electrode, it shall be buried at a depth below the earth's surface of not less than _____.

    (a) 18 in.
    (b) 24 in.
    (c) 30 in.
    (d) 8 ft

62. Buildings or structures supplied by multiple services or feeders must use the same _____ to ground enclosures and equipment in or on that building.

    (a) service
    (b) disconnect
    (c) grounding electrode system
    (d) any of these

63. Where used outside, aluminum or copper-clad aluminum grounding electrode conductors shall not be terminated within _____ of the earth.

    (a) 6 in.
    (b) 12 in.
    (c) 15 in.
    (d) 18 in.

64. Bare aluminum or copper-clad aluminum grounding electrode conductors shall not be used where in direct contact with _____ or where subject to corrosive conditions.

    (a) masonry or the earth
    (b) bare copper conductors
    (c) wooden framing members
    (d) all of these

65. Grounding electrode conductors shall be installed in one continuous length without a splice or joint, unless spliced by _____.

    (a) connecting together sections of a busbar
    (b) irreversible compression-type connectors listed as grounding and bonding equipment
    (c) the exothermic welding process
    (d) any of these

66. Ferrous metal raceways and enclosures for grounding electrode conductors shall be electrically continuous from the point of attachment to cabinets or equipment to the grounding electrode.

    (a) True
    (b) False

67. A service consisting of 12 AWG service-entrance conductors requires a grounding electrode conductor sized no less than _____.

    (a) 10 AWG
    (b) 8 AWG
    (c) 6 AWG
    (d) 4 AWG

68. The largest size grounding electrode conductor required is _____ copper.

    (a) 6 AWG
    (b) 1/0 AWG
    (c) 3/0 AWG
    (d) 250 kcmil

69. In an ac system, the size of the grounding electrode conductor to a concrete-encased electrode shall not be required to be larger than a(n) _____ copper conductor.

    (a) 10 AWG
    (b) 8 AWG
    (c) 6 AWG
    (d) 4 AWG

70. The connection of the grounding electrode conductor to a buried grounding electrode (driven ground rod) shall be made with a listed terminal device that is accessible.

    (a) True
    (b) False

71. Exothermic or irreversible compression connections, together with the mechanical means used to attach to fireproofed structural metal, shall not be required to be accessible.

    (a) True
    (b) False

72. Interior metal water piping located not more than _____ from the point of entrance to the building shall be permitted to be used as a conductor to interconnect electrodes that are part of the grounding electrode system.

    (a) 2 ft
    (b) 4 ft
    (c) 5 ft
    (d) 6 ft

73. Where conditions of maintenance and supervision ensure only qualified persons service the installation in _____ buildings, the entire length of the metal water piping system can be used for grounding purposes, provided the entire length, other than short sections passing through walls, floors, or ceilings, is exposed.

    (a) industrial
    (b) institutional
    (c) commercial
    (d) all of these

74. The grounding conductor connection to the grounding electrode shall be made by _____.

    (a) listed lugs
    (b) exothermic welding
    (c) listed pressure connectors
    (d) any of these

75. The normally noncurrent-carrying metal parts of service equipment, such as _____, shall be bonded together.

    (a) service raceways or service cable armor
    (b) service equipment enclosures containing service conductors, including meter fittings, boxes, or the like, interposed in the service raceway or armor
    (c) service cable trays
    (d) all of these

76. Electrical continuity at service equipment, service raceways, and service conductor enclosures shall be ensured by _____.

    (a) bonding equipment to the grounded service conductor
    (b) connections utilizing threaded couplings on enclosures, if made up wrenchtight
    (c) other listed bonding devices, such as bonding-type locknuts, bushings, or bushings with bonding jumpers
    (d) any of these

77. Service raceways threaded into metal service equipment such as bosses (hubs) are considered to be effectively _____ to the service metal enclosure.

    (a) attached
    (b) bonded
    (c) grounded
    (d) none of these

78. A means external to enclosures for connecting intersystem _____ conductors shall be provided at service equipment or metering equipment enclosure and disconnecting means of buildings or structures supplied by a feeder.

    (a) bonding
    (b) ungrounded
    (c) secondary
    (d) a and b

79. At existing buildings or structures, an intersystem bonding termination is not required if other acceptable means of bonding exits. An external accessible means for bonding communications systems together can be by the use of a(n) _____.

    (a) nonflexible metallic raceway
    (b) exposed grounding electrode conductor
    (c) connection to a grounded raceway or equipment approved by the authority having jurisdiction
    (d) any of these

80. For circuits over 250 volts-to-ground, electrical continuity can be maintained between a box or enclosure where no oversized, concentric or eccentric knockouts are encountered, and a metal conduit by _____.

    (a) threadless fittings for cables with metal sheaths
    (b) double locknuts on threaded conduit (one inside and one outside the box or enclosure)
    (c) fittings that have shoulders that seat firmly against the box with a locknut on the inside or listed fittings
    (d) all of these

81. Equipment bonding jumpers on the supply side of the service shall be no smaller than the sizes shown in _____.

    (a) Table 250.102(C)(1)
    (b) Table 250.122
    (c) Table 310.15(B)(16)
    (d) Table 310.15(B)(6)

82. What is the minimum size copper equipment bonding jumper for a 40A rated circuit?

    (a) 14 AWG
    (b) 12 AWG
    (c) 10 AWG
    (d) 8 AWG

83. An equipment bonding jumper can be installed on the outside of a raceway, providing the length of the equipment bonding jumper is not more than _____ and the equipment bonding jumper is routed with the raceway.

    (a) 12 in.
    (b) 24 in.
    (c) 36 in.
    (d) 72 in.

84. Metal water piping system(s) shall be bonded to the _____.

    (a) grounded conductor at the service
    (b) service equipment enclosure
    (c) equipment grounding bar or bus at any panelboard within a single occupancy building
    (d) a or b

85. The bonding jumper used to bond the metal water piping system shall be sized in accordance with _____.

    (a) Table 250.66
    (b) Table 250.122
    (c) Table 310.15(B)(16)
    (d) Table 310.15(B)(6)

86. Electrical equipment permanently mounted on skids, and the skids themselves, shall be connected to the equipment grounding conductor sized as required by _____.

    (a) 250.50
    (b) 250.66
    (c) 250.122
    (d) 310.15

87. Which of the following appliances installed in residential occupancies need not be connected to an equipment grounding conductor?

    (a) toaster
    (b) aquarium
    (c) dishwasher
    (d) refrigerator

88. The armor of Type AC cable containing an aluminum bonding strip is recognized by the *NEC* as an equipment grounding conductor.

    (a) True
    (b) False

89. Type MC cable provides an effective ground-fault current path and is recognized by the *NEC* as an equipment grounding conductor when _____.

    (a) it contains an insulated or uninsulated equipment grounding conductor in compliance with 250.118(1)
    (b) the combined metallic sheath and uninsulated equipment grounding/bonding conductor of interlocked metal tape–type MC cable is listed and identified as an equipment grounding conductor
    (c) only when it is hospital grade Type MC cable
    (d) a or b

90. An equipment grounding conductor shall be identified by _____.

    (a) a continuous outer finish that is green
    (b) being bare
    (c) a continuous outer finish that is green with one or more yellow stripes
    (d) any of these

91. A wire-type equipment grounding conductor is permitted to be used as a grounding electrode conductor if it meets all the requirements of Parts II, III, and IV of Article 250.

    (a) True
    (b) False

92. Where conductors are run in parallel in multiple raceways or cables and include an EGC of the wire type, the equipment grounding conductor must be installed in parallel in each raceway or cable, sized in compliance with 250.122.

    (a) True
    (b) False

93. A grounded circuit conductor is permitted to ground noncurrent-carrying metal parts of equipment, raceways, and other enclosures on the supply side or within the enclosure of the ac service-disconnecting means.

    (a) True
    (b) False

94. A(n) _____ shall be used to connect the grounding terminal of a grounding-type receptacle to a grounded box.

    (a) equipment bonding jumper
    (b) grounded conductor jumper
    (c) a or b
    (d) a and b

95. The arrangement of grounding connections shall be such that the disconnection or the removal of a receptacle, luminaire, or other device fed from the box does not interrupt the grounding continuity.

    (a) True
    (b) False

96. A connection between equipment grounding conductors and a metal box shall be by _____.

    (a) a grounding screw used for no other purpose
    (b) equipment listed for grounding
    (c) a listed grounding device
    (d) any of these

97. Article 285 covers surge protective devices rated over 1 kV.

    (a) True
    (b) False

98. The conductors used to connect the surge protective device to the line or bus and to ground shall not be any longer than _____ and shall avoid unnecessary bends.

    (a) 6 in.
    (b) 12 in.
    (c) 18 in.
    (d) necessary

99. A Type 2 surge protective device is permitted to be connected on either the line or load side of the service equipment.

    (a) True
    (b) False

100. Type 3 surge protective devices can be installed on the load side of a branch-circuit overcurrent device up to the equipment served. If _____, the Type 3 SPD connection must be a minimum 30 ft of conductor distance from the service or separately derived system disconnect.

    (a) voltage drop is excessive
    (b) installed in a metal raceway or cable
    (c) included in the manufacturer's instructions
    (d) b and c

RANDOM ORDER
[ARTICLES 90–285]

Please use the 2014 *Code* book to answer the following questions.

1. A 15A or 20A, 125V receptacle outlet shall be located within 25 ft of heating, air-conditioning, and refrigeration equipment for _____ occupancies.

   (a) dwelling
   (b) commercial
   (c) industrial
   (d) all of these

2. Foyers with an area greater than _____ sq ft must have a receptacle located in each wall space 3 ft or more in width unbroken by doorways, windows next to doors that extend to the floor, and similar openings.

   (a) 40
   (b) 60
   (c) 80
   (d) 100

3. The *NEC* does not apply to electric utility-owned wiring and equipment _____.

   (a) installed by an electrical contractor
   (b) installed on public property
   (c) consisting of service drops or service laterals
   (d) in a utility office building

4. Wiring shall be installed so that the completed system will be free from _____, other than as required or permitted elsewhere in the *Code*.

   (a) short circuits
   (b) ground faults
   (c) connections to the earth
   (d) all of these

5. An arc-fault circuit interrupter is a device intended to de-energize the circuit when it recognizes characteristics unique to _____.

   (a) overcurrent
   (b) arcing
   (c) a ground fault
   (d) harmonic fundamental

6. The service disconnecting means shall plainly indicate whether it is in the _____ position.

   (a) open or closed
   (b) tripped
   (c) up or down
   (d) correct

7. To guard live parts operating at 50V must be guarded by being _____.

    (a) located in a room accessible only to qualified persons
    (b) located on a balcony accessible only to qualified persons
    (c) elevated 8 ft or more above the floor or other working surface for 50V to 300V
    (d) any of these

8. There shall be no reduction in the size of the neutral or grounded conductor on _____ loads supplied from a 4-wire, wye-connected, three-phase system.

    (a) dwelling unit
    (b) hospital
    (c) nonlinear
    (d) motel

9. Overhead service conductors to a building shall maintain a vertical clearance of final spans above, or within, _____ ft measured horizontally from the platforms, projections, or surfaces from which they might be reached.

    (a) 3
    (b) 6
    (c) 8
    (d) 10

10. Surge protective devices shall be listed.

    (a) True
    (b) False

11. In dwelling units, lighting outlets can be controlled by occupancy sensors where equipped with a _____ that will allow the sensor to function as a wall switch.

    (a) manual override
    (b) photo cell
    (c) sensor
    (d) none of these

12. For a single separately derived system, the grounding electrode conductor connects the grounded conductor of the derived system to the grounding electrode at the same point on the separately derived system where the _____ is connected.

    (a) metering equipment
    (b) transfer switch
    (c) system bonding jumper
    (d) largest circuit breaker

13. The *NEC* defines a "_____" as all circuit conductors between the service equipment, the source of a separately derived system, or other power supply source and the final branch-circuit overcurrent device.

    (a) service
    (b) feeder
    (c) branch circuit
    (d) all of these

14. Where more than one concrete-encased electrode is present at a building or structure, it shall be permitted to connect to only one of them.

    (a) True
    (b) False

15. The size of the grounding electrode conductor for a building or structure supplied by a feeder shall not be smaller than that identified in _____, based on the largest ungrounded supply conductor.

    (a) 250.66
    (b) 250.122
    (c) Table 310.15(B)(16)
    (d) none of these

16. The *Code* covers underground mine installations and self-propelled mobile surface mining machinery and its attendant electrical trailing cable.

    (a) True
    (b) False

17. For a grounded system, an unspliced _____ shall be used to connect the equipment grounding conductor(s) and the service disconnecting means to the grounded conductor of the system within the enclosure for each service disconnect.

    (a) grounding electrode
    (b) main bonding jumper
    (c) busbar
    (d) insulated copper conductor

18. _____ shall not be used as grounding electrodes.

    (a) Metal underground gas piping systems
    (b) Aluminum
    (c) Metal well casings
    (d) a and b

19. Additional services shall be permitted for a single building or other structure sufficiently large to make two or more services necessary if permitted by _____.

    (a) the registered design professional
    (b) special permission
    (c) the engineer of record
    (d) master electricians

20. Each service disconnecting means shall be suitable for _____.

    (a) hazardous (classified) locations
    (b) wet locations
    (c) dry locations
    (d) the prevailing conditions

21. For a circuit to be considered a multiwire branch circuit, it shall have _____.

    (a) two or more ungrounded conductors with a voltage potential between them
    (b) a grounded conductor having equal voltage potential between it and each ungrounded conductor of the circuit
    (c) a grounded conductor connected to the neutral or grounded terminal of the system
    (d) all of these

22. The common grounding electrode conductor installed for multiple separately derived systems shall not be smaller than _____ copper when using a wire-type conductor.

    (a) 1/0 AWG
    (b) 2/0 AWG
    (c) 3/0 AWG
    (d) 4/0 AWG

23. Working space distances for enclosed live parts shall be measured from the _____ of equipment or apparatus, if the live parts are enclosed.

    (a) enclosure
    (b) opening
    (c) a or b
    (d) none of these

24. The disconnecting means for a building supplied by a feeder shall be installed at a(n) _____ location.

    (a) accessible
    (b) readily accessible
    (c) outdoor
    (d) indoor

25. The *Code* requires the installation of an equipment grounding conductor of the wire type in _____.

    (a) rigid metal conduit (RMC)
    (b) intermediate metal conduit (IMC)
    (c) electrical metallic tubing (EMT)
    (d) listed flexible metal conduit over 6 ft in length

26. Handles or levers of circuit breakers, and similar parts that may move suddenly in such a way that persons in the vicinity are likely to be injured by being struck by them, shall be _____.

    (a) guarded
    (b) isolated
    (c) a and b
    (d) a or b

27. Supplementary overcurrent protection ____.

    (a) shall not be used in luminaires
    (b) may be used as a substitute for a branch-circuit overcurrent device
    (c) may be used to protect internal circuits of equipment
    (d) shall be readily accessible

28. A separate portion of a raceway system that provides access through a removable cover(s) to the interior of the system, defines the term ____.

    (a) junction box
    (b) accessible raceway
    (c) conduit body
    (d) cutout box

29. Outline lighting may include an arrangement of ____ to outline or call attention to the shape of a building.

    (a) incandescent lamps
    (b) electric-discharge lighting
    (c) electrically powered light sources
    (d) any of these

30. When bonding enclosures, metal raceways, frames, and fittings, any nonconductive paint, enamel, or similar coating shall be removed at ____.

    (a) contact surfaces
    (b) threads
    (c) contact points
    (d) all of these

31. The grounding electrode conductor for a single separately derived system is used to connect the grounded conductor of the derived system to the grounding electrode.

    (a) True
    (b) False

32. Receptacles installed behind a bed in the guest rooms in hotels and motels shall be located to prevent the bed from contacting an attachment plug, or the receptacle shall be provided with a suitable guard.

    (a) True
    (b) False

33. When an underground metal water piping system is used as a grounding electrode, bonding shall be provided around insulated joints and around any equipment that is likely to be disconnected for repairs or replacement.

    (a) True
    (b) False

34. A branch circuit that supplies only one utilization equipment is a(n) ____ branch circuit.

    (a) individual
    (b) general-purpose
    (c) isolated
    (d) special-purpose

35. Overcurrent devices aren't permitted to be located in the bathrooms of ____.

    (a) dwelling units
    (b) dormitories
    (c) guest rooms or guest suites of hotels or motels
    (d) all of these

36. All 15A and 20A, 125V receptacles located outdoors or on rooftops in locations other than dwelling units must be GFCI protected except for a receptacle that's supplied by a branch circuit dedicated to ____ if the receptacle isn't readily accessible and the equipment or receptacle has ground-fault protection of equipment (GFPE) [426.28 and 427.22].

    (a) electric snow-melting or deicing equipment
    (b) pipeline and vessel heating equipment
    (c) holiday decorative lighting
    (d) a or b

37. Alternating-current systems of 50V to 1,000V that supply premises wiring systems shall be grounded where supplied by a three-phase, 4-wire, delta-connected system in which the midpoint of one phase winding is used as a circuit conductor.

    (a) True
    (b) False

38. For a separate building or structure supplied by a feeder or branch circuit, the grounded conductor can serve as the ground-fault return path for the building/structure disconnecting means for existing installations made in compliance with previous editions of the *Code* as long as the installation continues to meet the condition(s) that _____.

    (a) there are no continuous metallic paths between buildings and structures
    (b) ground-fault protection of equipment isn't installed on the supply side of the feeder
    (c) the neutral conductor is sized no smaller than the larger required by 220.61 or 250.122
    (d) all of these

39. Where a lighting outlet(s) is installed for interior stairways, there shall be a wall switch at each floor level and each landing level that includes an entryway where the stairway between floor levels has six risers or more unless remote, central, or automatic control is used.

    (a) True
    (b) False

40. Any current in excess of the rated current of equipment or the ampacity of a conductor is called "_____."

    (a) trip current
    (b) fault current
    (c) overcurrent
    (d) a short circuit

41. If a set of 120/240V overhead service conductors terminate at a through-the-roof raceway or approved support, with less than 6 ft of these conductors passing over the roof overhang, the minimum clearance above the roof for these service conductors shall be _____.

    (a) 12 in.
    (b) 18 in.
    (c) 2 ft
    (d) 5 ft

42. Flexible cord used in listed extension cord sets shall be considered protected against overcurrent when used _____.

    (a) in indoor installations
    (b) in unclassified locations
    (c) within the extension cord's listing requirements
    (d) within 50 ft of the branch-circuit panelboard

43. Circuit breakers used to switch high-intensity discharge lighting circuits shall be listed and marked as _____.

    (a) SWD
    (b) HID
    (c) a or b
    (d) a and b

44. Where two or more branch circuits supply devices or equipment on the same yoke or mounting strap, a means to disconnect simultaneously all ungrounded conductors that supply those devices or equipment shall be provided at the _____.

    (a) point where the branch circuit originates
    (b) location of the device or equipment
    (c) point where the feeder originates
    (d) none of these

45. Plug fuses of the Edison-base type shall have a maximum rating of _____.

    (a) 20A
    (b) 30A
    (c) 40A
    (d) 50A

46. The maximum unbalanced feeder load for household electric ranges, wall-mounted ovens, and counter-mounted cooking units shall be considered as _____ percent of the load on the ungrounded conductors.

    (a) 50
    (b) 70
    (c) 85
    (d) 115

47. Equipment grounding conductors, grounding electrode conductors, and bonding jumpers shall be connected by _____.

    (a) listed pressure connectors
    (b) terminal bars
    (c) exothermic welding
    (d) any of these

48. The _____ of any system is the ratio of the maximum demand of a system, or part of a system, to the total connected load of a system.

    (a) load
    (b) demand factor
    (c) minimum load
    (d) calculated factor

49. A conductor encased within material of composition or thickness that is not recognized by the *NEC* as electrical insulation is considered _____.

    (a) noninsulating
    (b) bare
    (c) covered
    (d) protected

50. Equipment bonding jumpers shall be of copper or other corrosion-resistant material.

    (a) True
    (b) False

PRACTICE QUIZ 7

STRAIGHT ORDER [ARTICLES 300–324]

Please use the 2014 *Code* book to answer the following questions.

1. All conductors of the same circuit, including the grounded and equipment grounding conductors, shall be contained within the same _____, unless otherwise permitted elsewhere in the *Code*.

   (a) raceway
   (b) cable
   (c) trench
   (d) all of these

2. Conductors of ac and dc circuits, rated 1,000V or less, shall be permitted to occupy the same _____ provided that all conductors have an insulation rating equal to the maximum voltage applied to any conductor.

   (a) enclosure
   (b) cable
   (c) raceway
   (d) any of these

3. Where Type NM cable passes through factory or field openings in metal members, it shall be protected by _____ bushings or _____ grommets that cover metal edges.

   (a) approved
   (b) identified
   (c) listed
   (d) none of these

4. Where cables and nonmetallic raceways are installed parallel to framing members, the nearest outside surface of the cable or raceway shall be _____ the nearest edge of the framing member where nails or screws are likely to penetrate.

   (a) not less than 1¼ in. from
   (b) immediately adjacent to
   (c) not less than ⅟₁₆ in. from
   (d) 90° away from

5. A cable, raceway, or box installed under metal-corrugated sheet roof decking shall be supported so the top of the cable, raceway, or box is not less than _____ from the lowest surface of the roof decking to the top of the cable, raceway, or box.

   (a) ½ in.
   (b) 1 in.
   (c) 1½ in.
   (d) 2 in.

6. When installing PVC conduit underground without concrete cover, there shall be a minimum of _____ in. of cover.

   (a) 6
   (b) 12
   (c) 18
   (d) 22

7. Type UF cable used with a 24V landscape lighting system can have a minimum cover of _____ in.

    (a) 6
    (b) 12
    (c) 18
    (d) 24

8. The interior of underground raceways shall be considered a _____ location.

    (a) wet
    (b) dry
    (c) damp
    (d) corrosive

9. Type MC Cable listed for _____ is permitted to be installed underground under a building without installation in a raceway.

    (a) direct burial
    (b) damp and wet locations
    (c) rough service
    (d) b and c

10. Direct-buried service conductors that are not encased in concrete and that are buried 18 in. or more below grade shall have their location identified by a warning ribbon placed in the trench at least _____ in. above the underground installation.

    (a) 6
    (b) 10
    (c) 12
    (d) 18

11. Backfill used for underground wiring shall not _____.

    (a) damage the wiring method
    (b) prevent compaction of the fill
    (c) contribute to the corrosion of the raceway
    (d) all of these

12. Each direct-buried single conductor cable must be located _____ in the trench to the other single conductor cables in the same parallel set of conductors, including equipment grounding conductors.

    (a) perpendicular
    (b) bundled together
    (c) in close proximity
    (d) spaced apart

13. Direct-buried conductors, cables, or raceways, which are subject to movement by settlement or frost, shall be arranged to prevent damage to the _____ or to equipment connected to the raceways.

    (a) siding of the building mounted on
    (b) landscaping around the cable or raceway
    (c) enclosed conductors
    (d) expansion fitting

14. Cables or raceways installed using directional boring equipment shall be _____ for this purpose.

    (a) marked
    (b) listed
    (c) labeled
    (d) approved

15. Raceways, cable trays, cablebus, auxiliary gutters, cable armor, boxes, cable sheathing, cabinets, elbows, couplings, fittings, supports, and support hardware shall be of materials suitable for _____.

    (a) corrosive locations
    (b) wet locations
    (c) the environment in which they are to be installed
    (d) none of these

16. Where corrosion protection is necessary for ferrous metal equipment and the conduit is threaded in the field, the threads shall be coated with a(n) _____ electrically conductive, corrosion-resistant compound.

    (a) marked
    (b) listed
    (c) labeled
    (d) approved

17. Which of the following metal parts shall be protected from corrosion?

    (a) Ferrous metal raceways.
    (b) Ferrous metal elbows.
    (c) Ferrous boxes.
    (d) all of these

18. Ferrous metal raceways, boxes, fittings, supports, and support hardware can be installed in concrete or in direct contact with the earth or other areas subject to severe corrosive influences, where _____ approved for the conditions.

    (a) the soil is
    (b) made of material
    (c) the qualified installer is
    (d) none of these

19. Aluminum raceways, cable trays, cablebus, auxiliary gutters, cable armor, boxes, cable sheathing, cabinets, elbows, couplings, nipples, fittings, supports, and support hardware _____ shall be provided with supplementary corrosion protection.

    (a) embedded or encased in concrete
    (b) in direct contact with the earth
    (c) likely to become energized
    (d) a or b

20. Where nonmetallic wiring methods are subject to exposure to chemical solvents or vapors, they shall be inherently resistant to chemicals based upon their being _____.

    (a) listed for the chemical
    (b) identified for the chemical
    (c) a and b
    (d) a or b

21. An exposed wiring system for indoor wet locations where walls are frequently washed shall be mounted so that there is at least a _____ between the mounting surface and the electrical equipment.

    (a) ¼ in. airspace
    (b) separation by insulated bushings
    (c) separation by noncombustible tubing
    (d) none of these

22. Raceways shall be provided with expansion fittings where necessary to compensate for thermal expansion and contraction.

    (a) True
    (b) False

23. Raceways, cable assemblies, boxes, cabinets, and fittings shall be securely fastened in place.

    (a) True
    (b) False

24. Where independent support wires of a ceiling assembly are used to support raceways, cable assemblies, or boxes above a ceiling, they shall be secured at _____ ends.

    (a) one
    (b) both
    (c) a or b
    (d) none of these

25. The independent support wires for supporting electrical wiring methods in a fire-rated ceiling assembly shall be distinguishable from fire-rated suspended-ceiling framing support wires by _____.

    (a) color
    (b) tagging
    (c) other effective means
    (d) any of these

26. Metal or nonmetallic raceways, cable armors, and cable sheaths _____ between cabinets, boxes, fittings, or other enclosures or outlets.

    (a) can be attached with electrical tape
    (b) are allowed gaps for expansion
    (c) shall be continuous
    (d) none of these

27. Conductors in raceways shall be _____ between outlets, boxes, devices, and so forth.

    (a) continuous
    (b) installed
    (c) copper
    (d) in conduit

28. When the opening to an outlet, junction, or switch point is less than 8 in. in any dimension, each conductor shall be long enough to extend at least _____ in. outside the opening of the enclosure.

    (a) 0
    (b) 3
    (c) 6
    (d) 12

29. Fittings and connectors shall be used only with the specific wiring methods for which they are designed and listed.

    (a) True
    (b) False

30. A bushing shall be permitted in lieu of a box or terminal where the conductors emerge from a raceway and enter or terminate at equipment such as open switchboards, unenclosed control equipment, or similar equipment.

    (a) True
    (b) False

31. The number and size of conductors permitted in a raceway is limited to _____.

    (a) permit heat to dissipate
    (b) prevent damage to insulation during installation
    (c) prevent damage to insulation during removal of conductors
    (d) all of these

32. Short sections of raceways used for _____ shall not be required to be installed complete between outlet, junction, or splicing points.

    (a) meter to service enclosure connection
    (b) protection of cables from physical damage
    (c) nipples
    (d) separately derived systems

33. Metal raceways shall not be _____ by welding to the raceway.

    (a) supported
    (b) terminated
    (c) connected
    (d) all of these

34. Conductors in ferrous metal raceways and enclosures shall be arranged so as to avoid heating the surrounding ferrous metal by alternating-current induction. To accomplish this, the _____ conductor(s) shall be grouped together.

    (a) phase
    (b) grounded
    (c) equipment grounding
    (d) all of these

35. _____ is a nonferrous, nonmagnetic metal that has no heating due to hysteresis heating.

    (a) Steel
    (b) Iron
    (c) Aluminum
    (d) all of these

36. Openings around electrical penetrations into or through fire-resistant-rated walls, partitions, floors, or ceilings shall _____ to maintain the fire-resistance rating.

    (a) be documented
    (b) not be permitted
    (c) be firestopped using approved methods
    (d) be enlarged

37. Equipment and devices shall only be permitted within ducts or plenum chambers specifically fabricated to transport environmental air if necessary for their direct action upon, or sensing of, the _____.

    (a) contained air
    (b) air quality
    (c) air temperature
    (d) none of these

38. _____ shall be permitted to support the wiring methods and equipment permitted to be used in other spaces used for environmental air (plenum).

    (a) Metal cable tray systems
    (b) Nonmetallic wireways
    (c) PVC conduit
    (d) Surface nonmetallic raceways

39. Wiring methods and equipment installed behind suspended-ceiling panels shall be arranged and secured to allow access to the electrical equipment.

    (a) True
    (b) False

40. Insulated conductors used in wet locations shall be _____.

    (a) moisture-impervious metal-sheathed
    (b) MTW, RHW, RHW-2, TW, THW, THW-2, THHW, THWN, THWN-2, XHHW, XHHW-2, or ZW
    (c) listed for wet locations
    (d) any of these

41. Parallel conductors shall have the same _____.

    (a) length
    (b) material
    (c) size in circular mil area
    (d) all of these

42. No conductor shall be used where its operating temperature exceeds that designated for the type of insulated conductor involved.

    (a) True
    (b) False

43. The ampacities listed in 310.15 do not take _____ into consideration.

    (a) continuous loads
    (b) voltage drop
    (c) insulation
    (d) wet locations

44. Where six current-carrying conductors are run in the same conduit or cable, the ampacity of each conductor shall be adjusted by a factor of _____ percent.

    (a) 40
    (b) 60
    (c) 80
    (d) 90

45. The ampacity adjustment factors of Table 310.15(B)(3)(a) do not apply to Type AC or Type MC cable without an overall outer jacket, if which of the following conditions are met?

    (a) Each cable has not more than three current-carrying conductors.
    (b) The conductors are 12 AWG copper.
    (c) No more than 20 current-carrying conductors are installed without maintaining spacing.
    (d) all of these

46. Where conductors are installed in raceways or cables exposed to direct sunlight on or above rooftops, the ambient temperature shall be increased by _____ where the conduits are less than ½ in. from the rooftop.

    (a) 30°F
    (b) 40°F
    (c) 50°F
    (d) 60°F

47. THW insulation has a _____ rating when installed within electric-discharge lighting equipment, such as through fluorescent luminaires.

    (a) 60°C
    (b) 75°C
    (c) 90°C
    (d) 105°C

48. Which conductor type has an insulation temperature rating of 90°C?

    (a) THWN
    (b) RHW
    (c) THHN
    (d) TW

49. Letters used to designate the number of conductors within a cable are _____.

    (a) D—Two insulated conductors laid parallel
    (b) M—Two or more insulated conductors twisted spirally
    (c) T—Two or more insulated conductors twisted in parallel
    (d) a and b

50. Cabinets, cutout boxes, and meter socket enclosures installed in wet locations shall be _____.

    (a) waterproof
    (b) raintight
    (c) weatherproof
    (d) watertight

51. Where raceways or cables enter above the level of uninsulated live parts of cabinets, cutout boxes, and meter socket enclosures in a wet location, a(n) _____ shall be used.

    (a) fitting listed for wet locations
    (b) explosionproof seal
    (c) fitting listed for damp locations
    (d) insulated fitting

52. Noncombustible surfaces that are broken or incomplete shall be repaired so there will be no gaps or open spaces greater than _____ in. at the edge of a cabinet or cutout box employing a flush-type cover.

    (a) $\frac{1}{32}$
    (b) $\frac{1}{16}$
    (c) $\frac{1}{8}$
    (d) $\frac{1}{4}$

53. Each cable entering a cutout box _____.

    (a) shall be secured to the cutout box
    (b) can be sleeved through a chase
    (c) shall have a maximum of two cables per connector
    (d) all of these

54. Cabinets, cutout boxes, and meter socket enclosures can be used for conductors feeding through, spliced, or tapping off to other enclosures, switches, or overcurrent devices where _____.

    (a) the total area of the conductors at any cross section doesn't exceed 40 percent of the cross-sectional area of the space
    (b) the total area of conductors, splices, and taps installed at any cross section doesn't exceed 75 percent of the cross-sectional area of that space
    (c) a warning label on the enclosure identifies the closest disconnecting means for any feed-through conductors
    (d) all of these

55. Boxes, conduit bodies, and fittings installed in wet locations shall be required to be listed for use in wet locations.

    (a) True
    (b) False

56. The total volume occupied by two internal cable clamps, six 12 AWG conductors, and a single-pole switch is _____ cu in.

    (a) 2.00
    (b) 4.50
    (c) 14.50
    (d) 20.25

57. When counting the number of conductors in a box, a conductor running through the box with an unbroken loop or coil not less than twice the minimum length required for free conductors shall be counted as _____ conductor(s).

    (a) one
    (b) two
    (c) three
    (d) four

58. Equipment grounding conductor(s), and not more than _____ fixture wires smaller than 14 AWG shall be omitted from the calculations where they enter the box from a domed luminaire or similar canopy and terminate within that box.

    (a) one
    (b) two
    (c) three
    (d) four

59. Where one or more internal cable clamps are present in the box, a single volume allowance in accordance with Table 314.16(b) shall be made based on the largest conductor present in the box.

    (a) True
    (b) False

60. Where a luminaire stud or hickey is present in the box, a _____ volume allowance in accordance with Table 314.16(b) shall be made for each type of fitting, based on the largest conductor present in the box.

(a) single
(b) double
(c) single allowance for each gang
(d) none of these

61. For the purposes of determining box fill, each device or utilization equipment in the box which is wider than a single device box counts as two conductors for each _____ required for the mounting.

(a) inch
(b) kilometer
(c) gang
(d) box

62. Where one or more equipment grounding conductors enter a box, a _____ volume allowance in accordance with Table 314.16(b) shall be made based on the largest equipment grounding conductor.

(a) single
(b) double
(c) triple
(d) none of these

63. Conduit bodies that are durably and legibly marked by the manufacturer with their volume can contain splices, taps, or devices.

(a) True
(b) False

64. Short-radius conduit bodies such as capped elbows, and service-entrance elbows that enclose conductors 6 AWG or smaller shall not contain _____.

(a) splices
(b) taps
(c) devices
(d) any of these

65. In noncombustible walls or ceilings, the front edge of a box, plaster ring, extension ring, or listed extender employing a flush-type cover, shall be set back not more than _____ in. from the finished surface.

(a) ⅛
(b) ¼
(c) ⅜
(d) ½

66. Surface extensions shall be made by mounting and mechanically securing an extension ring over the box, unless otherwise permitted.

(a) True
(b) False

67. A surface extension can be made from the cover of a box where the cover is designed so it is unlikely to fall off or be removed if its securing means becomes loose. The wiring method shall be _____ for an approved length that permits removal of the cover and provide access to the box interior, and arranged so that any grounding continuity is independent of the connection between the box and cover.

(a) solid
(b) flexible
(c) rigid
(d) cord

68. Surface-mounted outlet boxes shall be _____.

(a) rigidly and securely fastened in place
(b) supported by cables that protrude from the box
(c) supported by cable entries from the top and permitted to rest against the supporting surface
(d) none of these

69. _____ can be used to fasten boxes to a structural member using brackets on the outside of the enclosure.

(a) Nails
(b) Screws
(c) Bolts
(d) a and b

70. A wood brace used for supporting a box for structural mounting shall have a cross-section not less than nominal _____.

    (a) 1 in. x 2 in.
    (b) 2 in. x 2 in.
    (c) 2 in. x 3 in.
    (d) 2 in. x 4 in.

71. Outlet boxes can be secured to suspended-ceiling framing members by mechanical means such as _____, or by other means identified for the suspended-ceiling framing member(s).

    (a) bolts
    (b) screws
    (c) rivets
    (d) any of these

72. Two intermediate metal or rigid metal conduits threaded wrenchtight into an enclosure can be used to support an outlet box containing devices or luminaires, if each raceway is supported within _____ in. of the box.

    (a) 12
    (b) 18
    (c) 24
    (d) 36

73. In completed installations, each outlet box shall have a _____.

    (a) cover
    (b) faceplate
    (c) canopy
    (d) any of these

74. A vertically mounted luminaire weighing not more than _____ can be supported to a device box or plaster ring with no fewer than two No. 6 or larger screws.

    (a) 4 lb
    (b) 6 lb
    (c) 8 lb
    (d) 10 lb

75. Boxes used at luminaire or lampholder outlets in a ceiling shall be designed so that a luminaire or lampholder can be attached and the boxes shall be required to support a luminaire weighing a minimum of _____ lb.

    (a) 20
    (b) 30
    (c) 40
    (d) 50

76. A luminaire that weighs more than _____ lb can be supported by an outlet box that is listed and marked for the weight of the luminaire.

    (a) 20
    (b) 30
    (c) 40
    (d) 50

77. Floor boxes _____ specifically for the application shall be used for receptacles located in the floor.

    (a) identified
    (b) listed
    (c) approved
    (d) none of these

78. Listed outlet boxes to support ceiling-suspended fans that weigh more than _____ lb shall have the maximum allowable weight marked on the box.

    (a) 35
    (b) 50
    (c) 60
    (d) 70

79. Pull boxes or junction boxes with any dimension over _____ ft shall have all conductors cabled or racked in an approved manner.

    (a) 3
    (b) 6
    (c) 9
    (d) 12

80. Exposed live parts on the power distribution block are allowed when the junction box cover is removed.

    (a) True
    (b) False

81. Where the junction box contains a power distribution block, and it has conductors that don't terminate on the power distribution block(s), the through conductors must be arranged so the power distribution block terminals are _____ following installation.

    (a) unobstructed
    (b) above the through conductors
    (c) visible
    (d) labeled

82. Handhole enclosure covers shall have an identifying _____ that prominently identifies the function of the enclosure, such as "electric."

    (a) mark
    (b) logo
    (c) manual
    (d) a or b

83. For straight pulls, the length of a pull box shall not be less than _____ times the outside diameter, over the sheath, of the largest shielded or lead-covered conductor or cable entering the box on systems over 1,000V.

    (a) 12
    (b) 16
    (c) 24
    (d) 48

84. For angle or U-pulls, the distance between the shielded conductor entry (for systems over 1,000V, nominal) and the opposite wall of the box shall not be less than _____ times the outside diameter of the largest cable or conductor.

    (a) 12
    (b) 16
    (c) 24
    (d) 36

85. The distance between a shielded cable or conductor entry and its exit from the box shall not be less than _____ times the outside diameter of that cable or conductor on a system of over 1,000V.

    (a) 12
    (b) 16
    (c) 24
    (d) 36

86. Type AC cable shall be secured at intervals not exceeding 4½ ft and within _____ in. of every outlet box, cabinet, conduit body, or fitting.

    (a) 6
    (b) 8
    (c) 10
    (d) 12

87. Type AC cable installed horizontally through wooden or metal framing members is considered supported where support doesn't exceed _____ ft intervals.

    (a) 2
    (b) 3
    (c) 4½
    (d) 6

88. Type AC cable installed in thermal insulation shall have conductors that are rated at 90°C. The ampacity of the cable in this application shall not exceed that of a _____ rated conductor.

    (a) 60°C
    (b) 75°C
    (c) 90°C
    (d) none of these

89. Flat cable assemblies can supply tap devices for _____ loads.

    (a) lighting
    (b) small appliance
    (c) small power
    (d) any of these

90. Flat cable assemblies shall not be installed outdoors or in wet or damp locations unless _____ for the use.

    (a) special permission is granted
    (b) approved
    (c) identified
    (d) none of these

91. Extensions from flat cable assemblies shall be made by approved wiring methods, within the _____, installed at either end of the flat cable assembly runs.

    (a) end-caps
    (b) junction boxes
    (c) surface metal raceway
    (d) underfloor metal raceway

92. Flat cable assemblies shall consist of _____ conductors.

    (a) two
    (b) three
    (c) four
    (d) any of these

93. Type FCC systems shall be permitted for individual branch circuits.

    (a) True
    (b) False

94. General-purpose branch circuits wired with flat conductor cable shall not be rated more than _____.

    (a) 15A
    (b) 20A
    (c) 30A
    (d) 40A

95. Type FCC cable systems are permitted on wall surfaces in _____.

    (a) surface metal raceways
    (b) cable trays
    (c) busways
    (d) any of these

96. Use of Type FCC systems in damp locations is _____.

    (a) not permitted
    (b) permitted
    (c) permitted provided the system is encased in concrete
    (d) permitted by special permission only

97. No more than _____ layers of flat conductor cable can cross at any one point.

    (a) one
    (b) two
    (c) three
    (d) four

98. Bare Type FCC cable ends shall _____.

    (a) be sealed
    (b) be insulated
    (c) use listed insulating ends
    (d) all of these

99. Receptacles, receptacle housings, and self-contained devices used with flat conductor cable systems shall be _____.

    (a) rated a minimum of 20A
    (b) rated a minimum of 15A
    (c) identified for this use
    (d) none of these

100. Each Type FCC transition assembly shall incorporate means for _____.

    (a) facilitating the entry of the Type FCC cable into the assembly
    (b) connecting the Type FCC cable to the grounded conductors
    (c) electrically connecting the assembly to the metal cable shields and equipment grounding conductors
    (d) all of these

RANDOM ORDER
[ARTICLES 90–324]

Please use the 2014 *Code* book to answer the following questions.

1. In general, the minimum size conductor permitted for use in parallel installations is _____ AWG.

   (a) 10
   (b) 4
   (c) 1
   (d) 1/0

2. Where rock bottom is encountered when driving a ground rod at an angle up to 45 degrees, the electrode can be buried in a trench that is at least _____ deep.

   (a) 18 in.
   (b) 30 in.
   (c) 4 ft
   (d) 8 ft

3. The service conductors shall be connected to the service disconnecting means by _____ or other approved means.

   (a) pressure connectors
   (b) clamps
   (c) solder
   (d) a or b

4. The equipment grounding conductor shall not be required to be larger than the circuit conductors.

   (a) True
   (b) False

5. At least one wall switch-controlled lighting outlet must be installed in every habitable room and bathroom of a dwelling unit.

   (a) True
   (b) False

6. Where cables or nonmetallic raceways are installed through bored holes in joists, rafters, or wood members, holes shall be bored so that the edge of the hole is _____ the nearest edge of the wood member.

   (a) not less than 1¼ in. from
   (b) immediately adjacent to
   (c) not less than ¹⁄₁₆ in. from
   (d) 90° away from

7. Where direct-buried conductors and cables emerge from grade, they shall be protected by enclosures or raceways to a point at least _____ ft above finished grade.

   (a) 3
   (b) 6
   (c) 8
   (d) 10

8. For the purpose of determining the placement of receptacles in a dwelling unit kitchen, a(n) _____ countertop is measured from the connecting edge.

    (a) island
    (b) usable
    (c) peninsular
    (d) cooking

9. Alternating-current systems of 50V to 1,000V that supply premises wiring systems shall be grounded where the system is three-phase, 4-wire, wye connected with the neutral conductor used as a circuit conductor.

    (a) True
    (b) False

10. Grounding electrode conductors smaller than _____ shall be in rigid metal conduit, IMC, PVC conduit, electrical metallic tubing, or cable armor.

    (a) 10 AWG
    (b) 8 AWG
    (c) 6 AWG
    (d) 4 AWG

11. Overhead service conductors installed over roofs shall have a vertical clearance of _____ ft above the roof surface, unless a lesser distance is permitted by an exception.

    (a) 3
    (b) 8
    (c) 12
    (d) 15

12. THWN insulated conductors are rated _____.

    (a) 75°C
    (b) for wet locations
    (c) a and b
    (d) not enough information

13. Armored cable shall not be installed _____.

    (a) in damp or wet locations
    (b) where subject to physical damage
    (c) where exposed to corrosive conditions
    (d) all of these

14. The ground-fault protection system for service equipment shall be _____ when first installed on site.

    (a) a Class A device
    (b) identified
    (c) turned on
    (d) performance tested

15. Using the standard load calculation method, the feeder demand factor for five household clothes dryers is _____ percent.

    (a) 50
    (b) 70
    (c) 85
    (d) 100

16. The intersystem bonding termination shall _____.

    (a) be accessible for connection and inspection
    (b) consist of a set of terminals with the capacity for connection of not less than three intersystem bonding conductors
    (c) not interfere with opening the enclosure for a service, building/ structure disconnecting means, or metering equipment
    (d) all of these

17. Outside wiring shall not be installed beneath openings through which materials may be moved, and shall not be installed where they will obstruct entrance to these buildings' openings.

    (a) True
    (b) False

18. Where installed in raceways, conductors _____ AWG and larger shall be stranded.

    (a) 10
    (b) 8
    (c) 6
    (d) 4

19. Enclosures for overcurrent devices shall be mounted in a _____ position unless impracticable.

    (a) vertical
    (b) horizontal
    (c) vertical or horizontal
    (d) there are no requirements

20. Surface-type cabinets, cutout boxes, and meter socket enclosures in damp or wet locations shall be mounted so there is at least _____ in. airspace between the enclosure and the wall or supporting surface.

    (a) 1/16
    (b) 1/4
    (c) 1 1/4
    (d) 6

21. What size copper grounding electrode conductor is required for a service that has three sets of 600 kcmil copper conductors per phase?

    (a) 1 AWG
    (b) 1/0 AWG
    (c) 2/0 AWG
    (d) 3/0 AWG

22. The next higher standard rating overcurrent device above the ampacity of the ungrounded conductors being protected shall be permitted to be used, provided the _____.

    (a) conductors are not part of a branch circuit supplying more than one receptacle for cord-and-plug-connected portable loads
    (b) ampacity of the conductors doesn't correspond with the standard ampere rating of a fuse or circuit breaker
    (c) next higher standard rating selected doesn't exceed 800A
    (d) all of these

23. Where circuit conductors are spliced or terminated on equipment within a box, any equipment grounding conductors associated with those circuit conductors shall be connected to the box with devices suitable for the use.

    (a) True
    (b) False

24. The _____ of a circuit shall be selected and coordinated to permit the circuit protective devices to clear a fault without extensive damage to the electrical equipment of the circuit.

    (a) overcurrent devices
    (b) total circuit impedance
    (c) equipment short-circuit current ratings
    (d) all of these

25. Lightning protection system ground terminals _____ be bonded to the building or structure grounding electrode system.

    (a) shall
    (b) shall not
    (c) shall be permitted to
    (d) none of these

26. When bare conductors are installed with insulated conductors, their ampacities shall be limited to _____.

    (a) 60°C
    (b) 75°C
    (c) 90°C
    (d) the lowest temperature rating for any of the insulated conductors

27. Feeder and service loads for fixed electric space heating shall be calculated at _____ percent of the total connected load.

    (a) 80
    (b) 100
    (c) 125
    (d) 200

28. _____ is defined as the area between the top of direct-burial cable and the top surface of the finished grade.

    (a) Notch
    (b) Cover
    (c) Gap
    (d) none of these

29. Multiwire branch circuits shall _____.

    (a) supply only line-to-neutral loads
    (b) not be permitted in dwelling units
    (c) have their conductors originate from different panelboards
    (d) none of these

30. Flat cable assemblies shall not be installed _____.

    (a) where subject to corrosive vapors unless suitable for the application
    (b) in hoistways
    (c) in any hazardous (classified) location
    (d) all of these

31. The grounding of electrical systems, circuit conductors, surge arresters, surge-protective devices, and conductive normally noncurrent-carrying metal parts of equipment shall be installed and arranged in a manner that will prevent objectionable current.

    (a) True
    (b) False

32. If a set of 120/240V overhead feeder conductors terminates at a through-the-roof raceway or approved support, with less than 6 ft of these conductors passing over the roof overhang, the minimum clearance above the roof for these conductors is _____.

    (a) 12 in.
    (b) 18 in.
    (c) 2 ft
    (d) 5 ft

33. A system or circuit conductor that is intentionally grounded is called a(n) "_____."

    (a) grounding conductor
    (b) unidentified conductor
    (c) grounded conductor
    (d) grounding electrode conductor

34. Under the optional method for calculating a single-family dwelling service, general loads beyond the initial 10 kVA are assessed at a _____ percent demand factor.

    (a) 40
    (b) 50
    (c) 60
    (d) 75

35. An individual 20A branch circuit can supply a single dwelling unit bathroom for receptacle outlet(s) and other equipment within the same bathroom.

    (a) True
    (b) False

36. Armored cable used to connect recessed luminaires or equipment within an accessible ceiling can be unsecured for lengths up to _____ ft.

    (a) 2
    (b) 3
    (c) 4½
    (d) 6

37. When Type AC cable is run across the top of a floor joist in an attic without permanent ladders or stairs, guard strips within _____ of the scuttle hole or attic entrance shall protect the cable.

    (a) 3 ft
    (b) 4 ft
    (c) 5 ft
    (d) 6 ft

38. Grounded electrical systems shall be connected to earth in a manner that will _____.

    (a) limit voltages due to lightning, line surges, or unintentional contact with higher-voltage lines
    (b) stabilize the voltage-to-ground during normal operation
    (c) facilitate overcurrent device operation in case of ground faults
    (d) a and b

39. Where a supply-side bonding jumper of the wire type is run with the derived phase conductors from the source of a separately derived system to the first disconnecting means, it shall be sized in accordance with 250.102(C), based on _____.

    (a) the size of the primary conductors
    (b) the size of the secondary overcurrent protection
    (c) the size of the derived ungrounded conductors
    (d) one third the size of the primary grounded conductor

40. A receptacle connected to one of the dwelling unit small-appliance branch circuits can be used to supply an electric clock.

    (a) True
    (b) False

41. A neutral conductor is the conductor connected to the _____ of a system, which is intended to carry neutral current under normal conditions.

    (a) grounding electrode
    (b) neutral point
    (c) intersystem bonding termination
    (d) none of these

42. "_____" means that an object is not readily accessible to persons unless special means for access are used.

    (a) Isolated
    (b) Secluded
    (c) Protected
    (d) Locked

43. Metal shields for flat conductor cable shall be electrically continuous to the _____.

    (a) floor
    (b) cable
    (c) equipment grounding conductor
    (d) none of these

44. The radius of the curve of the inner edge of any bend shall not be less than _____ for Type AC cable.

    (a) five times the largest conductor within the cable
    (b) three times the diameter of the cable
    (c) five times the diameter of the cable
    (d) six times the outside diameter of the conductors

45. In rooms other than kitchens and bathrooms of dwelling units, one or more receptacles controlled by a wall switch shall be permitted in lieu of _____.

    (a) lighting outlets
    (b) luminaires
    (c) the receptacles required by 210.52(b) and (D)
    (d) all of these

46. Listed FMC can be used as the equipment grounding conductor if the length in any ground return path does not exceed 6 ft and the circuit conductors contained in the conduit are protected by overcurrent devices rated at _____ or less.

    (a) 15A
    (b) 20A
    (c) 30A
    (d) 60A

47. Metal raceways, cable armor, and other metal enclosures shall be _____ joined together into a continuous electric conductor so as to provide effective electrical continuity.

    (a) electrically
    (b) permanently
    (c) metallically
    (d) none of these

48. A service is supplied by three metal raceways, each containing 600 kcmil ungrounded conductors. Determine the copper supply-side bonding jumper size for each service raceway.

    (a) 1/0 AWG
    (b) 3/0 AWG
    (c) 250 kcmil
    (d) 500 kcmil

49. Where conductors in parallel are run in separate raceways, the raceways shall have the same electrical characteristics.

    (a) True
    (b) False

50. Grounding and bonding connection devices that depend solely on _____ shall not be used.

    (a) pressure connections
    (b) solder
    (c) lugs
    (d) approved clamps

Mike Holt's NEC Exam Practice Questions, based on the 2014 NEC

Please use the 2014 *Code* book to answer the following questions.

1. Type MV cable is defined as a single or multiconductor solid dielectric insulated cable rated _____ volts or higher.

   (a) 601
   (b) 1,001
   (c) 2,001
   (d) 6,001

2. Smooth-sheath Type MC cable with an external diameter not greater than ¾ in. shall have a bending radius not more than _____ times the cable external diameter.

   (a) five
   (b) 10
   (c) 12
   (d) 13

3. Bends made in interlocked or corrugated sheath Type MC cable shall have a radius of at least _____ times the external diameter of the metallic sheath.

   (a) 5
   (b) 7
   (c) 10
   (d) 12

4. Type MC cable can be unsupported where the cable is _____.

   (a) fished between concealed access points in finished buildings or structures and support is impracticable
   (b) not more than 2 ft in length at terminals where flexibility is necessary
   (c) not more than 6 ft from the last point of support within an accessible ceiling for the connection of luminaires or other electrical equipment
   (d) a or c

5. The minimum size copper conductor permitted for Type MC cable is _____.

   (a) 18 AWG
   (b) 16 AWG
   (c) 14 AWG
   (d) 12 AWG

6. Type MI cable shall be supported and secured at intervals not exceeding _____ ft.

   (a) 3
   (b) 3½
   (c) 5
   (d) 6

7. Where single-conductor Type MI cables are used, all phase conductors and, when used, the _____ conductor, shall be grouped together to minimize induced voltage on the metal sheath.

    (a) larger
    (b) neutral
    (c) grounding
    (d) largest

8. Where the outer sheath of Type MI cable is made of copper, it shall provide an adequate path to serve as an equipment grounding conductor.

    (a) True
    (b) False

9. Type NM cable shall be _____.

    (a) marked
    (b) approved
    (c) identified
    (d) listed

10. Type NM and Type NMC cables shall be permitted in _____.

    (a) one- and two-family dwellings and their attached/detached garages and storage buildings
    (b) multifamily dwellings permitted to be of Types III, IV, and V construction
    (c) other structures permitted to be of Types III, IV, and V construction, except as prohibited in 334.12
    (d) any of these

11. Type NM cable can be installed as open runs in dropped or suspended ceilings in other than one- and two-family and multifamily dwellings.

    (a) True
    (b) False

12. Type NM cable shall not be used _____.

    (a) in other than dwelling units
    (b) in the air void of masonry block not subject to excessive moisture
    (c) for exposed work
    (d) embedded in poured cement, concrete, or aggregate

13. Type NM cable can be supported and secured by _____.

    (a) staples
    (b) cable ties
    (c) straps
    (d) any of these

14. Type NM cable protected from physical damage by a raceway shall not be required to be _____ within the raceway.

    (a) covered
    (b) insulated
    (c) secured
    (d) unspliced

15. Flat Type NM cables shall not be stapled on edge.

    (a) True
    (b) False

16. The difference in construction between Type NM cable and Type NMC cable is that Type NMC cable is _____, which Type NM is not.

    (a) corrosion resistant
    (b) flame retardant
    (c) fungus resistant
    (d) a and c

17. Type TC cable shall not be installed _____.

    (a) where it will be exposed to physical damage
    (b) outside of a raceway or cable tray system, unless permitted in 336.10(4) and 336.10(7)
    (c) direct buried unless identified for such use
    (d) all of these

18. Type _____ is a multiconductor cable identified for use as underground service-entrance cable.

    (a) SE
    (b) NM
    (c) UF
    (d) USE

19. Type SE cables shall be permitted to be used for branch circuits or feeders where the insulated conductors are used for circuit wiring and the uninsulated conductor is used only for _____ purposes.

    (a) grounded connection
    (b) equipment grounding
    (c) remote control and signaling
    (d) none of these

20. Type UF cable shall not be used where subject to physical damage.

    (a) True
    (b) False

21. IMC must be secured _____.

    (a) by fastening within 3 ft of each outlet box, junction box, device box, cabinet, conduit body, or other conduit termination
    (b) within 5 ft of a box or termination fitting when structural members don't permit the raceway to be secured within 3 ft of the termination
    (c) except when the IMC is within 3 ft of the service head for an above-the-roof termination of a mast
    (d) a, b, or c

22. Threadless couplings and connectors used on threaded IMC ends shall be listed for the purpose.

    (a) True
    (b) False

23. Threadless couplings approved for use with IMC in wet locations shall be _____.

    (a) rainproof
    (b) listed for wet locations
    (c) moistureproof
    (d) concrete-tight

24. Where IMC enters a box, fitting, or other enclosure, _____ shall be provided to protect the wire from abrasion unless the design of the box, fitting, or enclosure affords equivalent protection.

    (a) a bushing
    (b) duct seal
    (c) electrical tape
    (d) seal fittings

25. Aluminum fittings and enclosures can be used with _____ conduit where not subject to severe corrosive influences.

    (a) steel rigid metal
    (b) aluminum rigid metal
    (c) PVC-coated rigid conduit only
    (d) a and b

26. The minimum radius of a field bend on trade size 1¼ RMC is _____ in.

    (a) 7
    (b) 8
    (c) 10
    (d) 14

27. Cut ends of RMC shall be _____ or otherwise finished to remove rough edges.

    (a) threaded
    (b) reamed
    (c) painted
    (d) galvanized

28. Threadless couplings and connectors used with RMC buried in masonry or concrete shall be the _____ type.

    (a) raintight
    (b) wet and damp location
    (c) nonabsorbent
    (d) concrete tight

29. Running threads shall not be used on RMC for connection at _____.

    (a) boxes
    (b) cabinets
    (c) couplings
    (d) meter sockets

30. Each length of RMC shall be clearly and durably identified in every _____ ft.

    (a) 3
    (b) 5
    (c) 10
    (d) 20

31. FMC can be installed exposed or concealed where not subject to physical damage.

    (a) True
    (b) False

32. Bends in FMC _____ between pull points.

    (a) shall not be made
    (b) need not be limited (in degrees)
    (c) shall not exceed 360 degrees
    (d) shall not exceed 180 degrees

33. Flexible metal conduit shall not be required to be _____ where fished between access points through concealed spaces in finished buildings or structures and supporting is impracticable.

    (a) secured
    (b) supported
    (c) complete
    (d) a and b

34. For flexible metal conduit, if flexibility is necessary after installation, unsecured lengths from the last point the raceway is securely fastened must not exceed _____.

    (a) 3 ft for trade sizes ½ through 1¼
    (b) 4 ft for trade sizes 1½ through 2
    (c) 5 ft for trade sizes 2½ and larger
    (d) all of these

35. The use of LFMC shall be permitted for _____.

    (a) direct burial where listed and marked for the purpose
    (b) exposed work
    (c) concealed work
    (d) all of these

36. LFMC shall be supported and secured _____.

    (a) at intervals not exceeding 4½ ft
    (b) within 8 in. on each side of a box where fished
    (c) where fished
    (d) at intervals not exceeding 6 ft

37. PVC conduit shall be permitted for exposed work where subject to physical damage if identified for such use.

    (a) True
    (b) False

38. Bends in PVC conduit shall _____ between pull points.

    (a) not be made
    (b) not be limited in degrees
    (c) be limited to 360 degrees
    (d) be limited to 180 degrees

39. The cut ends of PVC conduit must be trimmed to remove the burrs and rough edges.

    (a) True
    (b) False

40. PVC conduit shall be securely fastened within _____ in. of each box.

    (a) 6
    (b) 12
    (c) 24
    (d) 36

41. Joints between PVC conduit, couplings, fittings, and boxes shall be made by _____.

    (a) the authority having jurisdiction
    (b) set screw fittings
    (c) an approved method
    (d) expansion fittings

42. PVC conduit and fittings for use above ground shall be_____.

    (a) flame retardant
    (b) resistant to low temperatures and sunlight
    (c) resistant to distortion from heat
    (d) all of these

43. HDPE shall be permitted in _____.

    (a) discrete lengths
    (b) continuous lengths from a reel
    (c) 20-foot lengths
    (d) a or b

44. Bends shall be made in HDPE conduit _____.

    (a) in a manner that will not damage the raceway
    (b) so as not to significantly reduce the internal diameter of the raceway
    (c) with mechanical bending tools
    (d) a and b

45. Each length of HDPE conduit shall be clearly and durably marked not less than every _____ ft.

    (a) 3
    (b) 5
    (c) 10
    (d) 20

46. NUCC and its associated fittings shall be _____.

    (a) listed
    (b) metallic
    (c) identified
    (d) none of these

47. NUCC shall not be used _____.

    (a) in exposed locations
    (b) inside buildings
    (c) in hazardous (classified) locations
    (d) all of these

48. In order to _____ NUCC, the conduit shall be trimmed away from the conductors or cables using an approved method that will not damage the conductor or cable insulation or jacket.

    (a) facilitate installing
    (b) enhance the appearance of the installation of
    (c) terminate
    (d) provide safety to the persons installing

49. Joints between NUCC, fittings, and boxes shall be made by _____.

    (a) a qualified person
    (b) set screw fittings
    (c) an approved method
    (d) exothermic welding

50. When LFNC is used, and equipment grounding is required, a separate _____ shall be installed in the conduit.

    (a) equipment grounding conductor
    (b) expansion fitting
    (c) flexible nonmetallic connector
    (d) none of these

51. EMT couplings and connectors shall be made up _____.

    (a) of metal
    (b) in accordance with industry standards
    (c) tight
    (d) none of these

52. FMT can be used _____.

    (a) in dry and damp locations
    (b) for direct burial
    (c) in lengths over 6 ft
    (d) for a maximum of 1,000V

53. The maximum trade size FMT is _____.

    (a) ⅜
    (b) ½
    (c) ¾
    (d) 1

54. ENT and fittings can be_____, provided fittings identified for this purpose are used.

    (a) encased in poured concrete
    (b) embedded in a concrete slab on grade where the tubing is placed on sand or approved screenings
    (c) a or b
    (d) none of these

55. Unbroken lengths of electric nonmetallic tubing shall not be required to be secured where fished between access points for _____ work in finished buildings or structures and supporting is impractical.

    (a) concealed
    (b) exposed
    (c) hazardous
    (d) completed

56. Bushings or adapters shall be provided at ENT terminations to protect the conductors from abrasion, unless the box, fitting, or enclosure design provides equivalent protection.

    (a) True
    (b) False

57. Joints between lengths of ENT, couplings, fittings, and boxes shall be made by _____.

    (a) a qualified person
    (b) set screw fittings
    (c) an approved method
    (d) exothermic welding

58. The _____ of conductors used in prewired ENT manufactured assemblies shall be identified by means of a printed tag or label attached to each end of the manufactured assembly.

    (a) type
    (b) size
    (c) quantity
    (d) all of these

59. Bare conductors in auxiliary gutters shall be securely and rigidly supported so that the minimum clearance between bare current-carrying metal parts of different potential mounted on the same surface will not be less than 2 in., nor less than _____ in. for parts in free air.

    (a) ¼
    (b) ½
    (c) 1
    (d) 2

60. Busways shall not be installed _____.

    (a) where subject to severe physical damage
    (b) outdoors or in wet or damp locations unless identified for such use
    (c) in hoistways
    (d) all of these

61. When devices or plug-in connections for tapping off feeders or branch circuits from a busway include an externally operable fusible switch that is out of reach, _____ shall be provided for operation of the disconnecting means from the floor.

    (a) ropes
    (b) chains
    (c) hook sticks
    (d) any of these

62. Busways shall be securely supported, unless otherwise designed and marked as such, at intervals not to exceed _____ ft.

    (a) 3
    (b) 5
    (c) 8
    (d) 10

63. Cablebus is ordinarily assembled at the _____.

    (a) point of installation
    (b) manufacturer's location
    (c) distributor's location
    (d) none of these

64. The current-carrying conductors in cablebus shall be sized in accordance with the design of the cablebus, and in no case smaller than _____ AWG.

    (a) 1/0
    (b) 2/0
    (c) 3/0
    (d) 4/0

65. Cablebus framework that is _____ shall be permitted as the equipment grounding conductor for branch circuits and feeders.

    (a) bonded
    (b) welded
    (c) protected
    (d) galvanized

66. A cablebus system shall include approved fittings for dead ends.

    (a) True
    (b) False

67. The header on a cellular concrete floor raceway shall be installed _____ to the cells.

    (a) in a straight line
    (b) at right angles
    (c) a and b
    (d) none of these

68. Connections from cellular concrete floor raceway headers to cabinets shall be made by means of _____.

    (a) listed metal raceways
    (b) PVC raceways
    (c) listed fittings
    (d) a and c

69. For cellular concrete floor raceways, junction boxes shall be _____ the floor grade and sealed against the free entrance of water or concrete.

    (a) leveled to
    (b) above
    (c) below
    (d) perpendicular to

70. When an outlet is _____ from a cellular concrete floor raceway, the sections of circuit conductors supplying the outlet shall be removed from the raceway.

    (a) discontinued
    (b) abandoned
    (c) removed
    (d) any of these

71. Loop wiring _____ in a cellular metal raceway.

    (a) shall not be permitted
    (b) shall not be considered a splice or tap
    (c) shall be considered a splice or tap when used
    (d) none of these

72. Wireways shall be permitted for _____.

    (a) exposed work
    (b) totally concealed work
    (c) wet locations if listed for the purpose
    (d) a and c

73. Wireways can pass transversely through a wall _____.

    (a) if the length passing through the wall is unbroken
    (b) if the wall is of fire-rated construction
    (c) in hazardous (classified) locations
    (d) if the wall is not of fire-rated construction

74. Expansion fittings for nonmetallic wireways shall be provided to compensate for thermal expansion and contraction, where the length change is expected to be _____ in. or greater in a straight run.

    (a) 1/16
    (b) 1/4
    (c) 1/2
    (d) 6

75. Conductors, including splices and taps, shall not fill the non-metallic wireway to more than _____ percent of its area at that point.

    (a) 25
    (b) 75
    (c) 80
    (d) 125

76. A multioutlet assembly shall not be installed _____.

    (a) in hoistways
    (b) where subject to severe physical damage
    (c) where subject to corrosive vapors
    (d) all of these

77. Metal multioutlet assemblies can pass through a dry partition, provided no receptacle is concealed in the partition and the cover of the exposed portion of the system can be removed.

    (a) True
    (b) False

78. A strut-type channel raceway shall not be installed _____.

    (a) in concealed locations
    (b) where subject to corrosive influences, if enamel is the only protection from corrosion of ferrous channel raceways and fittings
    (c) a or b
    (d) none of these

79. The ampacity adjustment factors of 310.15(B)(3)(a) shall not apply to conductors installed in strut-type channel raceways where _____.

    (a) the cross-sectional area of the raceway exceeds 4 sq in.
    (b) the number of current-carrying conductors does not exceed 30
    (c) the sum of the cross-sectional areas of all contained conductors does not exceed 20 percent of the interior cross-sectional area of the strut-type channel raceway
    (d) all of these

80. Strut-type channel raceway shall be permitted as an equipment grounding conductor in accordance with 250.118(13).

    (a) True
    (b) False

81. Surface metal raceways shall not be used _____.

    (a) where subject to severe physical damage
    (b) where subject to corrosive vapors
    (c) in hoistways
    (d) all of these

82. The maximum number of conductors permitted in any surface raceway shall be _____.

    (a) no more than 30 percent of the inside diameter
    (b) no greater than the number for which it was designed
    (c) no more than 75 percent of the cross-sectional area
    (d) that which is permitted in Table 312.6(A)

83. Surface metal raceways and associated fittings shall be supported _____.

    (a) in accordance with the manufacturer's installation instructions
    (b) at intervals appropriate for the building design
    (c) at intervals not exceeding 4 ft
    (d) at intervals not exceeding 8 ft

84. The conductors, including splices and taps, in a metal surface raceway having a removable cover shall not fill the raceway to more than _____ percent of its cross-sectional area at that point.

    (a) 38
    (b) 40
    (c) 53
    (d) 75

85. Surface metal raceway enclosures providing a transition from other wiring methods shall have a means for connecting a(n) _____.

    (a) grounded conductor
    (b) ungrounded conductor
    (c) equipment grounding conductor
    (d) all of these

86. Where combination surface metal raceways are used for both signaling conductors and lighting and power circuits, the different systems shall be run in separate compartments identified by _____ of the interior finish.

    (a) stamping
    (b) imprinting
    (c) color coding
    (d) any of these

87. Cable trays can be used as a support system for _____.

    (a) service conductors, feeders, and branch circuits
    (b) communications circuits
    (c) control and signaling circuits
    (d) all of these

88. Where exposed to the direct rays of the sun, insulated conductors and jacketed cables installed in cable trays shall be _____ as being sunlight resistant.

    (a) listed
    (b) approved
    (c) identified
    (d) none of these

89. Cable trays and their associated fittings shall be _____ for the intended use.

    (a) listed
    (b) approved
    (c) identified
    (d) none of these

90. _____ wiring methods can be installed in a cable tray.

    (a) Metal raceway
    (b) Nonmetallic raceway
    (c) Cable
    (d) all of these

91. Cable tray systems shall not be used _____.

    (a) in hoistways
    (b) where subject to severe physical damage
    (c) in hazardous (classified) locations
    (d) a or b

92. In industrial facilities where conditions of maintenance and supervision ensure that only qualified persons will service the installation, cable tray systems can be used to support _____.

    (a) raceways
    (b) cables
    (c) boxes and conduit bodies
    (d) all of these

93. For raceways terminating at a cable tray, a(n) _____ cable tray clamp or adapter shall be used to securely fasten the raceway to the cable tray system.

    (a) listed
    (b) approved
    (c) identified
    (d) none of these

94. A box shall not be required where cables or conductors from cable trays are installed in bushed conduit and tubing used as support or for protection against _____.

    (a) abuse
    (b) unauthorized access
    (c) physical damage
    (d) tampering

95. The conductor ampacity adjustment factors only apply to the number of current-carrying conductors in the cable and not to the number of conductors in the cable tray.

    (a) True
    (b) False

96. Supports for concealed knob-and-tube wiring shall be installed within _____ in. of each side of each tap or splice and at intervals not exceeding _____ ft.

    (a) 2, 3½
    (b) 3, 2½
    (c) 4, 6½
    (d) 6, 4½

97. The messenger of messenger-supported wiring shall be supported at dead ends and at intermediate locations so as to eliminate _____ on the circuit conductors.

    (a) static
    (b) magnetism
    (c) tension
    (d) induction

98. Open wiring on insulators within _____ ft from the floor shall be considered exposed to physical damage.

    (a) 2
    (b) 4
    (c) 7
    (d) 8

99. Conductors smaller than 8 AWG for open wiring on insulators shall be supported within _____ in. of a tap or splice.

    (a) 6
    (b) 8
    (c) 10
    (d) 12

100. When nails are used to mount knobs for the support of open wiring on insulators, they shall not be smaller than _____-penny.

    (a) six
    (b) eight
    (c) ten
    (d) twelve

Please use the 2014 *Code* book to answer the following questions.

1. Where exposed to sunlight, nonmetallic raceways, cable trays, boxes, cables with a nonmetallic outer jacket, fittings, and support hardware shall be _____.

   (a) listed as sunlight resistant
   (b) identified as sunlight resistant
   (c) a and b
   (d) a or b

2. Floor-mounted flat conductor cable and fittings shall be covered with carpet squares no larger than _____.

   (a) 24 inches square
   (b) 30 sq in. area
   (c) 36 sq in. area
   (d) 39.37 inches square

3. A grounding electrode shall be required if a building or structure is supplied by a feeder.

   (a) True
   (b) False

4. In ungrounded systems, electrical equipment, wiring, and other electrically conductive material likely to become energized shall be installed in a manner that creates a low-impedance circuit from any point on the wiring system to the electrical supply source to facilitate the operation of overcurrent devices should a(n) _____ fault from a different phase occur on the wiring system.

   (a) isolated ground
   (b) second ground
   (c) arc
   (d) high impedance

5. When Type NM cable is used with nonmetallic boxes not larger than 2¼ x 4 in., securing the cable to the box shall not be required if the cable is fastened within _____ in. of that box.

   (a) 6
   (b) 8
   (c) 10
   (d) 12

6. In general, areas where acids and alkali chemicals are handled and stored may present corrosive conditions, particularly when wet or damp.

   (a) True
   (b) False

7. Where more than two Type NM cables are installed through the same opening in wood framing that is to be sealed with thermal insulation, caulk, or sealing foam, the allowable ampacity of each conductor shall be ____.

    (a) no more than 20A
    (b) adjusted in accordance with Table 310.15(B)(3)(a)
    (c) limited to 30A
    (d) calculated by an engineer

8. Service-entrance conductors can be spliced or tapped by clamped or bolted connections at any time as long as ____.

    (a) the free ends of conductors are covered with an insulation that is equivalent to that of the conductors or with an insulating device identified for the purpose
    (b) wire connectors or other splicing means installed on conductors that are buried in the earth are listed for direct burial
    (c) no splice is made in a raceway
    (d) all of these

9. Type USE cable used for service laterals shall be permitted to emerge from the ground if terminated in an enclosure at an outside location and protected in accordance with 300.5(D).

    (a) True
    (b) False

10. Raceways shall be ____ between outlet, junction, or splicing points prior to the installation of conductors.

    (a) installed complete
    (b) tested for ground faults
    (c) a minimum of 80 percent complete
    (d) none of these

11. When LFMC is used to connect equipment where flexibility is necessary to minimize the transmission of vibration from equipment of for equipment requiring movement after installation, a(n) ____ conductor shall be installed.

    (a) main bonding
    (b) grounded
    (c) equipment grounding
    (d) none of these

12. The service drop is defined as the overhead conductors between the utility electric supply system and the ____.

    (a) service equipment
    (b) service point
    (c) grounding electrode
    (d) equipment grounding conductor

13. Steel or aluminum cable tray systems shall be permitted to be used as an equipment grounding conductor, provided the cable tray sections and fittings are identified as ____, among other requirements.

    (a) an equipment grounding conductor
    (b) special
    (c) industrial
    (d) all of these

14. Overhead service conductors are the conductors between the ____ and the first point of connection to the service-entrance conductors at the building or other structure.

    (a) service disconnect
    (b) service point
    (c) grounding electrode
    (d) equipment grounding conductor

15. Exposed runs of Type AC cable can be installed on the underside of joists where supported at each joist and located so it is not subject to physical damage.

    (a) True
    (b) False

16. Where PVC conduit enters a box, fitting, or other enclosure, a bushing or adapter shall be provided to protect the conductor from abrasion unless the design of the box, fitting, or enclosure affords equivalent protection.

    (a) True
    (b) False

17. Nonmetallic cable trays shall be made of ____ material.

    (a) fire-resistant
    (b) waterproof
    (c) corrosive
    (d) flame-retardant

18. A building or structure shall have the interior metal water piping system bonded with a conductor sized in accordance with _____.

    (a) Table 250.66
    (b) Table 250.122
    (c) Table 310.15(B)(16)
    (d) none of these

19. The ampacity of a conductor can be different along the length of the conductor. The higher ampacity can be used beyond the point of transition for a distance of no more than _____ ft, or no more than _____ percent of the circuit length figured at the higher ampacity, whichever is less.

    (a) 10, 10
    (b) 10, 20
    (c) 15, 15
    (d) 20, 10

20. Where portions of a cable raceway or sleeve are subjected to different temperatures and condensation is known to be a problem, the _____ shall be filled with an approved material to prevent the circulation of warm air to a colder section of the raceway or sleeve.

    (a) raceway
    (b) sleeve
    (c) a or b
    (d) none of these

21. A(n) _____ shall be considered equivalent to an overcurrent trip unit for the purpose of providing overcurrent protection of conductors.

    (a) current transformer
    (b) overcurrent relay
    (c) a and b
    (d) a or b

22. Type AC cable installed through, or parallel to, framing members shall be protected against physical damage from penetration by screws or nails.

    (a) True
    (b) False

23. Type _____ cable is a factory assembly of insulated circuit conductors within an armor of interlocking metal tape, or a smooth or corrugated metallic sheath.

    (a) AC
    (b) MC
    (c) NM
    (d) b and c

24. The *NEC* defines a(n) "_____" as a structure that stands alone or that is cut off from adjoining structures by fire walls or fire barriers, with all openings therein protected by approved fire doors.

    (a) unit
    (b) apartment
    (c) building
    (d) utility

25. All 15A and 20A, 125V receptacles located outdoors of dwelling units, including receptacles installed under the eaves of roofs, must be GFCI protected except for a receptacle that's supplied by a branch circuit dedicated to _____ if the receptacle isn't readily accessible and the equipment or receptacle has ground-fault protection of equipment (GFPE) [426.28 or 427.22].

    (a) electric snow-melting or deicing equipment
    (b) pipeline and vessel heating equipment
    (c) holiday decorative lighting
    (d) a or b

26. The grounded conductor brought to service equipment shall be routed with the phase conductors and shall not be smaller than specified in Table _____ when the service-entrance conductors are 1,100 kcmil copper and smaller.

    (a) 250.102(C)(1)
    (b) 250.122
    (c) 310.16
    (d) 430.52

27. Conduit bodies containing conductors larger than 6 AWG shall have a cross-sectional area at least twice that of the largest conduit to which they can be attached.

    (a) True
    (b) False

28. Utilization equipment is equipment that utilizes electricity for _____ purposes.

    (a) electromechanical
    (b) heating
    (c) lighting
    (d) any of these

29. Surface nonmetallic raceways and associated fittings shall be supported in accordance with the _____ installation instructions.

    (a) vendor's
    (b) supplier's
    (c) manufacturer's
    (d) engineer's

30. Electrical equipment that depends on _____ for cooling of exposed surfaces shall be installed so that airflow over such surfaces is not prevented by walls or by adjacent installed equipment.

    (a) outdoor air
    (b) natural circulation of air and convection principles
    (c) artificial cooling and circulation
    (d) magnetic induction

31. Where practicable, contact of dissimilar metals shall be avoided in an IMC raceway installation to prevent _____.

    (a) corrosion
    (b) galvanic action
    (c) shorts
    (d) none of these

32. The space above a hung ceiling used for environmental air-handling purposes is an example of _____, and the wiring limitations of _____ apply.

    (a) a specifically fabricated duct used for environmental air, 300.22(B)
    (b) other space used for environmental air (plenum), 300.22(C)
    (c) a supply duct used for environmental air, 300.22(B)
    (d) none of these

33. Conductors, splices or terminations in a handhole enclosure shall be listed as suitable for _____.

    (a) wet locations
    (b) damp locations
    (c) direct burial in the earth
    (d) none of these

34. Type MC cable installed through, or parallel to, framing members shall be protected against physical damage from penetration by screws or nails by 1¼ in. separation or protected by a suitable metal plate.

    (a) True
    (b) False

35. Tap devices used in Type FC assemblies shall be rated not less than _____ or more than 300 volts-to-ground.

    (a) 15A
    (b) 20A
    (c) 30A
    (d) 40A

36. The intersystem bonding termination shall _____.

    (a) be securely mounted and electrically connected to service equipment, the meter enclosure, or exposed nonflexible metallic service raceway, or be mounted at one of these enclosures and be connected to the enclosure or grounding electrode conductor with a minimum 6 AWG copper conductor
    (b) be securely mounted to the building/structure disconnecting means, or be mounted at the disconnecting means and be connected to the metallic enclosure or grounding electrode conductor with a minimum 6 AWG copper conductor
    (c) have terminals that are listed as grounding and bonding equipment
    (d) all of these

37. There shall be no more than _____ switches or circuit breakers to serve as the disconnecting means for a building supplied by a feeder.

    (a) two
    (b) four
    (c) six
    (d) eight

38. Where run horizontally, nonmetallic wireways shall be supported at each end, at intervals not to exceed _____ ft, and at each joint, unless listed for other support intervals.

    (a) 3
    (b) 6
    (c) 8
    (d) 10

39. Noncombustible surfaces that are broken or incomplete around boxes employing a flush-type cover or faceplate shall be repaired so there will be no gaps or open spaces larger than _____ in. at the edge of the box.

    (a) ¹⁄₁₆
    (b) ⅛
    (c) ¼
    (d) ½

40. When an outlet from an underfloor raceway is discontinued, the circuit conductors supplying the outlet _____.

    (a) may be spliced
    (b) may be reinsulated
    (c) may be cut and capped off
    (d) shall be removed from the raceway

41. Two or more _____ small-appliance branch circuits shall be provided to supply power for receptacle outlets in the dwelling unit kitchen, dining room, breakfast room, pantry, or similar dining areas.

    (a) 15A
    (b) 20A
    (c) 30A
    (d) either 20A or 30A

42. PVC conduit shall not be used _____, unless specifically permitted.

    (a) in hazardous (classified) locations
    (b) for the support of luminaires or other equipment
    (c) where subject to physical damage unless identified for such use
    (d) all of these

43. ENT shall be permitted for direct earth burial when used with fittings listed for this purpose.

    (a) True
    (b) False

44. The temperature rating associated with the ampacity of a _____ shall be selected and coordinated so as not to exceed the lowest temperature rating of any connected termination, conductor, or device.

    (a) terminal
    (b) conductor
    (c) device
    (d) all of these

45. In walls or ceilings constructed of wood or other combustible surface material, boxes, plaster rings, extension rings, or listed extenders shall _____.

    (a) be flush with the surface
    (b) project from the surface
    (c) a or b
    (d) be set back no more than ¼ in.

46. Electrical equipment such as switchboards, switchgear, panelboards, industrial control panels, meter socket enclosures, and motor control centers, that are in other than dwelling units, and are likely to require _____ while energized, shall be field or factory marked to warn qualified persons of potential electric arc flash hazards.

    (a) examination
    (b) adjustment
    (c) servicing or maintenance
    (d) any of these

47. When IMC is cut in the field, reaming is required to remove the burrs and rough edges.

    (a) True
    (b) False

48. Handhole enclosure covers shall require the use of tools to open, or they shall weigh over _____.

    (a) 45 lb
    (b) 70 lb
    (c) 100 lb
    (d) 200 lb

49. The grounding electrode for a separately derived system shall be as near as practicable to, and preferably in the same area as, the grounding electrode conductor connection to the system.

    (a) True
    (b) False

50. Receptacles shall have the terminal intended for connection to the grounded conductor identified by a metal or metal coating that is substantially _____ in color.

    (a) green
    (b) white
    (c) gray
    (d) b or c

51. Outside secondary conductors can be of unlimited length without overcurrent protection at the point they receive their supply if the conductors _____.

    (a) are suitably protected from physical damage
    (b) terminate at a single circuit breaker or a single set of fuses that limits the load to the ampacity of the conductors
    (c) a and b
    (d) none of these

52. For indoor installations, heating, cooling, or ventilating equipment shall not be installed in the dedicated space above a panelboard or switchboard.

    (a) True
    (b) False

53. When installing direct-buried cables, a _____ shall be used at the end of a conduit that terminates underground.

    (a) splice kit
    (b) terminal fitting
    (c) bushing
    (d) b or c

54. The maximum size conductors permitted in a nonmetallic surface raceway shall not be larger than that for which the wireway is designed.

    (a) True
    (b) False

55. The insulation temperature rating of conductors in Type NM cable shall be _____.

    (a) 60°C
    (b) 75°C
    (c) 90°C
    (d) 105°C

56. Admitting close approach not guarded by locked doors, elevation, or other effective means, is referred to as _____.

    (a) accessible (as applied to equipment)
    (b) accessible (as applied to wiring methods)
    (c) accessible, readily
    (d) all of these

57. Circuit breakers used to switch 120V or 277V fluorescent lighting circuits shall be listed and marked _____.

    (a) UL
    (b) SWD or HID
    (c) Amps
    (d) VA

58. Openings in cabinets, cutout boxes, and meter socket enclosures through which conductors enter shall be _____.

    (a) closed in an approved manner
    (b) made using concentric knockouts only
    (c) centered in the cabinet wall
    (d) identified

59. Power distribution blocks installed in metal wireways shall _____.

    (a) allow for sufficient wire-bending space at terminals
    (b) not have uninsulated exposed live parts
    (c) a or b
    (d) a and b

60. Conductors with the color _____ insulation shall not be used for ungrounded or grounded conductors.

    (a) green
    (b) green with one or more yellow stripes
    (c) a or b
    (d) white

61. When ungrounded circuit conductors are increased in size from the minimum size that has sufficient ampacity for the intended installation, the equipment grounding conductor must be proportionately increased in size according to the _____ of the ungrounded conductors.

    (a) ampacity
    (b) circular mil area
    (c) diameter
    (d) none of these

62. Where RMC enters a box, fitting, or other enclosure, _____ shall be provided to protect the wire from abrasion, unless the design of the box, fitting, or enclosure affords equivalent protection.

    (a) a bushing
    (b) duct seal
    (c) electrical tape
    (d) seal fittings

63. Flexible metal conduit must be securely fastened by a means approved by the authority having jurisdiction within _____ of termination.

    (a) 6 in.
    (b) 10 in.
    (c) 1 ft
    (d) 10 ft

64. Horizontal runs of IMC supported by openings through framing members at intervals not exceeding 10 ft and securely fastened within 3 ft of terminations shall be permitted.

    (a) True
    (b) False

65. Metal parts of cord-and-plug-connected equipment shall be connected to an equipment grounding conductor that terminates to a grounding-type attachment plug.

    (a) True
    (b) False

66. EMT, elbows, couplings, and fittings can be installed in concrete, in direct contact with the earth, or in areas subject to severe corrosive influences if _____.

    (a) protected by corrosion protection
    (b) approved as suitable for the condition
    (c) a and b
    (d) listed for wet locations

67. The frame of a vehicle-mounted generator shall not be required to be connected to a(n) _____ if the generator only supplies equipment mounted on the vehicle or cord-and-plug connected equipment, using receptacles mounted on the vehicle.

    (a) grounding electrode
    (b) grounded conductor
    (c) ungrounded conductor
    (d) equipment grounding conductor

68. A box or conduit body shall not be required for conductors in handhole enclosures, except where connected to electrical equipment.

    (a) True
    (b) False

69. The additional service disconnecting means for fire pumps, emergency systems, legally required standby, or optional standby services, shall be installed remote from the one to six service disconnecting means for normal service to minimize the possibility of _____ interruption of supply.

    (a) intentional
    (b) accidental
    (c) simultaneous
    (d) prolonged

70. Where service equipment consists of more than one enclosure, grounding electrode conductor connections shall be permitted to be _____.

    (a) multiple individual grounding electrode conductors
    (b) one grounding electrode conductor at a common location
    (c) a common grounding electrode conductor and taps
    (d) any of these

71. Overcurrent devices shall be readily accessible and installed so the center of the grip of the operating handle of the switch or circuit breaker, when in its highest position, is not more than _____ above the floor or working platform.

    (a) 2 ft
    (b) 4 ft 6 in.
    (c) 5 ft
    (d) 6 ft 7 in.

72. When locating lighting outlets in dwelling units, a vehicle door in a garage shall be considered an outdoor entrance.

    (a) True
    (b) False

73. Materials such as straps, bolts, screws, and so forth, which are associated with the installation of IMC in wet locations shall be _____.

    (a) weatherproof
    (b) weathertight
    (c) corrosion resistant
    (d) none of these

74. The radius of the inner edge of any bend in Type MI cable shall not be less than _____ times the external diameter of the metallic sheath for any cable having an external diameter greater than ¾ in., but not more than 1 in.

    (a) three
    (b) six
    (c) eight
    (d) 10

75. Nonmetallic cables can enter the top of surface-mounted cabinets, cutout boxes, and meter socket enclosures through non-flexible raceways not less than 18 in. or more than _____ ft in length if all of the required conditions are met.

    (a) 3
    (b) 10
    (c) 25
    (d) 100

76. Type _____ fuse adapters shall be designed so that once inserted in a fuseholder they cannot be removed.

    (a) A
    (b) E
    (c) S
    (d) P

77. For a separate building or structure supplied by a separately derived system when overcurrent protection isn't provided for the supply conductors to the building/structure as permitted by 240.21(C)(4), the installation must be _____ in accordance with 250.30(A).

    (a) AFCI protected
    (b) grounded and bonded
    (c) isolated
    (d) all of these

78. _____ can be installed in messenger-supported wiring.

    (a) Multiconductor service-entrance cable
    (b) Mineral-insulated (Type MI) cable
    (c) Multiconductor underground feeder cable
    (d) all of these

79. Listed FMC and LFMC shall contain an equipment grounding conductor if the raceway is installed for the reason of _____.

    (a) physical protection
    (b) flexibility after installation
    (c) minimizing transmission of vibration from equipment
    (d) b or c

80. A _____ is the total components and subsystem that, in combination, convert solar energy into electric energy suitable for connection to a utilization load.

    (a) photovoltaic system
    (b) solar array
    (c) a and b
    (d) neither a nor b

81. A "_____" is a building or portion of a building in which one or more self-propelled vehicles can be kept for use, sale, storage, rental, repair, exhibition, or demonstration purposes.

    (a) garage
    (b) residential garage
    (c) service garage
    (d) commercial garage

82. Electrical wiring within the cavity of a fire-rated floor-ceiling or roof-ceiling assembly shall not be supported by the ceiling assembly or ceiling support wires.

    (a) True
    (b) False

83. Flat cable assemblies shall have conductors of _____ AWG special stranded copper conductors.

    (a) 14
    (b) 12
    (c) 10
    (d) all of these

84. For liquidtight flexible metal conduit, if flexibility is necessary after installation, unsecured lengths from the last point the raceway is securely fastened must not exceed _____.

    (a) 3 ft for trade sizes ½ through 1¼
    (b) 4 ft for trade sizes 1½ through 2
    (c) 5 ft for trade sizes 2½ and larger
    (d) all of these

85. Listed boxes and handhole enclosures designed for underground installation can be directly buried when covered by _____, if their location is effectively identified and accessible.

    (a) concrete
    (b) gravel
    (c) noncohesive granulated soil
    (d) b or c

86. Conductors are considered outside a building when they are installed _____.

    (a) under not less than 2 in. of concrete beneath a building or structure
    (b) within a building or structure in a raceway encased in not less than a 2 in. thickness of concrete or brick
    (c) installed in a vault that meets the construction requirements of Article 450, Part III
    (d) all of these

87. A listed exposed work cover can be the grounding and bonding means when the device is attached to the cover with at least _____ permanent fastener(s) and the cover mounting holes are located on a non-raised portion of the cover.

    (a) one
    (b) two
    (c) three
    (d) none of these

88. The maximum size conductors permitted in a metal surface raceway shall not be larger than that for which the wireway is designed.

    (a) True
    (b) False

89. Single-pole breakers with identified handle ties can be used to protect each ungrounded conductor for line-to-line connected loads.

    (a) True
    (b) False

90. Loop wiring in an underfloor raceway _____ to be a splice or tap.

(a) shall be considered
(b) shall not be considered
(c) shall not be permitted
(d) none of these

91. A reliable conductor that ensures electrical conductivity between metal parts of the electrical installation that are required to be electrically connected is called a(n) "_____."

(a) grounding electrode
(b) auxiliary ground
(c) bonding conductor or jumper
(d) tap conductor

92. Type NM cable shall be protected from physical damage by _____.

(a) EMT
(b) Schedule 80 PVC conduit
(c) RMC
(d) any of these

93. Surge protective devices shall be marked with a short-circuit current rating and shall not be installed where the available fault current is in excess of that rating.

(a) True
(b) False

94. The metallic sheath of metal-clad cable shall be continuous and _____.

(a) flame-retardant
(b) weatherproof
(c) close fitting
(d) all of these

95. Type AC cable is permitted in _____ installations.

(a) wet
(b) cable trays
(c) exposed
(d) b and c

96. Bends in NUCC shall _____ between termination points.

(a) not be made
(b) not be limited in degrees
(c) be limited to 360 degrees
(d) be limited to 180 degrees

97. Where a main bonding jumper is a screw only, the screw shall be identified by a(n) _____ that shall be visible with the screw installed.

(a) silver or white finish
(b) etched ground symbol
(c) hexagonal head
(d) green finish

98. Auxiliary gutters shall be constructed and installed so that adequate _____ continuity of the complete system is secured.

(a) mechanical
(b) electrical
(c) a or b
(d) a and b

99. The receptacle grounding terminal of an isolated ground receptacle shall be connected to a(n) _____ equipment grounding conductor run with the circuit conductors.

(a) insulated
(b) covered
(c) bare
(d) solid

100. Liquidtight flexible metal conduit must be securely fastened by a means approved by the authority having jurisdiction within _____ of termination.

(a) 6 in.
(b) 10 in.
(c) 1 ft
(d) 10 ft

STRAIGHT ORDER
[ARTICLES 400–427]

Please use the 2014 *Code* book to answer the following questions.

1. HPD cord shall be permitted for _____.

   (a) not hard usage
   (b) hard usage
   (c) extra-hard usage
   (d) all of these

2. Conductors within flexible cords and cables shall not be associated together in such a way that the _____ temperature of the conductors is exceeded.

   (a) operating
   (b) governing
   (c) ambient
   (d) limiting

3. Flexible cords and cables can be used for _____.

   (a) wiring of luminaires
   (b) connection of portable luminaires or appliances
   (c) connection of utilization equipment to facilitate frequent interchange
   (d) all of these

4. Flexible cords and cables shall not be used where _____.

   (a) run through holes in walls, ceilings, or floors
   (b) run through doorways, windows, or similar openings
   (c) attached to building surfaces, unless permitted by 368.56(B)
   (d) all of these

5. Flexible cords and cables shall not be concealed behind building _____, or run through doorways, windows, or similar openings.

   (a) structural ceilings
   (b) suspended or dropped ceilings
   (c) floors or walls
   (d) all of these

6. Flexible cords and cables shall be connected to fittings so that tension will not be transmitted to joints or terminal screws by _____.

   (a) knotting the cord
   (b) winding the cord with tape
   (c) fittings designed for the purpose
   (d) any of these

7. The allowable ampacity of 18 TFFN is _____.

   (a) 6A
   (b) 8A
   (c) 10A
   (d) 14A

8. The number of fixture wires in a single conduit or tubing shall not exceed the percentage fill specified in _____.

   (a) Chapter 9, Table 1
   (b) Table 250.66
   (c) Table 310.15(B)(16)
   (d) 240.6

9. When grouping conductors of switch loops in the same raceway, it is not required to include a grounded conductor in every switch loop.

   (a) True
   (b) False

10. As a general rule, the grounded circuit conductor for the controlled lighting circuit shall be provided at the location where switches control lighting loads that are supplied by a grounded general-purpose branch circuit.

    (a) True
    (b) False

11. Switches controlling line-to-neutral lighting loads must have a grounded conductor provided at the switch location unless the _____.

    (a) conductors enter the device box through a raceway that has sufficient area to accommodate a grounded conductor
    (b) box enclosing the switch is accessible for the installation of an additional or replacement cable without removing finish materials
    (c) lighting consists of all fluorescent fixtures with integral disconnects for the ballasts
    (d) a or b

12. Surface-mounted switches or circuit breakers in a damp or wet location shall be enclosed in a _____ enclosure or cabinet that complies with 312.2.

    (a) weatherproof
    (b) rainproof
    (c) watertight
    (d) raintight

13. Which of the following switches must indicate whether they are in the open (off) or closed (on) position?

    (a) General-use switches
    (b) Motor-circuit switches
    (c) Circuit breakers
    (d) all of these

14. Switches and circuit breakers used as switches can be mounted _____ if they are installed adjacent to motors, appliances, or other equipment that they supply and are accessible by portable means.

    (a) not higher than 6 ft 7 in.
    (b) higher than 6 ft 7 in.
    (c) in the mechanical equipment room
    (d) up to 8 ft high

15. A multipole, general-use snap switch shall not be fed from more than a single circuit unless it is listed and marked as a _____ switch.

    (a) 2-circuit
    (b) 3-circuit
    (c) a or b
    (d) none of these

16. Snap switches in listed assemblies aren't required to be connected to an equipment grounding conductor if _____.

    (a) the device is provided with a nonmetallic faceplate that cannot be installed on any other type of device and the device does not have mounting means to accept other configurations of faceplates
    (b) the device is equipped with a nonmetallic yoke
    (c) all parts of the device that are accessible after installation of the faceplate are manufactured of nonmetallic material
    (d) all of these

17. Snap switches installed in boxes shall have the _____ seated against the finished wall surface.

    (a) extension plaster ears
    (b) body
    (c) toggle
    (d) all of these

18. Nonmetallic boxes for switches shall be installed with a wiring method that provides or includes _____.

    (a) a grounded conductor
    (b) an equipment grounding conductor
    (c) an inductive balance
    (d) none of these

19. Snap switches rated _____ or less directly connected to aluminum conductors shall be listed and marked CO/ALR.

    (a) 15A
    (b) 20A
    (c) 25A
    (d) 30A

20. General-use _____ switches shall be used only to control permanently installed incandescent luminaires unless listed for control of other loads and installed accordingly.

    (a) dimmer
    (b) fan speed control
    (c) timer
    (d) all of these

21. A child care facility is a building or structure, or portion thereof, used for educational, supervision, or personal care services for more than _____ children seven years in age or less.

    (a) two
    (b) three
    (c) four
    (d) six

22. Receptacles and cord connectors shall be rated not less than _____ at 125V, or at 250V, and shall be of a type not suitable for use as lampholders.

    (a) 10A
    (b) 15A
    (c) 20A
    (d) 30A

23. Receptacles rated _____ or less directly connected to aluminum conductors shall be listed and marked CO/ALR.

    (a) 15A
    (b) 20A
    (c) 25A
    (d) 30A

24. Where a grounding means exists in the receptacle enclosure a(n) _____-type receptacle shall be used.

    (a) isolated ground
    (b) grounding
    (c) GFCI
    (d) dedicated

25. Effective January 1, 2014, where a receptacle outlet is supplied by a branch circuit that requires arc-fault circuit-interrupter protection [210.12(A)], a replacement receptacle at this outlet shall be _____.

    (a) a listed (receptacle) outlet branch circuit type arc-fault circuit-interrupter receptacle
    (b) a receptacle protected by a listed (receptacle) outlet branch-circuit type arc-fault circuit-interrupter type receptacle
    (c) a receptacle protected by a listed combination type arc-fault circuit-interrupter type circuit breaker
    (d) all of these

26. Listed tamper-resistant receptacles shall be provided where replacements are made at receptacle outlets that are required to be tamper resistant elsewhere in this *Code*.

    (a) True
    (b) False

27. Receptacles mounted in boxes flush with the finished surface or projecting beyond it shall be installed so that the mounting yoke or strap of the receptacle is _____.

    (a) held rigidly against the box or box cover
    (b) mounted behind the wall surface
    (c) held rigidly at the finished surface
    (d) none of these

28. Receptacles mounted to and supported by a cover shall be secured by more than one screw unless listed and identified for securing by a single screw.

    (a) True
    (b) False

29. Receptacles in countertops and similar work surfaces shall not be installed _____, unless listed as receptacle assemblies for countertop applications.

    (a) in the sides of cabinets
    (b) in a face-up position
    (c) on GFCI circuits
    (d) on the kitchen small-appliance circuit

30. Receptacles shall not be grouped or ganged in enclosures unless the voltage between adjacent devices does not exceed _____.

    (a) 100V
    (b) 200V
    (c) 300V
    (d) 400V

31. Metal faceplates for receptacles shall be grounded.

    (a) True
    (b) False

32. Attachment plugs and cord connectors shall be listed and marked with the _____.

    (a) manufacturer's name or identification
    (b) voltage rating
    (c) amperage rating
    (d) all of these

33. An outdoor receptacle in a location protected from the weather, or in another damp location, shall be installed in an enclosure that is weatherproof when the receptacle is _____.

    (a) covered
    (b) enclosed
    (c) protected
    (d) none of these

34. Receptacles installed outdoors, in a location protected from the weather or other damp locations, shall be in an enclosure that is _____ when the receptacle is covered.

    (a) raintight
    (b) weatherproof
    (c) rainproof
    (d) weathertight

35. A receptacle is considered to be in a location protected from the weather when located under roofed open porches, canopies, marquees, and the like, where it will not be subjected to _____.

    (a) spray from a hose
    (b) a direct lightning hit
    (c) beating rain or water runoff
    (d) falling or wind-blown debris

36. A receptacle shall not be installed within, or directly over, a bathtub or shower space.

    (a) True
    (b) False

37. A receptacle installed in an outlet box flush-mounted in a finished surface in a damp or wet location shall be made weatherproof by means of a weatherproof faceplate assembly that provides a _____ connection between the plate and the finished surface.

    (a) sealed
    (b) weathertight
    (c) sealed and protected
    (d) watertight

38. Nongrounding, nonlocking type, 15A and 20A, 125V receptacles used for replacements in a dwelling unit shall not be required to be listed as tamper resistant.

    (a) True
    (b) False

39. Nonlocking type 15A and 20A, 125V receptacles in _____ must be listed as tamper resistant.

    (a) restaurants
    (b) guest rooms and guest suites of hotels and motels
    (c) office buildings
    (d) b and c

40. Panelboards supplied by a three-phase, 4-wire, delta-connected system shall have the phase with higher voltage-to-ground (high-leg) connected to the _____ phase.

    (a) A
    (b) B
    (c) C
    (d) any of these

41. The purpose or use of panelboard circuits and circuit _____, including spare positions, shall be legibly identified on a circuit directory located on the face or inside of the door of a panelboard, and at each switch or circuit breaker in a switchboard.

    (a) manufacturers
    (b) conductors
    (c) feeders
    (d) modifications

42. Noninsulated busbars shall have a minimum space of _____ in. between the bottom of a switchboard enclosure and busbars or other obstructions.

    (a) 6
    (b) 8
    (c) 10
    (d) 12

43. A panelboard shall be protected by an overcurrent device within the panelboard, or at any point on the _____ side of the panelboard.

    (a) load
    (b) supply
    (c) a or b
    (d) none of these

44. Each _____ conductor shall terminate within the panelboard at an individual terminal that is not used for another conductor.

    (a) grounded
    (b) ungrounded
    (c) grounding
    (d) all of these

45. Pilot lights, instruments, voltage (potential) transformers, current transformers, and other switchboard devices with potential coils shall be supplied by a circuit that is protected by overcurrent devices rated _____.

    (a) 10A or less
    (b) 15A or less
    (c) 15A or more
    (d) 20A or less

46. A panelboard shall be provided with physical means to prevent the installation of more _____ devices than that number for which the panelboard was designed, rated, and listed.

    (a) overcurrent
    (b) equipment
    (c) circuit breaker
    (d) all of these

47. Article 410 covers luminaires, portable luminaires, lampholders, pendants, incandescent filament lamps, arc lamps, electric-discharge lamps, and _____, and the wiring and equipment forming part of such products and lighting installations.

    (a) decorative lighting products
    (b) lighting accessories for temporary seasonal and holiday use
    (c) portable flexible lighting products
    (d) all of these

48. Lampholders installed over highly combustible material shall be of the _____ type.

    (a) industrial
    (b) switched
    (c) unswitched
    (d) residential

49. Surface-mounted fluorescent luminaires in clothes closets shall be permitted on the wall above the door, or on the ceiling, provided there is a minimum clearance of _____ in. between the luminaire and the nearest point of a storage space.

    (a) 3
    (b) 6
    (c) 9
    (d) 12

50. In clothes closets, recessed incandescent or LED luminaires with a completely enclosed light source can be installed in the wall or the ceiling, provided there is a minimum clearance of _____ in. between the luminaire and the nearest point of a storage space.

    (a) 3
    (b) 6
    (c) 9
    (d) 12

51. The maximum weight of a luminaire permitted to be supported by the screw shell of a lampholder is _____ lb.

    (a) 2
    (b) 3
    (c) 4
    (d) 6

52. Poles over 20 ft in height above grade, without a hinged base, that support luminaires shall _____.

    (a) have an accessible handhole (sized 2 x 4 in.) with a cover suitable for use in wet locations
    (b) have an equipment grounding terminal that is accessible from the handhole
    (c) a and b
    (d) none of these

53. Luminaires attached to the framing of a suspended ceiling shall be secured to the framing member(s) by mechanical means such as _____.

    (a) bolts
    (b) screws
    (c) rivets
    (d) any of these

54. Luminaires and equipment must be mechanically connected to an equipment grounding conductor as specified in 250.118 and must be sized in accordance with _____.

    (a) Table 250.66
    (b) Table 250.122
    (c) Table 310.16
    (d) a and c

55. Replacement luminaires aren't required to be connected to an equipment grounding conductor if no equipment grounding conductor exists at the outlet box and the luminaire is _____.

    (a) more than 20 years old
    (b) mounted to the box using nonmetallic fittings and screws
    (c) mounted more than 6 ft above the floor
    (d) GFCI protected

56. Fixture wires used as pendant conductors for incandescent luminaires with intermediate or candelabra-base lampholders shall not be smaller than _____ AWG.

    (a) 22
    (b) 18
    (c) 16
    (d) 14

57. Splices and taps shall not be located within luminaire _____.

    (a) arms or stems
    (b) bases or screw shells
    (c) a and b
    (d) a or b

58. Wiring on luminaire chains and other movable parts shall be _____.

    (a) rated for 110°C
    (b) stranded
    (c) hard-usage rated
    (d) none of these

59. Luminaires can be used as a raceway for circuit conductors only when listed and marked for use as a raceway.

    (a) True
    (b) False

60. Luminaires identified for _____, with an integral outlet box in accordance with 410.21 shall be permitted to be used as a conductor raceway.

    (a) through-wiring
    (b) wet locations
    (c) Class 1, Division 1 locations
    (d) b and c

61. Luminaires shall be marked with the maximum lamp wattage, manufacturer's _____, trademark, or other suitable means of identification.

    (a) address
    (b) name
    (c) phone number
    (d) none of these

62. Portable luminaires shall be wired with _____ recognized by 400.4, and have an attachment plug of the polarized or grounding type.

    (a) flexible cable
    (b) flexible cord
    (c) nonmetallic flexible cable
    (d) nonmetallic flexible cord

63. Lampholders installed in wet locations shall be listed for use in _____ locations.

    (a) damp
    (b) wet
    (c) dry
    (d) any of these

64. Luminaires installed in _____ shall comply with 410.115 through 410.122.

    (a) recessed cavities in walls or ceilings
    (b) suspended ceilings
    (c) Class I classified locations
    (d) a and b

65. Recessed incandescent luminaires shall have _____ protection and shall be identified as thermally protected.

    (a) physical
    (b) corrosion
    (c) thermal
    (d) all of these

66. The minimum distance that an outlet box containing tap supply conductors is permitted to be placed from a recessed luminaire is _____ ft.

    (a) 1
    (b) 2
    (c) 3
    (d) 4

67. The raceway or cable for tap conductors to recessed luminaires shall have a minimum length of _____ in.

    (a) 6
    (b) 12
    (c) 18
    (d) 24

68. Luminaires containing a metal halide lamp (other than a thick-glass PAR lamp) shall be provided with a containment barrier that encloses the lamp, or shall be provided with a physical means that only allows the use of a(n) _____.

    (a) Type O lamp
    (b) Type CB lamp
    (c) a or b
    (d) inert gas

69. For existing installed luminaires in indoor locations, other than dwellings and associated accessory structures, a disconnecting means _____ in fluorescent luminaires that utilize double-ended lamps (typical fluorescent lamps) at the time a ballast is replaced.

    (a) shall be installed
    (b) is not required to be added
    (c) shall not be installed
    (d) can be a screw terminal

70. Lighting track fittings can be equipped with general-purpose receptacles.

    (a) True
    (b) False

71. Lighting track shall not be installed within the zone measured 3 ft horizontally and _____ ft vertically from the top of the bathtub rim or shower stall threshold.

    (a) 2
    (b) 3
    (c) 4
    (d) 8

72. Lighting track shall have two supports for a single section of _____ ft or shorter in length and each individual section of not more than 4 ft attached to it shall have one additional support, unless the track is identified for supports at greater intervals.

    (a) 2
    (b) 4
    (c) 6
    (d) 8

73. Exposed secondary circuits of lighting systems operating at 30V or less shall be _____.

    (a) installed in a Chapter 3 wiring method
    (b) supplied by a Class 2 power source and shall use Class 2 cable in accordance with Article 725
    (c) at least 7 ft above the finished floor unless listed for a lower installation height
    (d) any of these

74. A vending machine is defined as any self-service device that dispenses products or merchandise without the necessity of replenishing the device between each vending operation and designed to require insertion of a _____.

    (a) coin or paper currency
    (b) token or card
    (c) key or payment by other means
    (d) all of these

75. An in-sink waste disposer can be cord-and-plug-connected, but the cord shall not be less than 18 in. or more than _____ in. in length.

    (a) 30
    (b) 36
    (c) 42
    (d) 48

76. The length of the cord for a dishwasher or trash compactor shall not be longer than _____ ft, measured from the rear of the appliance.

    (a) 2
    (b) 4
    (c) 6
    (d) 8

77. Wall-mounted ovens and counter-mounted cooking units shall be permitted to be _____.

    (a) permanently connected
    (b) cord-and-plug-connected
    (c) a or b
    (d) none of these

78. For permanently connected appliances rated over _____, the branch-circuit switch or circuit breaker can serve as the disconnecting means where the switch or circuit breaker is within sight from the appliance, or is lockable in accordance with 110.25.

    (a) 200 VA
    (b) 300 VA
    (c) 400 VA
    (d) 500 VA

79. For permanently connected motor-operated appliances with motors rated over _____, a switch or circuit breaker located within sight from the motor operated appliance can serve as the appliance disconnect.

    (a) ⅛ hp
    (b) ¼ hp
    (c) 15A
    (d) b and c

80. If an appliance of more than ⅛ hp is provided with a unit switch that complies with 422.34(A), (B), (C), or (D), the switch or circuit breaker serving as the other disconnecting means shall be permitted to be out of sight from the appliance.

    (a) True
    (b) False

81. For cord-and-plug-connected household electric ranges, an attachment plug and receptacle connection at the rear base of the range can serve as the disconnecting means, if it is _____.

    (a) less than 40A
    (b) a flush-mounted receptacle
    (c) GFCI-protected
    (d) accessible from the front by the removal of a drawer

82. Appliances that have a unit switch with a marked_____ position that disconnects all the ungrounded conductors can serve as the appliance disconnecting means.

    (a) on
    (b) off
    (c) on/off
    (d) all of these

83. Electric drinking fountains shall be _____ protected.

    (a) GFCI
    (b) AFCI
    (c) a or b
    (d) none of these

84. Fixed electric space-heating equipment and motors shall be considered a _____ load for branch circuit sizing.

    (a) noncontinuous
    (b) intermittent
    (c) continuous
    (d) none of these

85. Fixed electric space-heating equipment shall be installed to provide the _____ spacing between the equipment and adjacent combustible material, unless it is listed for direct contact with combustible material.

    (a) required
    (b) minimum
    (c) maximum
    (d) safest

86. A unit switch with a marked _____ position that is part of a fixed space heater, and disconnects all ungrounded conductors, shall be permitted to serve as the required disconnecting means.

    (a) on
    (b) closed
    (c) off
    (d) none of these

87. Electric space-heating equipment employing resistance-type heating elements rated more than _____ shall have the heating elements subdivided.

    (a) 24A
    (b) 36A
    (c) 48A
    (d) 60A

88. Electric space-heating cables shall be furnished complete with factory-assembled nonheating leads at least _____ in length.

    (a) 6 in.
    (b) 18 in.
    (c) 3 ft
    (d) 7 ft

89. On electric space-heating cables, blue leads indicate a cable rated for use on a nominal circuit voltage of _____.

    (a) 120V
    (b) 208V
    (c) 240V
    (d) 277V

90. Conductors located above an electric space-heated ceiling are considered to be operating in an ambient temperature of _____.

    (a) 20°C
    (b) 30°C
    (c) 50°C
    (d) 86°C

91. Electric space-heating cables shall not be installed over cabinets whose clearance from the ceiling is less than the minimum _____ dimension of the cabinet to the nearest cabinet edge that is open to the room or area.

    (a) horizontal
    (b) vertical
    (c) overall
    (d) depth

92. Duct heater controller equipment shall have a disconnecting means installed within _____ the controller except as allowed by 424.19(A).

    (a) 25 ft of
    (b) sight from
    (c) the side of
    (d) none of these

93. When installing duct heaters, sufficient clearance shall be maintained to permit replacement and adjustment of controls and heating elements.

    (a) True
    (b) False

94. A heating panel is a complete assembly provided with a junction box or length of flexible conduit for connection to a(n) _____.

    (a) wiring system
    (b) service
    (c) branch circuit
    (d) approved conductor

95. Examples of snow-melting resistance heaters include _____.

    (a) tubular heaters and strip heaters
    (b) heating panels
    (c) heating cables or heating tape
    (d) all of these

96. All fixed outdoor deicing and snow-melting equipment shall be provided with a means for simultaneous disconnection from all _____ conductors.

    (a) grounded
    (b) grounding
    (c) ungrounded
    (d) all of these

97. Pipeline resistance heating elements include heating _____.

    (a) blankets
    (b) tape
    (c) cables
    (d) all of these

98. Fixed electric heating equipment for pipelines and vessels shall be considered a(n) _____ load.

    (a) noncontinuous
    (b) insignificant
    (c) continuous
    (d) proprietary

99. Ground-fault protection of equipment shall be provided for electric heat tracing and heating panels installed on pipelines or vessels except in certain industrial installations where there is alarm indication of ground faults.

    (a) True
    (b) False

100. For a skin-effect heating installation complying with Article 427, the provisions of 300.20 shall apply to the installation of a single conductor in a ferromagnetic envelope (metal enclosure).

    (a) True
    (b) False

RANDOM ORDER
[ARTICLES 90–427]

Please use the 2014 *Code* book to answer the following questions.

1. _____ clips identified for use with the type of ceiling framing member(s) and luminaires shall be permitted to be used to secure luminaires to the ceiling framing members.

   (a) Marked
   (b) Labeled
   (c) Identified
   (d) listed

2. Type MC cable containing four or fewer conductors, sized no larger than 10 AWG, shall be secured within _____ in. of every box, cabinet, fitting, or other cable termination.

   (a) 8
   (b) 12
   (c) 18
   (d) 24

3. Service metal raceways and metal-clad cables are considered effectively bonded when using threadless couplings and connectors that are _____.

   (a) nonmetallic
   (b) made up tight
   (c) sealed
   (d) classified

4. HDPE conduit shall be resistant to _____.

   (a) moisture
   (b) chemical atmospheres
   (c) impact and crushing
   (d) all of these

5. Electric-discharge and LED luminaires supported independently of the outlet box shall be connected to the branch circuit through _____.

   (a) raceways
   (b) Type MC, AC, MI, or NM cable
   (c) flexible cords
   (d) any of these

6. The requirement for maintaining a 3-foot vertical clearance from the edge of the roof shall not apply to the final feeder conductor span where the conductors are attached to _____.

   (a) a building pole
   (b) the side of a building
   (c) an antenna
   (d) the base of a building

7. Bonding shall be provided where necessary to ensure _____ and the capacity to conduct safely any fault current likely to be imposed.

    (a) electrical continuity
    (b) fiduciary responsibility
    (c) listing requirements
    (d) electrical demand

8. Where single conductor cables comprising each phase, neutral, or grounded conductor of a circuit are connected in parallel in a cable tray, the conductors shall be installed _____, to prevent current unbalance in the paralleled conductors due to inductive reactance.

    (a) in groups consisting of not more than three conductors per phase or neutral
    (b) in groups consisting of not more than one conductor per phase or neutral
    (c) as individual conductors securely bound to the cable tray
    (d) in separate groups

9. If a protective device rating is marked on an appliance, the branch-circuit overcurrent device rating shall not exceed _____ percent of the protective device rating marked on the appliance.

    (a) 50
    (b) 80
    (c) 100
    (d) 115

10. Underground service-entrance conductors shall be protected against physical damage.

    (a) True
    (b) False

11. HDPE conduit shall be permitted only in trade sizes _____.

    (a) ¾ to 4
    (b) ½ to 6
    (c) 1 to 5
    (d) 1 to 3

12. Isolated ground receptacles installed in nonmetallic boxes shall be covered with a nonmetallic faceplate, unless the box contains a feature or accessory that permits the effective grounding of the faceplate.

    (a) True
    (b) False

13. The standard length of RMC shall _____.

    (a) be 10 ft
    (b) include a coupling on each length
    (c) be threaded on each end
    (d) all of these

14. In other than dwelling locations, GFCI protection is required in _____.

    (a) indoor wet locations
    (b) locker rooms with associated showering facilities
    (c) garages, service bays, and similar areas other than vehicle exhibition halls and showrooms
    (d) all of these

15. Luminaires shall be wired with conductors having insulation suitable for the environmental conditions and _____ to which the conductors will be subjected.

    (a) temperature
    (b) voltage
    (c) current
    (d) all of these

16. The number of conductors permitted in PVC conduit shall not exceed the percentage fill specified in _____.

    (a) Chapter 9, Table 1
    (b) Table 250.66
    (c) Table 310.15(B)(16)
    (d) 240.6

17. The *NEC* allows a lighting outlet on the wall in a clothes closet when it is at least 6 in. away from storage space.

    (a) True
    (b) False

18. Knife switches rated for more than 1,200A at 250V or less _____.

    (a) can be used only as isolating switches
    (b) shall not be opened under load
    (c) shall be placed so that gravity tends to close them
    (d) a and b

19. Ground-fault protection that functions to open the service disconnect _____ protect(s) from faults on the line side of the protective element.

    (a) will
    (b) will not
    (c) adequately
    (d) totally

20. Enclosures not over 100 cu in. having threaded entries and not containing a device shall be considered to be adequately supported where _____ or more conduits are threaded wrenchtight into the enclosure and each conduit is secured within 3 ft of the enclosure.

    (a) one
    (b) two
    (c) three
    (d) none of these

21. Track lighting shall not be installed _____.

    (a) where likely to be subjected to physical damage
    (b) in wet or damp locations
    (c) a and b
    (d) none of these

22. Electric space-heating cables shall not extend beyond the room or area in which they _____.

    (a) provide heat
    (b) originate
    (c) terminate
    (d) are connected

23. Surge arrestors 1,000V or less are also known as Type 1 surge protective devices (SPDs).

    (a) True
    (b) False

24. An insulated grounded conductor of _____ or smaller shall be identified by a continuous white or gray outer finish, or by three continuous white or gray stripes along its entire length on other than green insulation.

    (a) 8 AWG
    (b) 6 AWG
    (c) 4 AWG
    (d) 3 AWG

25. Type UF cable shall not be used in _____.

    (a) motion picture studios
    (b) storage battery rooms
    (c) hoistways
    (d) all of these

26. The maximum voltage permitted between ungrounded conductors of flat conductor cable systems is _____.

    (a) 150V
    (b) 250V
    (c) 300V
    (d) 600V

27. Means shall be provided to simultaneously disconnect the _____ of all fixed electric space-heating equipment from all ungrounded conductors.

    (a) heater
    (b) motor controller(s)
    (c) supplementary overcurrent device(s)
    (d) all of these

28. Inserts for cellular metal floor raceways shall be leveled to the floor grade and sealed against the entrance of _____.

    (a) concrete
    (b) water
    (c) moisture
    (d) all of these

29. In dwelling unit bathrooms, not less than one 15A or 20A, 125V receptacle outlet must be installed within _____ from the outside edge of each bathroom basin.

    (a) 20 in.
    (b) 3 ft
    (c) 4 ft
    (d) 6 ft

30. A(n) _____ is a device, or group of devices, by which the conductors of a circuit can be disconnected from their source of supply.

    (a) feeder
    (b) enclosure
    (c) disconnecting means
    (d) conductor interrupter

31. Receptacles and cord connectors having equipment grounding conductor contacts shall have those contacts connected to a(n) _____ conductor.

    (a) grounded
    (b) ungrounded
    (c) equipment grounding
    (d) neutral

32. Utilization equipment weighing not more than 6 lb can be supported to any box or plaster ring secured to a box, provided the equipment is secured with at least two _____ or larger screws.

    (a) No. 6
    (b) No. 8
    (c) No. 10
    (d) self-tapping

33. Auxiliary grounding electrodes can be connected to the _____.

    (a) equipment grounding conductor
    (b) grounded conductor
    (c) a and b
    (d) none of these

34. Receptacle outlet assemblies listed for the application can be installed in countertops of dwelling unit bathrooms.

    (a) True
    (b) False

35. In a multiple-occupancy building, each occupant shall have access to his or her own _____.

    (a) disconnecting means
    (b) building drops
    (c) building-entrance assembly
    (d) lateral conductors

36. "Continuous duty" is defined as _____.

    (a) when the load is expected to continue for five hours or more
    (b) operation at a substantially constant load for an indefinitely long time
    (c) operation at loads and for intervals of time, both of which may be subject to wide variations
    (d) operation at which the load may be subject to maximum current for six hours or more

37. Raceways or cable trays containing electric conductors shall not contain any pipe or tube for steam, water, air, gas, drainage, or any service other than _____.

    (a) as permitted by the authority having jurisdiction
    (b) electrical
    (c) pneumatic
    (d) as designed by the engineer

38. If neutral conductors of different voltage systems are installed in the same raceway, cable, or enclosure, the means of identification of the different neutrals shall be documented in a manner that's _____ or be permanently posted where the conductors of different systems originate.

    (a) available to the AHJ
    (b) available through the engineer
    (c) readily available
    (d) included in the as-built drawings

39. Where practicable, rod, pipe, and plate electrodes shall be installed _____.

    (a) directly below the electrical meter
    (b) on the north side of the building
    (c) below permanent moisture level
    (d) all of these

40. Edison-base fuseholders shall be used only if they are made to accept _____ fuses by the use of adapters.

    (a) Edison-base
    (b) medium-base
    (c) heavy-duty base
    (d) Type S

41. Unless an individual switch is provided for each luminaire located over combustible material, lampholders shall be located at least _____ ft above the floor, or shall be located or guarded so that the lamps cannot be readily removed or damaged.

    (a) 3
    (b) 6
    (c) 8
    (d) 10

42. In multiwire branch circuits, the continuity of the _____ conductor shall not be dependent upon the device connections.

    (a) ungrounded
    (b) grounded
    (c) grounding electrode
    (d) a and b

43. Where NUCC enters a box, fitting, or other enclosure, a bushing or adapter shall be provided to protect the conductor or cable from abrasion unless the design of the box, fitting, or enclosure provides equivalent protection.

    (a) True
    (b) False

44. Nonlocking type 15A and 20A, 125V receptacles in _____ must be listed as tamper resistant.

    (a) theatres
    (b) arcades
    (c) child care facilities
    (d) major repair garages

45. The minimum point of attachment of overhead service conductors to a building shall not be less than _____ above finished grade.

    (a) 8 ft
    (b) 10 ft
    (c) 12 ft
    (d) 15 ft

46. Where flexible cords are used in ambient temperatures other than _____ the temperature correction factors from Table 310.15(B)(2)(a) shall be applied to the ampacity in Table 400.5(A)(1) and Tables 400.5(A)(2).

    (a) 30°C
    (b) 60°C
    (c) 75°C
    (d) 90°C

47. All 15A or 20A, 120V branch circuits that supply outlets or devices in dwelling unit kitchens, family rooms, dining rooms, living rooms, parlors, libraries, dens, bedrooms, sunrooms, recreation rooms, closets, hallways, laundry areas, or similar rooms or areas shall be AFCI protected by a listed arc-fault circuit interrupter.

    (a) True
    (b) False

48. When the fluorescent luminaire disconnecting means for fluorescent luminaires that utilize double-ended lamps (typical fluorescent lamps) is external to the luminaire, it shall be _____.

    (a) accessible to qualified persons
    (b) a single device
    (c) located in sight of the disconnecting means
    (d) all of these

49. LFMC shall not be required to be secured or supported where fished between access points through _____ spaces in finished buildings or structures and supporting is impractical.

    (a) concealed
    (b) exposed
    (c) hazardous
    (d) completed

50. Decorative lighting and similar accessories used for holiday lighting and similar purposes shall be _____.

    (a) marked
    (b) listed
    (c) arc fault protected
    (d) GFCI protected

51. Rigid metal conduit that is directly buried outdoors shall have at least _____ in. of cover.

    (a) 6
    (b) 12
    (c) 18
    (d) 24

52. Conduits and raceways, including end fittings, shall not rise more than _____ in. above the bottom of a switchboard enclosure.

    (a) 3
    (b) 4
    (c) 5
    (d) 6

53. GFCI protection shall be provided for all 15A and 20A, 125V receptacles _____ in dwelling unit kitchens.

    (a) installed to serve the countertop surfaces
    (b) within 6 ft of the sink
    (c) for all receptacles
    (d) that are readily accessible

54. _____ in dwelling units shall supply only loads within that dwelling unit or loads associated only with that dwelling unit.

    (a) Service-entrance conductors
    (b) Ground-fault protection
    (c) Branch circuits
    (d) none of these

55. In indoor locations other than dwellings and associated accessory buildings, fluorescent luminaires that utilize double-ended lamps and contain ballast(s) and can be serviced in place shall have a disconnecting means either internal or external to each luminaire.

    (a) True
    (b) False

56. Unbroken lengths of surface nonmetallic raceways can be run through dry _____.

    (a) walls
    (b) partitions
    (c) floors
    (d) all of these

57. Plug-in-type circuit breakers that are backfed shall be _____ by an additional fastener that requires more than a pull to release.

    (a) grounded
    (b) secured in place
    (c) shunt tripped
    (d) none of these

58. A communications raceway is an enclosed channel of nonmetallic materials designed for holding communications wires and cables in _____ applications.

    (a) plenum
    (b) riser
    (c) general-purpose
    (d) all of these

59. Galvanized steel, stainless steel, and red brass RMC shall be permitted in or under cinder fill subject to permanent moisture, when protected on all sides by a layer of noncinder concrete not less than _____ in. thick.

    (a) 2
    (b) 4
    (c) 6
    (d) 18

60. Where a mast is used for overhead branch-circuit or feeder conductor support, it shall be of adequate strength or be supported by braces or guy wire to withstand safely the strain imposed by the conductors.

    (a) True
    (b) False

61. Type FC cable is an assembly of parallel conductors with an insulating material specifically designed for field installation in surface metal raceways.

    (a) True
    (b) False

62. A demand factor of _____ percent applies to a multifamily dwelling with ten units if the optional calculation method is used.

    (a) 43
    (b) 50
    (c) 60
    (d) 75

63. The *Code* contains provisions considered necessary for safety, which will not necessarily result in _____.

    (a) efficient use
    (b) convenience
    (c) good service or future expansion of electrical use
    (d) all of these

64. Type UF cable is permitted to be used for inside wiring.

    (a) True
    (b) False

65. Lighting systems operating at 30V or less shall be listed or assembled with listed components.

    (a) True
    (b) False

66. When 15A and 20A receptacles are installed in a wet location, the outlet box _____ must be listed for extra-duty use.

    (a) sleeve
    (b) hood
    (c) threaded entry
    (d) mounting

67. Type MC cable installed horizontally through wooden or metal framing members are considered secured and supported where such support doesn't exceed _____ ft intervals.

    (a) 3
    (b) 4
    (c) 6
    (d) 8

68. Type S fuses, fuseholders, and adapters shall be designed so that _____ would be difficult.

    (a) installation
    (b) tampering
    (c) shunting
    (d) b or c

69. Each current-carrying conductor of a paralleled set of conductors shall be counted as a current-carrying conductor for the purpose of applying the adjustment factors of 310.15(B)(3)(a).

    (a) True
    (b) False

70. According to the *NEC*, the volume of a 3 x 2 x 2 in. device box is _____ cu in.

    (a) 8
    (b) 10
    (c) 12
    (d) 14

71. In cellular concrete floor raceways, a grounding conductor shall connect the insert receptacles to a _____.

    (a) negative ground connection provided in the raceway
    (b) negative ground connection provided on the header
    (c) positive ground connection provided on the header
    (d) grounded terminal located within the insert

72. A "_____" is an accommodation with two or more contiguous rooms comprising a compartment that provides living, sleeping, sanitary, and storage facilities.

    (a) guest room
    (b) guest suite
    (c) dwelling unit
    (d) single-family dwelling

73. The _____ rating of a conductor is the maximum temperature, at any location along its length, which the conductor can withstand over a prolonged period of time without serious degradation.

    (a) ambient
    (b) temperature
    (c) maximum withstand
    (d) short-circuit

74. Short sections of metal enclosures or raceways used to provide support or protection of _____ from physical damage shall not be required to be connected to the equipment grounding conductor.

    (a) conduit
    (b) feeders under 600V
    (c) cable assemblies
    (d) none of these

75. A luminaire marked "Suitable for Wet Locations" _____ be permitted to be used in a damp location.

    (a) shall
    (b) shall not
    (c) a or b
    (d) none of these

76. Grommets or bushings for the protection of Type NM cable shall be _____ for the purpose.

    (a) marked
    (b) approved
    (c) identified
    (d) listed

77. The upper end of a ground rod electrode shall be _____ ground level unless the aboveground end and the grounding electrode conductor attachment are protected against physical damage.

    (a) above
    (b) flush with
    (c) below
    (d) b or c

78. Where insulated conductors are deflected within a metal wireway, the wireway shall be sized to meet the bending requirements corresponding to _____ wire per terminal in Table 312.6(A).

    (a) one
    (b) two
    (c) three
    (d) four

79. Metal cable trays containing only non-power conductors (such as communication, data, and signal conductors and cables) must be electrically continuous through approved connections or the use of a(n) _____.

    (a) grounding electrode conductor
    (b) bonding jumper
    (c) equipment grounding conductor
    (d) grounded conductor

80. Wiring methods installed behind panels that allow access shall be _____ according to their applicable articles.

    (a) supported
    (b) painted
    (c) in a metal raceway
    (d) all of these

81. At Type AC cable terminations, a(n) _____ shall be provided.

    (a) fitting (or box design) that protects the conductors from abrasion
    (b) insulating bushing between the conductors and the cable armor
    (c) a and b
    (d) none of these

82. Electric-discharge luminaires having an open-circuit voltage exceeding _____ shall not be installed in or on dwelling occupancies.

    (a) 120V
    (b) 250V
    (c) 600V
    (d) 1,000V

83. Underground raceways and cable assemblies entering a handhole enclosure shall extend into the enclosure, but they are not required to be _____.

    (a) bonded
    (b) insulated
    (c) mechanically connected to the handhole enclosure
    (d) below minimum cover requirements after leaving the handhole

84. Surge protective devices shall only be located outdoors.

    (a) True
    (b) False

85. Individual circuits for nonmotor-operated appliances that are continuously loaded shall have the branch-circuit rating sized not less than _____ percent of the appliance marked ampere rating, unless otherwise listed.

    (a) 80
    (b) 100
    (c) 125
    (d) 150

86. Grounding-type attachment plugs shall be used only with a cord having a(n) _____ conductor.

    (a) equipment grounding
    (b) isolated
    (c) computer circuit
    (d) insulated

87. Lampholders installed in damp locations shall be listed for use in _____ locations.

    (a) damp
    (b) wet
    (c) dry
    (d) a or b

88. Electrical equipment with _____ and having adequate fire-resistant and low-smoke-producing characteristics can be installed within an air-handling space (plenum).

    (a) a metal enclosure
    (b) a nonmetallic enclosure listed for use within an air-handling (plenum) space
    (c) any type of enclosure
    (d) a or b

89. The rating of a branch circuit shall be determined by the rating of the _____.

    (a) ampacity of the largest device connected to the circuit
    (b) average of the ampacity of all devices
    (c) branch-circuit overcurrent device
    (d) ampacity of the branch-circuit conductors according to Table 310.15(B)(16)

90. There are four principal determinants of conductor operating temperature, one of which is _____ generated internally in the conductor as the result of load current flow, including fundamental and harmonic currents.

    (a) friction
    (b) magnetism
    (c) heat
    (d) none of these

91. The minimum clearance for overhead service conductors not exceeding 600V that pass over commercial areas subject to truck traffic is _____ ft.

    (a) 10
    (b) 12
    (c) 15
    (d) 18

92. For Type NM and NMC cable, the conductor ampacity used for ambient temperature correction [310.15(B)(2)(a)], conductor bundling adjustment [310.15(B)(3)(a)], or both, is based on the 90ºC conductor insulation rating [310.15(B)(2)], provided the adjusted or corrected ampacity doesn't exceed that of a _____ rated conductor.

    (a) 60°C
    (b) 75°C
    (c) 90°C
    (d) 120°C

93. The minimum size conductor permitted for branch circuits under 600V is _____ AWG.

    (a) 14
    (b) 12
    (c) 10
    (d) 8

94. The point of attachment of overhead premises wiring to a building shall in no case be less than _____ above finished grade.

    (a) 8 ft
    (b) 10 ft
    (c) 12 ft
    (d) 15 ft

95. Cable trays used to support service-entrance conductors shall contain only service-entrance conductors _____.

    (a) unless a solid fixed barrier separates the service-entrance conductors from other conductors
    (b) under 300V
    (c) in industrial locations
    (d) over 600V

96. The sum of the cross-sectional areas of all contained conductors at any cross-section of a metal wireway shall not exceed _____ percent.

    (a) 50
    (b) 20
    (c) 25
    (d) 80

97. Fixed electric space-heating equipment requiring supply conductors with insulation rated over _____ shall be clearly and permanently marked.

    (a) 60°C
    (b) 75°C
    (c) 90°C
    (d) all of these

98. Handholds in poles supporting luminaires shall not be required for poles _____ ft or less in height above finished grade, if the pole is provided with a hinged base.

    (a) 5
    (b) 10
    (c) 15
    (d) 20

99. One conductor of flexible cords intended to be used as a(n) _____ conductor shall have a continuous marker readily distinguishing it from the other conductors. One means of identification is a braid finished to show a white or gray color on one conductor.

    (a) grounded circuit
    (b) equipment grounding
    (c) ungrounded
    (d) all of these

100. Bends in LFNC shall be made so that the conduit will not be damaged and the internal diameter of the conduit will not be effectively reduced. Bends can be made _____.

    (a) manually without auxiliary equipment
    (b) with bending equipment identified for the purpose
    (c) with any kind of conduit bending tool that will work
    (d) by the use of an open flame torch

STRAIGHT ORDER
[ARTICLES 430–504]

Please use the 2014 *Code* book to answer the following questions.

1. For general motor applications, the motor branch-circuit short-circuit and ground-fault protection device shall be sized based on the _____ values.

   (a) motor nameplate
   (b) NEMA standard
   (c) *NEC* Table
   (d) Factory Mutual

2. The motor _____ currents listed in Tables 430.247 through 430.250 shall be used to determine the ampacity of motor circuit conductors and short-circuit and ground-fault protection devices.

   (a) nameplate
   (b) full-load
   (c) power factor
   (d) service factor

3. Motor controllers and terminals of control circuit devices shall be connected with copper conductors unless identified for use with a different conductor.

   (a) True
   (b) False

4. A motor terminal housing enclosing rigidly mounted motor terminals shall have a minimum of _____ in. between line terminals for a 230V motor.

   (a) ¼
   (b) ⅜
   (c) ½
   (d) ⅝

5. Open motors having commutators or collector rings shall be located or protected so that sparks cannot reach adjacent combustible material. This shall not prohibit the installation of these motors _____.

   (a) on wooden floors
   (b) over combustible fiber
   (c) under combustible material
   (d) none of these

6. In determining the highest rated motor for purposes of 430.24, the highest rated motor shall be based on the rated full-load current as selected _____.

   (a) from the motor nameplate
   (b) from Tables 430.247, 430.248, 430.249, and 430.250
   (c) from taking the horsepower times 746 watts
   (d) using the largest horsepower motor

7. Feeder tap conductors supplying motor circuits, with an ampacity at least one-third that of the feeder, shall not exceed _____ ft in length.

   (a) 10
   (b) 15
   (c) 20
   (d) 25

8. Overload relays and other devices for motor overload protection that are not capable of _____ shall be protected by fuses, circuit breakers, or motor short-circuit protector.

   (a) opening short circuits
   (b) clearing overloads
   (c) opening ground faults
   (d) a or c

9. If a(n) _____ shutdown is necessary to reduce hazards to persons, the overload sensing devices can be connected to a supervised alarm instead of causing immediate interruption of the motor circuit.

   (a) emergency
   (b) normal
   (c) orderly
   (d) none of these

10. The motor branch-circuit short-circuit and ground-fault protective device shall be capable of carrying the _____ current of the motor.

    (a) varying
    (b) starting
    (c) running
    (d) continuous

11. Where the motor short-circuit and ground-fault protection devices determined by Table 430.52 do not correspond to the standard sizes or ratings, a higher rating that does not exceed the next higher standard ampere rating shall be permitted.

    (a) True
    (b) False

12. A motor can be provided with combined overcurrent protection using a single protective device to provide branch-circuit _____ protection where the rating of the device provides the overload protection specified in 430.32.

    (a) short-circuit
    (b) ground-fault
    (c) motor overload
    (d) all of these

13. Overcurrent protection for motor control circuits shall not exceed _____ percent if the conductor is based on Table 310.15(B)(17) and does not extend beyond the motor control equipment enclosure.

    (a) 100
    (b) 150
    (c) 300
    (d) 400

14. Motor control circuit transformers, with a primary current rating of less than 2A, can have the primary protection device set at no more than _____ percent of the rated primary current rating.

    (a) 150
    (b) 200
    (c) 400
    (d) 500

15. Motor control circuits shall be arranged so they will be disconnected from all sources of supply when the disconnecting means is in the open position.

    (a) True
    (b) False

16. The motor controller shall have horsepower ratings at the application voltage not _____ the horsepower rating of the motor.

    (a) lower than
    (b) higher than
    (c) equal to
    (d) none of these

17. For stationary motors of 2 hp or less and 300V or less on ac circuits, the controller can be an ac-rated only general-use snap switch where the motor full-load current rating is not more than _____ percent of the rating of the switch.

    (a) 50
    (b) 60
    (c) 70
    (d) 80

18. A motor controller shall open all conductors to the motor where not used as a disconnecting means.

    (a) True
    (b) False

19. Each motor shall be provided with an individual controller.

    (a) True
    (b) False

20. The motor disconnecting means shall not be required to be in sight from the motor and the driven machinery location, provided _____.

    (a) the controller disconnecting means is lockable, in accordance with 110.25
    (b) locating the motor disconnecting means within sight of the motor is impractical
    (c) locating the motor disconnecting means within sight of the motor introduces additional or increased hazards to people or property
    (d) all of these

21. Where more than one motor disconnecting means is provided in the same motor branch circuit, at least one of the disconnecting means shall be readily accessible.

    (a) True
    (b) False

22. If a motor disconnecting means is a motor-circuit switch, it shall be rated in _____.

    (a) horsepower
    (b) watts
    (c) amperes
    (d) locked-rotor current

23. A switch or circuit breaker can be used as both the controller and disconnecting means if it _____.

    (a) opens all ungrounded conductors
    (b) is protected by an overcurrent device in each ungrounded conductor
    (c) is manually operable, or both power and manually operable
    (d) all of these

24. An oil switch can be used as both the motor controller and disconnecting means on a circuit whose rating _____ or 100A.

    (a) does not exceed 240V
    (b) does not exceed 300V
    (c) does not exceed 1,000V
    (d) exceeds 1,000V

25. Exposed live parts of motors and controllers operating at _____ or more between terminals shall be guarded against accidental contact by enclosure or by location.

    (a) 24V
    (b) 50V
    (c) 60V
    (d) 150V

26. Disconnecting means for air-conditioning or refrigerating equipment can be installed _____ the air-conditioning or refrigerating equipment, but not on panels that are designed to allow access to the equipment, and not over the equipment nameplate.

    (a) on
    (b) within
    (c) a or b
    (d) none of these

27. A hermetic motor-compressor controller shall have a _____ current rating not less than the respective nameplate rating(s) on the compressor.

    (a) continuous-duty full-load
    (b) locked-rotor
    (c) a or b
    (d) a and b

28. The rating of the attachment plug and receptacle shall not exceed _____ at 250V for a cord-and-plug-connected air-conditioner motor-compressor.

    (a) 15A
    (b) 20A
    (c) 30A
    (d) 40A

29. An attachment plug and receptacle can serve as the disconnecting means for a single-phase room air conditioner rated 250 volts or less if _____.

    (a) the manual controls on the room air conditioner are readily accessible and located within 6 ft of the floor
    (b) an approved manually operable disconnecting means is installed in a readily accessible location within sight from the room air conditioner
    (c) a or b
    (d) a and b

30. Article 445 contains installation and other requirements for generators.

    (a) True
    (b) False

31. Constant-voltage generators, except ac generator exciters, shall be protected from overload by _____ or other acceptable overcurrent protective means suitable for the conditions of use.

    (a) inherent design
    (b) circuit breakers
    (c) fuses
    (d) any of these

32. The ampacity of the conductors from the generator terminals to the first distribution device containing overcurrent protection shall not be less than _____ percent of the nameplate rating of the generator.

    (a) 75
    (b) 115
    (c) 125
    (d) 140

33. Separately derived system generators must have the _____ conductor sized not smaller than required to carry the maximum unbalanced current as determined by 220.61.

    (a) neutral
    (b) grounding
    (c) a and b
    (d) none of these

34. Transformers with ventilating openings shall be installed so that the ventilating openings are _____.

    (a) a minimum 18 in. above the floor
    (b) not blocked by walls or obstructions
    (c) aesthetically located
    (d) vented to the exterior of the building

35. Transformer vaults shall be located where they can be ventilated to the outside air without using flues or ducts, where _____.

    (a) permitted
    (b) practicable
    (c) required
    (d) all of these

36. Ventilation openings for transformer vaults must be located as far as possible from _____.

    (a) doors
    (b) windows
    (c) combustible material
    (d) any of these

37. Transformer vaults containing more than _____ total kVA transformer capacity shall be provided with a drain or other means that will carry off any accumulation of oil or water in the vault, unless impracticable.

    (a) 100
    (b) 150
    (c) 200
    (d) 250

38. For phase converters serving variable loads, the ampacity of the single-phase supply conductors shall not be less than _____ percent of the single-phase input full-load amperes listed on the phase converter nameplate.

    (a) 75
    (b) 100
    (c) 125
    (d) 150

39. Means shall be provided to simultaneously disconnect all _____ supply conductors to a phase converter.

    (a) ungrounded
    (b) grounded
    (c) grounding
    (d) all of these

40. The phase converter disconnecting means shall be _____ and located in sight from the phase converter.

    (a) protected from physical damage
    (b) readily accessible
    (c) easily visible
    (d) clearly identified

41. Capacitors containing more than _____ gallons of flammable liquid shall be enclosed in vaults or outdoor fenced enclosures.

    (a) 3
    (b) 5
    (c) 10
    (d) 11

42. Capacitors shall be _____ so that persons cannot come into accidental contact or bring conducting materials into accidental contact with exposed energized parts, terminals, or buses associated with them.

    (a) enclosed
    (b) located
    (c) guarded
    (d) any of these

43. A separate overcurrent device shall not be required for a capacitor connected on the load side of a motor overload protective device.

    (a) True
    (b) False

44. A separate disconnecting means shall be installed where a capacitor is connected on the load side of a motor controller.

    (a) True
    (b) False

45. Where a motor installation includes a capacitor connected on the load side of the motor overload device, the rating or setting of the motor overload device shall be based on the improved power factor of the motor circuit.

    (a) True
    (b) False

46. A capacitor operating at over 1,000V shall be provided with means to reduce the residual voltage to 50V or less within _____ minute(s) after it is disconnected from the source of supply.

    (a) one
    (b) three
    (c) five
    (d) seven

47. Resistors and reactors rated over 1,000V shall be isolated by _____ to protect personnel from accidental contact with energized parts.

    (a) an enclosure
    (b) elevation
    (c) a or b
    (d) a and b

48. Nominal battery voltage, as it relates to storage batteries, is the value of a(n) _____ of a given voltage class for convenient designation.

    (a) cell or battery
    (b) container
    (c) electrolyte
    (d) intertier connector

49. Racks (rigid frames designed to support battery cells or trays) must be made of which of the following?

    (a) Metal, treated to be resistant to deteriorating action by the electrolyte and provided with nonconducting or continuous insulating material members directly supporting the cells.
    (b) Fiberglass.
    (c) Other suitable nonconductive materials.
    (d) any of these

50. The required working space for battery systems is measured from the edge of the battery _____.

    (a) terminals
    (b) enclosure
    (c) rack or cabinet
    (d) any of these

51. Combustible dust is defined as dust particles that are 500 microns or smaller in diameter and _____ when dispersed and ignited in air.

    (a) present a fire hazard
    (b) present an explosion hazard
    (c) can't be extinguished
    (d) a or b

52. Class I, Division 1 locations are those in which ignitible concentrations of _____ can exist under normal operating conditions.

    (a) combustible dust
    (b) easily ignitible fibers or flyings
    (c) flammable gases or flammable liquid-produced vapors
    (d) pyrotechnics

53. When determining a Class I, Division 2 location, the _____ is a factor that should be considered in determining the classification and extent of the location.

    (a) quantity of flammable material that might escape in case of an accident
    (b) adequacy of ventilating equipment
    (c) record of the industry or business with respect to explosions or fires
    (d) all of these

54. Class II locations are those that are hazardous because of the presence of _____.

    (a) combustible dust
    (b) easily ignitible fibers/flyings
    (c) flammable gases or vapors
    (d) flammable liquids or gases

55. In Class _____ locations for Groups A, B, C, and D, the classification involves determinations of maximum explosion pressure and maximum safe clearance between parts of a clamped joint in an enclosure.

    (a) I
    (b) II
    (c) III
    (d) all of these

56. Equipment in an area containing ignitible concentrations of acetylene under normal operating conditions shall be classified as a Class I, Group A location.

    (a) True
    (b) False

57. An atmosphere containing ignitible concentrations of _____ is an example of a typical Class I, Group C hazardous (classified) location.

    (a) hydrogen
    (b) ethylene
    (c) gasoline
    (d) all of these

58. An atmosphere classified as hazardous Group E contains combustible metal dusts.

    (a) True
    (b) False

59. An atmosphere classified as hazardous Group G contains combustible dusts such as flour, grain, wood, plastic, and chemicals that are not included in Group E or Group F.

    (a) True
    (b) False

60. Acceptable protection techniques for electrical and electronic equipment in hazardous (classified) locations includes: _____.

    (a) Explosionproof Equipment
    (b) Dust-Ignitionproof
    (c) Dusttight
    (d) all of these

61. Threaded conduits or fittings installed in hazardous (classified) locations shall be made wrenchtight to _____.

    (a) prevent sparking when a fault current flows through the conduit system
    (b) ensure the explosionproof integrity of the conduit system where applicable
    (c) a and b
    (d) none of these

62. Equipment used in hazardous (classified) locations with metric threaded entries shall be installed using _____.

    (a) NPT threaded fittings
    (b) listed conduit fittings
    (c) listed cable fittings
    (d) b or c

63. Where optical fiber cable is capable of carrying current (composite optical fiber cable), the optical fiber cable must be installed in accordance with Articles 500, 501, 502, or 503.

    (a) True
    (b) False

64. MI cable terminated with fittings listed for the location is allowed in Class I, Division 1 locations.

    (a) True
    (b) False

65. In industrial establishments with restricted public access, where the conditions of maintenance and supervision ensure that only qualified persons service the installation, Type ITC-HL cable is allowed to be used in a Class I, Division 1 location if it _____ and installed in accordance with the provisions of Article 727.

    (a) is listed for use in Class I, Zone 1, or Division 1 locations
    (b) has a gas/vaportight continuous corrugated metallic sheath and an overall jacket of suitable polymeric material
    (c) is terminated with fittings listed for the application
    (d) all of these

66. Wiring methods permitted in Class I, Division 1 locations are permitted in Class I, Division 2 locations.

    (a) True
    (b) False

67. In Class I, Division 2 locations, where metallic conduit doesn't provide sufficient corrosion resistance, reinforced thermosetting resin conduit with the suffix –XW and Schedule 80 PVC conduit can be used, but only in industrial establishments where maintenance and supervision ensure that only qualified persons service the installation.

    (a) True
    (b) False

68. In a Class I, Division 2 location, if flexibility is necessary, _____ are some of the wiring methods that are permitted.

    (a) listed flexible metal fittings
    (b) flexible metal conduit, liquidtight flexible metal conduit and liquidtight nonmetallic conduit, all with listed fittings
    (c) interlocked armor Type MC cable with listed fittings
    (d) all of these

69. When provisions for flexibility are necessary in Class I, Division 2 locations, FMC with listed fittings can be used.

    (a) True
    (b) False

70. In a Class I, Division 2 location, switches and circuit breakers shall be installed in explosionproof enclosures meeting the requirements for Class I, Division 1 locations.

    (a) True
    (b) False

71. The minimum thickness of sealing compound in Class I locations shall not be less than the trade size of the conduit or sealing fitting and, in no case, shall the thickness of the compound be less than _____ in.

    (a) ⅛
    (b) ¼
    (c) ⅜
    (d) ⅝

72. In Class I locations, the locknut-bushing and double-locknut types of contacts shall not be depended on for bonding purposes.

    (a) True
    (b) False

73. Transformers and capacitors installed in Class I, Division 1 locations containing a liquid that will burn shall be installed in vaults.

    (a) True
    (b) False

74. Transformers and capacitors installed in Class I, Division 1 locations that do not contain flammable liquids shall not be required to be installed in vaults if they are identified for Class I locations.

    (a) True
    (b) False

75. Meters, instruments, instrument transformers, resistors, rectifiers, and thermionic tubes in Class I, Division 1 locations shall be installed in enclosures identified for use in Class I, Division 1 locations.

    (a) True
    (b) False

76. Meters, instruments and relays installed in Class I, Division 2 locations can have switches, circuit breakers, and make-and-break contacts installed in general-purpose enclosures if current-interrupting contacts are _____.

    (a) immersed in oil
    (b) enclosed within a hermetically sealed chamber
    (c) a or b
    (d) a and b

77. In Class I, Division 2 locations, fused or unfused disconnect and isolating switches for transformers or capacitor banks that are not intended to interrupt current in normal performance can be installed in general-purpose enclosures.

    (a) True
    (b) False

78. Luminaires installed in Class I, Division 1 locations shall be identified as a complete assembly for the Class I, Division 1 location and shall be clearly marked to indicate the _____.

    (a) maximum wattage of lamps
    (b) minimum conductor size
    (c) maximum overcurrent protection permitted
    (d) all of these

79. Pendant luminaires in a Class I, Division 1 location shall be suspended by and supplied through threaded rigid metal conduit stems or threaded steel intermediate conduit stems, and threaded joints shall be provided with _____ or other effective means to prevent loosening.

    (a) set-screws
    (b) welded joints
    (c) expansion joints
    (d) explosionproof flex

80. Boxes, box assemblies, or fittings used to support luminaires in Class I, Division 1 locations shall be identified for Class I locations.

    (a) True
    (b) False

81. Luminaires installed in Class I, Division 2 locations shall be protected from physical damage by a suitable _____.

    (a) warning label
    (b) pendant
    (c) guard or by location
    (d) all of these

82. Raceways permitted as a wiring method in Class II, Division 1 locations include _____.

    (a) threaded RMC and steel IMC
    (b) PVC conduit
    (c) electrical metallic tubing
    (d) any of these

83. Where flexibility is required, the following wiring methods are permitted in a Class II, Division 1 location _____.

    (a) dusttight flexible connectors
    (b) liquidtight flexible metal conduit with listed fittings
    (c) flexible cords listed for extra-hard usage with listed dusttight cord connectors
    (d) any of these

84. Seals in Class II hazardous (classified) locations shall be explosionproof.

    (a) True
    (b) False

85. Where LFMC is used in a Class II, Division 1 location as permitted in 502.10, it shall _____.

    (a) not be unsupported
    (b) not exceed 6 ft in length
    (c) include an equipment bonding jumper of the wire type
    (d) be listed for use in Class I locations

86. In Class II, Division 1 locations, control transformers, solenoids, impedance coils and resistors, and any overcurrent devices or switching mechanisms associated with them, shall have enclosures identified for _____.

    (a) Class I, Division 1 locations
    (b) control transformer duty
    (c) general duty
    (d) Class II, Division 1 locations

87. In Class II, Division 1 locations, motors, generators, and other rotating electrical machinery shall be _____.

    (a) identified for the location
    (b) totally enclosed pipe-ventilated
    (c) general duty
    (d) a or b

88. Luminaires installed in Class II, Division 1 locations shall be identified for the location and shall be clearly marked to indicate the _____.

    (a) maximum wattage and type of lamps for which they're designed
    (b) minimum conductor size
    (c) maximum overcurrent protection permitted
    (d) all of these

89. Luminaires installed in Class II, Division 1 locations shall be protected from physical damage by a suitable _____.

    (a) warning label
    (b) pendant
    (c) guard or by location
    (d) all of these

90. Pendant luminaires installed in Class II, Division 1 locations shall be suspended by threaded RMC or steel IMC conduit stems, by chains with approved fittings, or by other approved means. Stems shall be provided with _____ or other effective means to prevent loosening.

    (a) set-screws
    (b) welded joints
    (c) expansion joints
    (d) explosionproof flex

91. Raceways permitted in a Class III location include _____.

    (a) RMC and IMC
    (b) Type MC cable with listed termination fittings
    (c) electrical metallic tubing
    (d) any of these

92. Boxes and fittings shall be _____ where installed in a Class III location.

    (a) explosionproof
    (b) dust-ignitionproof
    (c) dusttight
    (d) weatherproof

93. Where LFMC is used in a Class III location as permitted in 503.10, it shall _____.

    (a) not be unsupported
    (b) not exceed 6 ft in length
    (c) include an equipment bonding jumper of the wire type
    (d) be listed for use in a Class I hazardous (classified) location

94. Luminaires for fixed lighting in Class III locations shall have enclosures for lamps and lampholders that are designed to prevent the escape of _____.

    (a) sparks
    (b) burning material
    (c) hot metal
    (d) all of these

95. Intrinsically safe apparatus, associated apparatus, and other equipment must be installed in accordance with the _____ drawing(s).

    (a) approved
    (b) control
    (c) identified
    (d) any of these

96. Conductors of intrinsically safe circuits shall not be placed in any _____ with conductors of any nonintrinsically safe system.

    (a) raceway
    (b) cable tray
    (c) cable
    (d) any of these

97. Intrinsically safe apparatus, metal enclosures, and metal raceways shall be connected to the equipment grounding conductor.

    (a) True
    (b) False

98. In hazardous (classified) locations, intrinsically safe apparatus shall be _____ in accordance with 250.100.

    (a) secured
    (b) bonded
    (c) painted
    (d) not be used

99. Intrinsically safe circuits must be identified at _____ locations to prevent unintentional interference with the circuits during testing and servicing.

    (a) terminal
    (b) junction
    (c) a or b
    (d) a and b

100. Conduits, cable trays, and other wiring methods used for intrinsically safe systems shall be identified by permanently affixed labels with the wording "Intrinsic Safety Wiring." The labels shall be visible after installation and the spacing between labels shall not exceed _____ ft.

    (a) 3
    (b) 10
    (c) 25
    (d) 50

RANDOM ORDER
[ARTICLES 90–504]

Please use the 2014 *Code* book to answer the following questions.

1. Underfloor raceways shall be laid so that a straight line from the center of one _____ to the center of the next _____ coincides with the centerline of the raceway system.

   (a) termination point, termination point
   (b) junction box, junction box
   (c) receptacle, receptacle
   (d) panelboard, panelboard

2. Generators must have a disconnecting means that is lockable in the open position, except where the _____.

   (a) driving means for the generator can be readily shut down, is rendered incapable of restarting, and is lockable in the OFF position
   (b) generator isn't arranged to operate in parallel with another generator or other source of voltage
   (c) a and b
   (d) a or b

3. The required working space for battery systems is measured from the edge of the battery _____.

   (a) terminals
   (b) enclosure
   (c) rack or cabinet
   (d) any of these

4. Cut ends of FMC shall be trimmed or otherwise finished to remove rough edges, except where fittings _____.

   (a) are the crimp-on type
   (b) thread into the convolutions
   (c) contain insulated throats
   (d) are listed for grounding

5. Motors shall be located so that adequate _____ is provided and so that maintenance, such as lubrication of bearings and replacing of brushes, can be readily accomplished.

   (a) space
   (b) ventilation
   (c) protection
   (d) all of these

6. If a branch circuit supplies a single nonmotor-operated appliance, the rating of overcurrent protection shall not exceed _____ percent of the appliance rated current if the overcurrent protection rating is not marked and the appliance is rated over 13.30A.

   (a) 100
   (b) 125
   (c) 150
   (d) 160

7. What's the minimum cover requirement for Type UF cable supplying power to a 120V, 15A GFCI-protected circuit outdoors under a driveway of a one-family dwelling?

   (a) 6 in.
   (b) 12 in.
   (c) 16 in.
   (d) 24 in.

8. Electrically conductive materials that are likely to _____ in ungrounded systems shall be connected together and to the supply system grounded equipment in a manner that creates a low-impedance path for ground-fault current that is capable of carrying the maximum fault current likely to be imposed on it.

   (a) become energized
   (b) require service
   (c) be removed
   (d) be coated with paint or nonconductive materials

9. AC or dc general-use snap switches may be used for control of inductive loads not exceeding _____ percent of the ampere rating of the switch at the applied voltage.

   (a) 50
   (b) 75
   (c) 90
   (d) 100

10. Class III locations are those that are hazardous because of the presence of _____.

   (a) combustible dust
   (b) easily ignitible fibers or materials producing combustible flyings
   (c) flammable gases or vapors
   (d) flammable liquids or gases

11. No _____ splices or taps shall be made within or on a luminaire.

   (a) unapproved
   (b) untested
   (c) uninspected
   (d) unnecessary

12. Flexible cords shall not be used as a substitute for _____ wiring.

   (a) temporary
   (b) fixed
   (c) overhead
   (d) none of these

13. Equipment grounding conductors for motor branch circuits shall be sized in accordance with Table 250.122, based on the rating of the _____ device.

   (a) motor overload
   (b) motor over-temperature
   (c) branch-circuit short-circuit and ground-fault protective
   (d) feeder overcurrent protection

14. A switchboard or panelboard containing an ungrounded ac electrical system is required to be legibly and permanently field-marked to caution that the system is ungrounded and include the _____.

   (a) contact information for the power supplier
   (b) contact information for emergency services
   (c) operating voltage between conductors
   (d) transformer impedance rating

15. A branch-circuit overcurrent device can serve as the disconnecting means for a stationary motor of ⅛ hp or less.

   (a) True
   (b) False

16. Currents that introduce noise or data errors in electronic equipment are considered objectionable currents in the context of 250.6(d) of the *NEC*.

   (a) True
   (b) False

17. Each appliance shall have a means that _____ disconnects all ungrounded circuit conductors.

   (a) sequentially
   (b) automatically
   (c) simultaneously
   (d) all of these

18. Ground-fault circuit-interrupter protection for personnel shall be provided for cables installed in electrically heated floors of _____.

    (a) bathrooms
    (b) hydromassage bathtub locations
    (c) kitchens
    (d) all of these

19. An enclosure for either surface mounting or flush mounting provided with a frame in which a door can be hung is called a(n) "_____."

    (a) enclosure
    (b) outlet box
    (c) cutout box
    (d) cabinet

20. Barriers shall be placed in all service switchboards such that no uninsulated, ungrounded service _____ or service terminal is exposed to inadvertent contact by persons or maintenance equipment while servicing load terminations.

    (a) busbar
    (b) conductors
    (c) cables
    (d) none of these

21. Premises wiring includes _____ wiring from the service point or power source to the outlets.

    (a) interior
    (b) exterior
    (c) underground
    (d) a and b

22. The supply-side bonding jumper on the supply side of services shall be sized according to the _____.

    (a) overcurrent device rating
    (b) ungrounded supply conductor size
    (c) service-drop size
    (d) load to be served

23. Wooden plugs driven into holes in _____ or similar materials shall not be used for securing electrical equipment.

    (a) masonry
    (b) concrete
    (c) plaster
    (d) all of these

24. In Class I, Division 1 locations, control transformers, impedance coils, and resistors, along with any switching mechanism associated with them, shall be provided with enclosures identified for _____.

    (a) Class I, Division 1 locations
    (b) control transformer duty
    (c) general duty
    (d) NEMA 3R

25. Central heating equipment, other than fixed electric space-heating equipment, shall be supplied by a(n) _____ branch circuit.

    (a) multiwire
    (b) individual
    (c) multipurpose
    (d) small-appliance

26. Cable wiring methods shall not be used as a means of support for _____.

    (a) other cables
    (b) raceways
    (c) nonelectrical equipment
    (d) all of these

27. Receptacles mounted in boxes set back from the wall surface shall be installed so that the mounting _____ of the receptacle is held rigidly at the finished surface.

    (a) screws or nails
    (b) yoke or strap
    (c) faceplate
    (d) none of these

28. The circuit conductors between the final overcurrent device protecting the circuit and the outlet(s) are known as "_____ conductors."

    (a) feeder
    (b) branch-circuit
    (c) home run
    (d) none of these

29. Luminaires must maintain a minimum clearance from the closet storage space of _____.

    (a) 12 in. for surface-mounted incandescent or LED luminaires with a completely enclosed light source
    (b) 6 in. for surface-mounted fluorescent luminaires
    (c) 6 in. for recessed fluorescent luminaires or recessed incandescent or LED luminaires with a completely enclosed light source
    (d) all of these

30. In Class II locations, a permitted method of bonding is the use of bonding jumpers with proper fittings.

    (a) True
    (b) False

31. In order for a metal underground water pipe to be used as a grounding electrode, it shall be in direct contact with the earth for _____.

    (a) 5 ft
    (b) 10 ft or more
    (c) less than 10 ft
    (d) 20 ft or more

32. Type FCC cable shall be clearly and durably marked _____.

    (a) on the top side at intervals not exceeding 30 in.
    (b) on both sides at intervals not exceeding 24 in.
    (c) with conductor material, maximum temperature, and ampacity
    (d) b and c

33. _____ enclosures are constructed so that dust will not enter under specific test conditions.

    (a) Dust-ignitionproof
    (b) Dusttight
    (c) a or b
    (d) a and

34. Totally enclosed motors of the types specified in 501.125(A)(2) or (A)(3) shall have a device to de-energize the motor or provide an alarm if there is any increase in temperature of the motor beyond designed limits when operating in Class I, Division 1 locations.

    (a) True
    (b) False

35. Conductor adjustment factors shall not apply to conductors in raceways having a length not exceeding _____ in.

    (a) 12
    (b) 24
    (c) 36
    (d) 48

36. Intrinsically safe conduit or cable runs that leave a Class I or II location shall be sealed. The seal shall be _____.

    (a) explosionproof or flameproof
    (b) flameproof
    (c) a and b
    (d) none of these

37. A 30A, 208V receptacle installed in a wet location, where the product intended to be plugged into it is not attended while in use, shall have an enclosure that is weatherproof with the attachment plug cap inserted or removed.

    (a) True
    (b) False

38. Each switchboard or panelboard used as service equipment shall be provided with a main bonding jumper within the panelboard, or within one of the sections of the switchboard, for connecting the grounded service-entrance conductor on its _____ side to the switchboard or panelboard frame.

    (a) load
    (b) supply
    (c) phase
    (d) high-leg

39. The residual voltage of a capacitor, rated not over 1,000V, shall be reduced to 50V or less within _____ after the capacitor is disconnected from the source of supply.

    (a) 15 seconds
    (b) 45 seconds
    (c) one minute
    (d) two minutes

40. In Class III locations, motors, generators, and other rotating machinery shall be totally enclosed _____.

    (a) nonventilated
    (b) pipe ventilated
    (c) fan cooled
    (d) any of these

41. A recessed luminaire shall be installed so that adjacent combustible material will not be subjected to temperatures in excess of _____°C.

    (a) 75
    (b) 90
    (c) 125
    (d) 150

42. The metal mounting yoke of a replacement switch isn't required to be connected to an equipment grounding conductor if the wiring at the existing switch doesn't contain an equipment grounding conductor, and _____.

    (a) the switch faceplate is nonmetallic with nonmetallic screws
    (b) the replacement switch is GFCI protected
    (c) a or b
    (d) the circuit is AFCI protected

43. In Class II, Division 2 locations, motors, generators, and other rotating electrical equipment shall be _____.

    (a) totally enclosed nonventilated or pipe-ventilated
    (b) totally enclosed water-air-cooled or fan-cooled
    (c) dust-ignitionproof
    (d) any of these

44. Lighting track shall not be installed less than _____ ft above the finished floor except where protected from physical damage or where the track operates at less than 30V rms, open-circuit voltage.

    (a) 4
    (b) 5
    (c) 5½
    (d) 6

45. In Class III locations, locknut-bushing and double-locknut types of fittings may be depended on for bonding purposes.

    (a) True
    (b) False

46. PVC conduit can support nonmetallic conduit bodies not larger than the largest entering raceway, but the conduit bodies shall not contain devices, luminaires, or other equipment.

    (a) True
    (b) False

47. Grounding electrode conductor taps from a separately derived system to a common grounding electrode conductor are permitted when a building or structure has multiple separately derived systems, provided that the taps terminate at the same point as the system bonding jumper.

    (a) True
    (b) False

48. _____ on equipment to be grounded shall be removed from contact surfaces to ensure good electrical continuity.

    (a) Paint
    (b) Lacquer
    (c) Enamel
    (d) any of these

49. A strut-type channel raceway can be installed _____.

    (a) where exposed
    (b) as a power pole
    (c) unbroken through walls, partitions, and floors
    (d) all of these

50. Metal enclosures and raceways for other than service conductors shall be connected to the neutral conductor.

    (a) True
    (b) False

51. Fixture wires shall not be used for branch-circuit wiring, except as permitted in other articles of the *Code*.

    (a) True
    (b) False

52. Circuit directories can include labels that depend on transient conditions of occupancy.

    (a) True
    (b) False

53. Where used, the surge protective device shall be connected to the grounded conductor of the circuit.

    (a) True
    (b) False

54. Receptacle yokes designed and _____ as self-grounding can, in conjunction with the supporting screws, establish the equipment bonding between the device yoke and a flush-type box.

    (a) approved
    (b) advertised
    (c) listed
    (d) installed

55. If a permanently installed electric baseboard heater has factory-installed receptacle outlets, the receptacle is permitted to be connected to the heater circuits.

    (a) True
    (b) False

56. The two to six disconnects for a disconnecting means for a building supplied by a feeder shall be _____.

    (a) the same size
    (b) grouped
    (c) in the same enclosure
    (d) none of these

57. Luminaires for fixed lighting in Class II, Division 2 locations shall be equipped with enclosures that are _____ or otherwise identified for the location.

    (a) dust-ignitionproof
    (b) dusttight
    (c) dustproof
    (d) explosionproof

58. When sealing fittings are required for Class I locations, they shall comply with which of the following rule(s)?

    (a) They shall be listed for Class I locations and shall be accessible.
    (b) The minimum thickness of the sealing compound shall not be less than the trade size of the sealing fitting and, in no case, shall the thickness of the compound be less than ⅝ in.
    (c) Splices and taps shall not be made in the conduit seal.
    (d) all of these

59. Type AC cable shall be supported and secured by _____.

    (a) staples
    (b) cable ties
    (c) straps
    (d) any of these

60. Fixture wires are used to connect luminaires to the _____ conductors supplying the luminaires.

    (a) service
    (b) branch-circuit
    (c) feeder
    (d) none of these

61. When mounting an enclosure in a finished surface, the enclosure shall be _____ secured to the surface by clamps, anchors, or fittings identified for the application.

    (a) temporarily
    (b) partially
    (c) never
    (d) rigidly

62. Horizontal runs of RMC supported by openings through _____ at intervals not exceeding 10 ft and securely fastened within 3 ft of termination points shall be permitted.

    (a) walls
    (b) trusses
    (c) rafters
    (d) framing members

63. Article 503 covers the requirements for electrical and electronic equipment and wiring in Class III locations where fire or explosion hazards may exist due to ignitible _____.

    (a) gases or vapors
    (b) fibers/flyings
    (c) dust
    (d) all of these

64. 20A, 125V receptacles subject to _____ can have an enclosure that is weatherproof when the attachment plug is removed.

    (a) shower spray
    (b) beating rain
    (c) corrosive conditions
    (d) routine high-pressure spray washing

65. The radius of the inner edge of any bend in Type MI cable shall not be less than five times the external diameter of the metallic sheath for cable not more than _____ in. in external diameter.

    (a) ½
    (b) ⅝
    (c) ¾
    (d) 1½

66. Closet storage space is defined as a volume bounded by the sides and back closet walls extending from the closet floor vertically to a height of _____ ft or the highest clothes-hanging rod at a horizontal distance of 2 ft from the sides and back of the closet walls.

    (a) 6
    (b) 7
    (c) 8
    (d) 9

67. A device comprised of _____ or more receptacles shall be calculated at not less than 90 VA per receptacle.

    (a) one
    (b) two
    (c) three
    (d) four

68. Panelboards equipped with snap switches rated at 30A or less shall have overcurrent protection not exceeding _____.

    (a) 30A
    (b) 50A
    (c) 100A
    (d) 200A

69. Ballasts for fluorescent lighting installed indoors shall have _____ protection.

    (a) AFCI
    (b) supplementary
    (c) integral thermal
    (d) none of these

70. External surfaces of pipeline and vessel heating equipment that operate at temperatures exceeding _____ shall be physically guarded, isolated, or thermally insulated to protect against contact by personnel in the area.

    (a) 110°F
    (b) 120°F
    (c) 130°F
    (d) 140°F

71. In Class 1, Division 2 locations, Schedule 80 PVC conduit or reinforced thermosetting resin conduit (RTRC) with the suffix -XW shall be permitted where _____.

    (a) metal conduit does not provide sufficient corrosion resistance
    (b) only qualified persons service the installation
    (c) installed in industrial locations
    (d) all of these

72. What is the minimum size copper supply-side bonding jumper for a service raceway containing 4/0 THHN aluminum conductors?

    (a) 6 AWG aluminum
    (b) 4 AWG aluminum
    (c) 4 AWG copper
    (d) 3 AWG copper

73. Concrete, brick, or tile walls are considered _____, as applied to working space requirements.

    (a) inconsequential
    (b) in the way
    (c) grounded
    (d) none of these

74. Color coding shall be permitted to identify intrinsically safe conductors where they are colored light _____ and where no other conductors colored light _____ are used.

    (a) red
    (b) blue
    (c) yellow
    (d) any of these

75. A conductor used to connect the system grounded conductor or the equipment to a grounding electrode or to a point on the grounding electrode system is called the "_____ conductor."

    (a) main grounding
    (b) common main
    (c) equipment grounding
    (d) grounding electrode

76. Where solid knobs are used for concealed knob-and-tube wiring, conductors shall be securely tied to them by _____ equivalent to that of the conductor.

    (a) tie wires having insulation
    (b) conductors having an AWG
    (c) nonconductive material
    (d) none of these

77. The disconnecting means for a motor controller shall be designed so that it cannot _____ automatically.

    (a) open
    (b) close
    (c) restart
    (d) shut down

78. Lampholders shall be constructed, installed, or equipped with shades or guards so that _____ isn't subjected to temperatures in excess of 90°C (194°F).

    (a) ferrous material
    (b) the shade or guard
    (c) combustible material
    (d) a or b

79. In Class III locations, flexible cords shall _____.

    (a) be listed as extra-hard usage
    (b) contain an equipment grounding conductor
    (c) terminate with a listed dusttight cord connector
    (d) all of these

80. Each electric appliance shall be provided with a(n) _____ giving the identifying name and the rating in volts and amperes, or in volts and watts.

    (a) pamphlet
    (b) nameplate
    (c) auxiliary statement
    (d) owner's manual

81. Conductors rated at a temperature _____ than the listed temperature rating of PVC conduit shall be permitted to be installed in PVC conduit, provided the conductors are not operated at a temperature above the raceway's listed temperature rating.

    (a) lower
    (b) the same as
    (c) higher
    (d) a or b

82. The maximum ampere rating of a 4 in. x ½ in. busbar 4 ft long and installed in an auxiliary gutter is _____.

    (a) 500A
    (b) 650A
    (c) 750A
    (d) 2,000A

83. Overhead service conductors shall have a horizontal clearance of not less than _____ ft from a pool.

    (a) 8
    (b) 10
    (c) 12
    (d) 14

84. A lighting system covered by Article 411 shall have a power supply output rated not more than _____ and not more than 30V.

    (a) 15A
    (b) 20A
    (c) 25A
    (d) 30A

85. A dwelling unit containing three 120V small-appliance branch circuits has a calculated load of _____VA for the small appliance circuits.

    (a) 1,500
    (b) 3,000
    (c) 4,500
    (d) 6,000

86. Exposed structural metal interconnected to form a metal building frame that is not intentionally grounded and is likely to become energized, shall be bonded to the _____.

    (a) service equipment enclosure or building disconnecting means
    (b) grounded conductor at the service
    (c) grounding electrode conductor where of sufficient size
    (d) any of these

87. Provisions appropriate to the battery technology shall be made for sufficient diffusion and ventilation of the gases from a storage battery to prevent the accumulation of a(n) _____ mixture.

    (a) corrosive
    (b) explosive
    (c) toxic
    (d) all of these

88. FMC shall be supported and secured _____.

    (a) at intervals not exceeding 4½ ft
    (b) within 8 in. on each side of a box where fished
    (c) where fished
    (d) at intervals not exceeding 6 ft

89. Outdoor luminaires and associated equipment can be supported by trees.

    (a) True
    (b) False

90. Chapters 1 through 4 of the *NEC* apply _____.

    (a) generally to all electrical installations
    (b) only to special occupancies and conditions
    (c) only to special equipment and material
    (d) all of these

91. Ungrounded alternating current systems from 50V to less than 1,000V must be legibly marked "Caution: Ungrounded System — Operating _____ Volts Between Conductors" at _____ of the system, with sufficient durability to withstand the environment involved.

    (a) the source
    (b) the first disconnecting means
    (c) every junction box
    (d) a or b

92. In Class II, Division 2 locations, enclosures for fuses, switches, circuit breakers, and motor controllers, including pushbuttons, relays, and similar devices shall be _____.

    (a) dusttight or otherwise identified for the location
    (b) raintight
    (c) rated as Class I, Division 1 explosionproof
    (d) general duty

93. When breaks occur in dwelling unit kitchen countertop spaces for range tops, refrigerators or sinks, each countertop surface shall be considered a separate counter space for determining receptacle placement.

    (a) True
    (b) False

94. Where angle or U pulls are made, the distance between each raceway entry inside the box or conduit body and the opposite wall of the box or conduit body shall not be less than _____ times the trade size of the largest raceway in a row plus the sum of the trade sizes of the remaining raceways in the same wall and row.

    (a) six
    (b) eight
    (c) twelve
    (d) none of these

95. Cable trays shall be _____ except as permitted by 392.10(D).

    (a) exposed
    (b) accessible
    (c) concealed
    (d) a and b

96. Conductors and busbars on a switchboard or panelboard shall be located so as to be free from _____ and shall be held firmly in place.

    (a) obstructions
    (b) physical damage
    (c) a and b
    (d) none of these

97. Electrical installations in hollow spaces, vertical shafts, and ventilation or air-handling ducts shall be made so that the possible spread of fire or products of combustion is not _____.

    (a) substantially increased
    (b) allowed
    (c) inherent
    (d) possible

98. An atmosphere containing carbon black, charcoal, coal, or coke dusts that have been sensitized by other materials so they present an explosion hazard is classified as Group F.

    (a) True
    (b) False

99. Branch-circuit conductors supplying a single air-conditioner motor-compressor shall have an ampacity not less than _____ percent of either the motor-compressor rated-load current or the branch-circuit selection current, whichever is greater.

    (a) 100
    (b) 125
    (c) 150
    (d) 200

100. Switches shall be marked with _____.

    (a) current
    (b) voltage
    (c) maximum horsepower, if horsepower rated
    (d) all of these

STRAIGHT ORDER
[ARTICLES 511–625]

Please use the 2014 *Code* book to answer the following questions.

1. A building or portions of a building where engine overhauls, painting, body and fender work, and repairs that require _____ of the motor vehicle fuel tank are performed defines the term "Major Repair Garage."

   (a) removal
   (b) replacement
   (c) filling
   (d) draining

2. In major repair garages where lighter-than-air gaseous fueled vehicles, such as vehicles fueled by natural gas or hydrogen, are repaired or stored, the area within _____ in. of the ceiling is classified as Class I, Division 2.

   (a) 6
   (b) 12
   (c) 18
   (d) 24

3. In major repair garages where ventilation is not provided in accordance with 511.3(C)(3)(a), any pit or depression below floor level shall be a Class I, _____ location that extends up to the floor level.

   (a) Division 1
   (b) Division 2
   (c) a or b
   (d) a and b

4. Any pit for which ventilation is not provided below a minor repair garage floor level of a lubrication or service room is considered to be a Class I, _____ location up to the floor level.

   (a) Division 1
   (b) Division 2
   (c) a or b
   (d) a and b

5. Portable lighting equipment used in commercial garages shall be identified for _____ locations, unless the lamp and its cord are supported or arranged in such a manner that they cannot be used in the locations classified in 511.3.

   (a) hard usage
   (b) Class I, Division 2
   (c) Class I, Division 1
   (d) general duty

6. Flexible cords for pendants installed above Class I locations in a commercial garage shall be _____.

   (a) suitable for the type of service
   (b) listed for hard usage
   (c) a and b
   (d) shall not be used

7. Fixed electrical equipment installed in spaces above a Class I location in a commercial garage shall be _____.

    (a) well ventilated
    (b) located above the level of any defined Class I location
    (c) identified for the location
    (d) b or c

8. Article 513 applies to buildings or structures in which service, repairs, or alterations are performed on _____.

    (a) boats
    (b) aircraft
    (c) automobiles
    (d) any of these

9. Any pit or depression below the level of an aircraft hangar floor shall be classified as a _____ location that extends up to said floor level.

    (a) Class I, Division 1
    (b) Class I, Division 2
    (c) Class II, Division 1
    (d) Class III

10. The entire area of an aircraft hangar, including any adjacent and communicating areas not suitably cut off from the hangar, shall be classified as a Class I, Division 2 or Zone 2 location up to a level of _____ in. above the floor.

    (a) 6
    (b) 12
    (c) 18
    (d) 24

11. Fixed wiring in an aircraft hangar not in a Class I location shall be _____.

    (a) installed in metal raceways
    (b) Type MI, TC, or MC cable
    (c) installed in nonmetallic raceways
    (d) a or b

12. For pendants in an aircraft hangar, not installed in Class I locations, flexible cords suitable for the type of service and identified for _____ shall be used.

    (a) hard usage
    (b) extra-hard usage
    (c) general duty
    (d) a or b

13. All wiring in or under the aircraft hangar floor shall comply with the requirements for _____ locations.

    (a) Class I, Division 1
    (b) Class I, Division 2
    (c) a or b
    (d) none of these

14. All 15A and 20A, 125V receptacles installed in aircraft hangars in areas where _____ is(are) used shall have GFCI protection for personnel.

    (a) electrical diagnostic equipment
    (b) electrical hand tools
    (c) portable lighting equipment
    (d) any of these

15. Article 514 applies to _____ and fleet vehicle motor fuel dispensing facilities.

    (a) motor fuel dispensing facilities
    (b) marine/motor fuel dispensing facilities
    (c) commercial gas stations for motor vehicles only
    (d) a and b

16. Locations where flammable liquids having a flash point _____, such as gasoline, will not be handled can be unclassified.

    (a) above 100°F
    (b) below 100°F
    (c) of 100°F
    (d) none of these

17. Underground wiring to motor fuel dispensers shall be installed in _____.

    (a) threaded rigid metal conduit
    (b) threaded steel IMC
    (c) PVC conduit when buried under not less than 2 ft of cover
    (d) any of these

18. The space between 5 ft and 10 ft from the open end of a vent, extending in all directions, shall be classified as _____ in a bulk storage plant.

    (a) Class I, Division 1
    (b) Class I, Division 2
    (c) Class II, Division 1
    (d) Class II, Division 2

19. Locations where flammable paints are dried, and provided with adequate positive ventilation, and the ventilating equipment is interlocked with the electrical equipment, may be designated _____ locations by the authority having jurisdiction.

    (a) Class I, Division 2
    (b) unclassified
    (c) Class II, Division 2
    (d) Class II, Division 1

20. Article 517 applies to electrical construction and installation criteria in health care facilities that provide services to _____.

    (a) human beings
    (b) animals
    (c) a and b
    (d) none of these

21. The patient care space is any space within a health care facility where patients are intended to be _____.

    (a) examined
    (b) treated
    (c) registered
    (d) a or b

22. The patient care space of a health care facility does not typically include business offices, corridors, lounges, day rooms, dining rooms, or similar areas.

    (a) True
    (b) False

23. Wiring methods used in health care locations must comply with the *NEC* Chapter 1 through 4 provisions, except as modified by Article 517.

    (a) True
    (b) False

24. In patient care areas, the grounding terminals of all receptacles, metal boxes and enclosures containing receptacles, and all non-current-carrying conductive surfaces of fixed electric equipment _____ shall be directly connected to an insulated copper equipment grounding conductor.

    (a) operating at over 100V
    (b) likely to become energized
    (c) subject to personal contact
    (d) all of these

25. In health care facilities, receptacles with insulated grounding terminals, as described in 250.146(d) shall be permitted in a patient care vicinity.

    (a) True
    (b) False

26. Each general care area patient bed location shall be provided with a minimum of _____ receptacle(s), which can be single, duplex, or any combination of these.

    (a) two
    (b) four
    (c) six
    (d) eight

27. Which of the following shall not be connected to the life safety branch in a hospital?

    (a) exit signs
    (b) elevators
    (c) general illumination
    (d) communications systems

28. Which of the following wiring methods are permitted in an assembly occupancy of fire-rated construction?

    (a) metal raceways
    (b) Type MC cable
    (c) Type AC cable
    (d) all of these

29. A "performance area" includes the stage and audience seating area associated with a _____ stage structure, whether indoors or outdoors.

    (a) temporary
    (b) permanent
    (c) a or b
    (d) a and b

30. The fixed wiring methods permitted in theaters, audience areas of motion picture and television studios, performance areas, and similar locations are _____.

    (a) any metal raceway
    (b) nonmetallic raceways encased in 2 in. of concrete
    (c) Type MC or AC cable containing an insulated equipment grounding conductor
    (d) any of these

31. On fixed stage equipment other than switchboards, portable strip lights and connector strips shall be wired with conductors having insulation rated suitable for the temperature but not less than _____.

    (a) 75°C
    (b) 90°C
    (c) 125°C
    (d) 200°C

32. The pilot light provided within a portable stage switchboard enclosure shall have overcurrent protection rated or set at not more than _____.

    (a) 10A
    (b) 15A
    (c) 20A
    (d) 30A

33. All lights and any receptacles installed in theater dressing rooms adjacent to the mirrors and above the dressing table counter(s), shall be controlled by wall switches in the dressing room(s).

    (a) True
    (b) False

34. Overhead wiring outside of tents and concession areas of carnivals and circuses which are accessible to pedestrians shall maintain a vertical clearance of _____ ft above finished grade, sidewalks, or from platforms, projections, or surfaces from which the wiring might be reached.

    (a) 3
    (b) 6
    (c) 8
    (d) 10

35. Electrical service equipment at carnivals and circuses shall not be accessible to unqualified persons, unless _____.

    (a) lockable
    (b) readily accessible
    (c) accessible
    (d) none of these

36. When installed indoors for carnivals, circuses, and fairs, flexible cords and flexible cables shall be listed for wet locations and shall be sunlight resistant.

    (a) True
    (b) False

37. Each portable structure at a carnival, circus, or fair shall be provided with a means to disconnect it from all ungrounded conductors within sight of and within _____ ft of the operator's station.

    (a) 3
    (b) 6
    (c) 8
    (d) 10

38. Wiring for lighting located inside tents and concession areas at carnivals, circuses, and fairs, where subject to physical damage shall be provided with mechanical protection.

    (a) True
    (b) False

39. Portable distribution and termination boxes installed outdoors at carnivals, circuses, or fairs shall be weatherproof and mounted so the bottom of the enclosure is not less than _____ in. above the ground.

    (a) 6
    (b) 8
    (c) 10
    (d) 12

40. GFCI protection for personnel shall be provided at carnivals, circuses, and fairs for all 15A and 20A, 125V nonlocking-type receptacle that are readily accessible to the general public.

    (a) True
    (b) False

41. A professional motion picture projector is one that uses _____ film and has on each edge 212 perforations per meter, or a type using carbon arc, xenon, or other light source equipment that develops hazardous gases, dust, or radiation.

    (a) 35 mm
    (b) 70 mm
    (c) 105 mm
    (d) a or b

42. Where the point of attachment is not known, service-entrance conductors for a manufactured building shall be installed _____.

    (a) after erection at the building site
    (b) before erection at the building site
    (c) a or b
    (d) none of these

43. In damp or wet locations of agricultural buildings, equipment enclosures and fittings shall be located or equipped to prevent moisture from _____ within the enclosure, box, conduit body, or fitting.

    (a) entering
    (b) accumulating
    (c) a or b
    (d) none of these

44. Where _____ may be present in an agricultural building, enclosures and fittings shall have corrosion-resistance properties suitable for the conditions.

    (a) wet dust
    (b) corrosive gases or vapors
    (c) other corrosive conditions
    (d) any of these

45. An equipotential plane shall be installed in all concrete floor confinement areas of livestock buildings, and all outdoor confinement areas with a concrete slab that contains metallic equipment accessible to livestock and that may become energized.

    (a) True
    (b) False

46. Equipotential planes shall be installed in outdoor concrete slabs where metallic equipment is located that may become energized and is accessible to livestock, other than poultry.

    (a) True
    (b) False

47. The equipotential plane in an agricultural building shall be connected to the electrical grounding system with a solid copper, insulated, covered, or bare conductor and not smaller than _____.

    (a) 10 AWG
    (b) 8 AWG
    (c) 6 AWG
    (d) 4 AWG

48. A _____ is a structure transportable in one or more sections that is built on a permanent chassis and designed to be used as a dwelling, with or without a permanent foundation.

    (a) manufactured home
    (b) mobile home
    (c) dwelling unit
    (d) all of these

49. GFCI protection in a mobile home shall be provided for _____.

    (a) receptacle outlets installed outdoors and in compartments accessible from outside
    (b) receptacles within 6 ft of a wet bar sink
    (c) all receptacles in bathrooms including receptacles in luminaires
    (d) all of these

50. Receptacle outlets over countertops in the kitchen in a mobile home shall _____.

    (a) be no more than 2 ft apart
    (b) be no more than 4 ft apart
    (c) be no more than 6 ft apart
    (d) include at least one receptacle outlet on each side of the sink

51. A receptacle outlet for mobile and manufactured home heat tape that is used to protect cold water inlet piping shall be _____ protected and it shall be connected to an interior branch circuit other than a small-appliance branch circuit where all of the outlets of the circuit are on the load side of the GFCI.

    (a) AFCI
    (b) GFCI
    (c) a or b
    (d) none of these

52. Aluminum conductors and copper-clad aluminum conductors shall be permitted for branch-circuit wiring in mobile homes.

    (a) True
    (b) False

53. Mobile home service equipment shall be located adjacent to the mobile home, located in sight from but not more than _____ ft from the exterior wall of the mobile home it serves.

    (a) 15
    (b) 20
    (c) 30
    (d) 40

54. Mobile home service equipment shall be rated not less than _____ at 120/240V.

    (a) 50A
    (b) 60A
    (c) 100A
    (d) 200A

55. Where feeder conductors are installed to serve a mobile home, an equipment grounding conductor shall be installed with the conductors, unless the premises wiring system is existing.

    (a) True
    (b) False

56. Electrical service and feeder loads for a recreational vehicle park shall be calculated at a minimum of _____ per site equipped with only 20A supply facilities (not including tent sites).

    (a) 1,200 VA
    (b) 2,400 VA
    (c) 3,500 VA
    (d) 9,600 VA

57. Feeders to floating buildings can be installed with _____ where flexibility is required.

    (a) extra-hard usage portable power cable listed for both wet locations and sunlight resistance
    (b) LFMC with approved fittings
    (c) LFNC with approved fittings
    (d) all of these

58. Private, noncommercial docking facilities constructed or occupied for the use of the owner or residents of the associated _____ are not covered by Article 555.

    (a) single-family dwelling
    (b) multifamily dwelling
    (c) a or b
    (d) none of these

59. At marinas and boatyards, the electrical datum plane, in land areas subject to tidal fluctuation, is a horizontal plane _____ ft above the highest high tide under normal circumstances.

    (a) 1
    (b) 2
    (c) 3
    (d) 4

60. The overcurrent protective device for the main marina feeder conductors must have ground-fault protection not exceeding _____. If ground-fault protection is provided for each individual marina branch or feeder circuit, ground-fault protection is not required for the main marina feeder conductors.

    (a) 6 mA
    (b) 20 mA
    (c) 30 mA
    (d) 100 mA

61. Electrical connections in marinas and boatyards shall be located _____ unless the conductor splices are contained within sealed wire connector systems listed and identified for submersion.

    (a) at least 12 in. above the deck of a floating pier
    (b) at least 12 in. above the deck of a fixed pier
    (c) not below the electrical datum plane of a fixed pier
    (d) all of these

62. The demand factor for marina load calculations of 45 shore power receptacles is _____ percent.

    (a) 40
    (b) 50
    (c) 60
    (d) 70

63. The equipment grounding conductor at a marina is required to be an insulated copper conductor for all circuits.

    (a) True
    (b) False

64. A _____ must be used to serve as the required shore power receptacle disconnecting means and it must be identified as to which receptacle it controls.

    (a) circuit breaker
    (b) switch
    (c) a and b
    (d) a or b

65. Temporary electrical power and lighting installations shall be permitted for a period not to exceed 90 days for _____ decorative lighting and similar purposes.

    (a) Christmas
    (b) New Year's
    (c) July 4th
    (d) holiday

66. Temporary wiring shall be _____ immediately upon the completion of construction or purpose for which the wiring was installed.

    (a) disconnected
    (b) removed
    (c) de-energized
    (d) any of these

67. Type NM cables can be used for feeder temporary installations without height limitation and without concealment.

    (a) True
    (b) False

68. Multiwire branch circuits for temporary wiring shall be provided with a means to disconnect simultaneously all _____ conductors where the branch circuit originates.

    (a) underground
    (b) overhead
    (c) ungrounded
    (d) grounded

69. At construction sites, boxes are not required for temporary wiring splices of _____.

    (a) multiconductor cords
    (b) multiconductor cables
    (c) a or b
    (d) none of these

70. Flexible cords and flexible cables used for temporary wiring shall _____.

    (a) be protected from accidental damage
    (b) be protected where passing through doorways
    (c) avoid sharp corners and projections
    (d) all of these

71. GFCI protection is required for 15A, 20A, and 30A, 125V receptacle outlets that are installed or existing as part of the permanent wiring of the building/structure when used during construction or remodeling. Listed cord sets or adapters that incorporate listed GFCI protection for portable use can be used to meet this requirement.

    (a) True
    (b) False

72. Fixed, mobile, or portable electric signs, section signs, outline lighting, and retrofit kits shall be _____.

    (a) approved by special permission
    (b) listed
    (c) identified for the location
    (d) a or b

73. Signs and outline lighting systems shall be marked with _____.

    (a) the manufacturer's name, trademark, or other means of identification
    (b) input voltage
    (c) current rating
    (d) all of these

74. The markings required on signs and outline lighting systems in 600.4(a) must be permanent, durable, and _____ when in wet locations.

    (a) weatherproof
    (b) laminated
    (c) rainproof
    (d) indelible

75. Metal or nonmetallic poles used to support signs can contain the sign circuit conductors, provided the installation complies with 410.30(B).

    (a) True
    (b) False

76. Each sign and outline lighting system shall be controlled by an externally operable switch or circuit breaker that opens all _____ conductors.

    (a) ungrounded
    (b) grounded
    (c) equipment grounding
    (d) all of these

77. Each sign and outline lighting system shall be controlled by an externally operable switch or circuit breaker that opens all ungrounded conductors simultaneously on _____ branch circuits.

    (a) 15A
    (b) 20A
    (c) multiwire
    (d) outdoor

78. For a sign, outline lighting system, or skeleton tubing system, the equipment grounding conductor size shall be in accordance with _____, based on the rating of the overcurrent device protecting the conductors supplying the sign or equipment.

    (a) 250.66
    (b) 250.122
    (c) 310.13
    (d) 310.16

79. Signs and outline lighting systems shall be installed so that adjacent combustible materials are not subjected to temperatures in excess of _____.

    (a) 60°C
    (b) 75°C
    (c) 90°C
    (d) 105°C

80. A working space not less than 3 ft high by 3 ft wide by _____ deep is required for each ballast, transformer, electronic power supply, and Class 2 power source where not installed in a sign.

    (a) 2 ft
    (b) 3 ft
    (c) 4 ft
    (d) 6 ft

81. Ballasts, transformers, electronic power supplies, and Class 2 power sources for signs can be located above a suspended ceiling, provided the enclosures _____.

    (a) are securely fastened in place
    (b) don't use the suspended-ceiling grid for support
    (c) a or b
    (d) a and b

82. A manufactured wiring system is a system assembled by a manufacturer, which cannot be inspected at the building site without _____.

    (a) a permit
    (b) a manufacturer's representative present
    (c) damage or destruction to the assembly
    (d) an engineer's supervision

83. Manufactured wiring systems shall be permitted in _____ locations.

    (a) accessible
    (b) dry
    (c) wet
    (d) a and b

84. Manufactured wiring systems shall be constructed with _____.

    (a) Type AC cable
    (b) Type MC cable
    (c) a or b
    (d) none of these

85. At least _____ 125V, single-phase, 15A or 20A, duplex receptacle(s) shall be provided in each elevator machine room and elevator machinery space.

    (a) one
    (b) two
    (c) three
    (d) four

86. The lighting switch for hoistway pits shall be readily accessible from the _____.

    (a) pit access door
    (b) elevator car
    (c) floor of the pit
    (d) machinery room

87. At least _____ 125V, single-phase, 15A or 20A, duplex receptacle(s) shall be provided in the elevator hoistway pit.

    (a) one
    (b) two
    (c) three
    (d) four

88. Only wiring, raceways, and cables used directly in connection with an elevator shall be permitted inside the hoistway and the machine room.

    (a) True
    (b) False

89. Where multiple driving machines are connected to a single elevator, escalator, moving walk, or pumping unit, there shall be one disconnecting means to disconnect the _____.

    (a) motors
    (b) control valve operating magnets
    (c) a and b
    (d) none of these

90. The disconnecting means for an elevator or escalator shall be an enclosed externally operable circuit breaker or fused motor circuit switch that is _____.

    (a) capable of interrupting six times the locked-rotor current
    (b) lockable
    (c) inherently protected
    (d) suitable for use as service equipment

91. Each 15A and 20A, 125V receptacle installed in pits, in hoistways, on elevator car tops, and in escalator and moving walk wellways shall be _____.

    (a) on a GFCI-protected circuit
    (b) of the GFCI type
    (c) a or b
    (d) none of these

92. Article 625 covers conductors and equipment external to an electric vehicle that connect an electric vehicle to a supply of electricity, and the installation of equipment and devices related to electric vehicle charging.

    (a) True
    (b) False

93. Off-road, self-propelled electric vehicles, such as _____ are not considered an electric vehicle.

    (a) industrial trucks, hoists, lifts
    (b) golf carts, airline ground support equipment
    (c) tractors, boats
    (d) all of these

94. The electric vehicle inlet is considered to be part of the electric vehicle supply equipment.

    (a) True
    (b) False

95. Where ventilation marking is required, the electric vehicle supply equipment shall be clearly field marked, that "ventilation is required."

    (a) True
    (b) False

96. Conductors that supply electric vehicle supply equipment shall have a rating of not less than 125 percent of the maximum load of the electric vehicle supply equipment.

    (a) True
    (b) False

97. Electric vehicle supply equipment rated more than _____ must have a disconnecting means installed in a readily accessible location that is capable of being locked in the open position.

    (a) 20A
    (b) 30A
    (c) 60A
    (d) 80A

98. The electric vehicle supply equipment located outdoors shall be located to permit direct electrical coupling of the EV connector to the electric vehicle.

    (a) True
    (b) False

99. The _____ of electric vehicle supply equipment located indoors shall be located not less than 18 in. above the floor level.

    (a) attachment plugs
    (b) fittings
    (c) power outlets
    (d) coupling

100. Unless specifically listed and marked for the location, the _____ of electric vehicle supply equipment shall be stored or located at a height of not less than 24 in. above the grade level for outdoor locations.

    (a) attachment plugs
    (b) fittings
    (c) power outlets
    (d) coupling means

PRACTICE QUIZ 16

RANDOM ORDER [ARTICLES 90–625]

Please use the 2014 *Code* book to answer the following questions.

1. All conductors of the same circuit shall be _____, unless otherwise specifically permitted in the *Code*.

   (a) in the same raceway or cable
   (b) in close proximity in the same trench
   (c) the same size
   (d) a or b

2. A box or conduit body shall not be required for splices and taps in direct-buried conductors and cables as long as the splice is made with a splicing device that is identified for the purpose.

   (a) True
   (b) False

3. Suitability of identified equipment for use in a hazardous (classified) location shall be determined by:

   (a) Equipment listing or labeling.
   (b) Evidence of equipment evaluation from a qualified testing laboratory or inspection agency concerned with product evaluation.
   (c) Evidence acceptable to the authority having jurisdiction, such as a manufacturer's self-evaluation or an owner's engineering judgment.
   (d) any of these

4. Class III, Division _____ locations include areas where easily ignitible fibers/flyings are handled, manufactured, or used.

   (a) 1
   (b) 2
   (c) 3
   (d) all of these

5. A(n) _____ shall be of such design that any alteration of its trip point (calibration) or the time required for its operation requires dismantling of the device or breaking of a seal for other than intended adjustments.

   (a) Type S fuse
   (b) Edison-base fuse
   (c) circuit breaker
   (d) fuseholder

6. A sealing fitting shall not be required if a metal conduit passes completely through a Class I, Division 2 location if the termination points of the unbroken conduit are located in unclassified locations and it has no fittings less than _____ in. of either side of the boundary of the hazardous (classified) location.

   (a) 6
   (b) 12
   (c) 18
   (d) 24

7. Three-way and four-way switches shall be wired so that all switching is done only in the _____ circuit conductor.

   (a) ungrounded
   (b) grounded
   (c) equipment ground
   (d) neutral

8. Raceways on exterior surfaces of buildings or other structures shall be arranged to drain, and be suitable for use in _____ locations.

   (a) damp
   (b) wet
   (c) dry
   (d) all of these

9. In a hospital where flammable anesthetics are employed, the entire area that extends _____ shall be classified as a Class I, Division 1 location.

   (a) upward to the structural ceiling
   (b) upward to a level 8 ft above the floor
   (c) upward to a level 5 ft above the floor
   (d) 10 ft in all directions

10. The conductors, including splices and taps, in a nonmetallic surface raceway having a cover capable of being opened in place, shall not fill the raceway to more than _____ percent of its cross-sectional area at that point.

    (a) 38
    (b) 40
    (c) 53
    (d) 75

11. The demand factors of Table 220.56 apply to space heating, ventilating, or air-conditioning equipment.

    (a) True
    (b) False

12. All branch circuits serving patient care areas shall be provided with an effective ground-fault current path by installation in a metal raceway system, or a cable having a metallic armor or sheath assembly. The metal raceway system, or metallic cable armor, or sheath assembly shall itself qualify as an equipment grounding conductor in accordance with 250.118.

    (a) True
    (b) False

13. Luminaires used in agricultural buildings shall _____.

    (a) minimize the entrance of dust, foreign matter, moisture, and corrosive material
    (b) be protected by a suitable guard if exposed to physical damage
    (c) be listed for use in wet locations when exposed to water
    (d) all of these

14. Branch-circuit conductors to individual appliances shall not be sized _____ than required by the appliance markings.

    (a) larger
    (b) smaller

15. The area used for _____ of alcohol-based windshield washer fluid in repair garages shall be unclassified.

    (a) storage
    (b) handling
    (c) dispensing into motor vehicles
    (d) any of these

16. In grounded systems, normally noncurrent-carrying electrically conductive materials that are likely to become energized shall be _____ in a manner that establishes an effective ground-fault current path.

    (a) connected together
    (b) connected to the electrical supply source
    (c) connected to the closest grounded conductor
    (d) a and b

17. For temporary installations, lamps shall be protected from accidental contact by a suitable _____ or by the use of a lampholder with a guard.

    (a) globe
    (b) luminaire
    (c) fitting
    (d) porcelain fitting

18. Trade size 1 IMC shall be supported at intervals not exceeding _____ ft.

    (a) 8
    (b) 10
    (c) 12
    (d) 14

19. ENT shall not be used where exposed to the direct rays of the sun, unless identified as _____.

    (a) high-temperature rated
    (b) sunlight resistant
    (c) Schedule 80
    (d) none of these

20. Indoor transformers rated over 35,000V, and insulated with nonflammable dielectric fluid identified as nonflammable, shall be installed in a vault furnished with a _____.

    (a) liquid confinement area
    (b) pressure-relief vent
    (c) means for absorbing or venting any gases generated by arcing
    (d) all of these

21. The removal of shielding material or the separation of the twisted pairs of shielded cables and twisted pair cables isn't required within the conduit seal fitting in a Class I, Division 2 hazardous (classified) location provided the termination is by an approved means to minimize the entrance of gases or vapors and prevent flame propagation.

    (a) True
    (b) False

22. The individual responsible for starting, stopping, and controlling an amusement ride or supervising a concession is known as the "_____."

    (a) operator
    (b) director
    (c) manager
    (d) facilitator

23. Ground clamps and fittings that are exposed to physical damage shall be enclosed in _____.

    (a) metal
    (b) wood
    (c) the equivalent of a or b
    (d) none of these

24. The conductors and electric vehicle connectors, _____ installed specifically for the purpose of transferring energy between the premises wiring and the electric vehicle.

    (a) attachment plugs
    (b) fittings
    (c) power outlets
    (d) any of these

25. Power distribution blocks shall be permitted in pull and junction boxes over 100 cubic inches when they comply with the provisions of 314.28(E)(1) through (5).

    (a) True
    (b) False

26. The motor disconnecting means for a motor shall _____ whether it is in the open (off) or closed (on) position.

    (a) plainly indicate
    (b) provide current
    (c) be in the upper position
    (d) none of these

27. An 800A fuse rated at 1,000V _____ on a 250V system.

    (a) shall not be used
    (b) shall be used
    (c) can be used
    (d) none of these

28. In patient care areas of health care facilities, secondary circuits of transformer-powered communications or signaling systems shall not be required to be enclosed in raceways unless required by Chapters 7 or 8.

    (a) True
    (b) False

29. When connected to multiwire branch circuits, the fluorescent luminaire disconnect must simultaneously break all circuit conductors of the ballast, including the grounded conductor.

    (a) True
    (b) False

30. Transformers and transformer vaults shall be readily accessible to qualified personnel for inspection and maintenance, except _____.

    (a) dry-type transformers 1,000V or less, located in the open on walls, columns, or structures
    (b) dry-type transformers rated not more than 50 kVA/1,000V installed in hollow spaces of buildings not permanently closed in by structure
    (c) a or b
    (d) none of these

31. ENT is not permitted in hazardous (classified) locations, unless permitted in other articles of the *Code*.

    (a) True
    (b) False

32. Equipment or materials to which a label, symbol, or other identifying mark of a product evaluation organization that is acceptable to the authority having jurisdiction has been attached is known as "_____."

    (a) listed
    (b) labeled
    (c) approved
    (d) identified

33. The term mobile home includes manufactured homes, unless otherwise indicated.

    (a) True
    (b) False

34. The top shield installed over all floor-mounted Type FCC cable shall completely _____ all cable runs, corners, connectors, and ends.

    (a) cover
    (b) encase
    (c) protect
    (d) none of these

35. What's the park electrical wiring system load, after applying the demand factors, for a mobile home park having six mobile homes?

    (a) 4,640 VA
    (b) 27,840 VA
    (c) 96,000 VA
    (d) 144,000 VA

36. Conductors supplying outlets for arc and xenon projectors of the professional type shall not be smaller than _____ and shall have an ampacity not less than the projector rating.

    (a) 12 AWG
    (b) 10 AWG
    (c) 8 AWG
    (d) 6 AWG

37. An assembly of interconnected intrinsically safe apparatus, associated apparatus, and interconnecting cables designed so that they are intrinsically safe circuits is a(n) _____.

    (a) intrinsically safe system
    (b) safe location
    (c) reclassified location
    (d) associated system

38. Where the electric vehicle supply equipment located indoors is listed as suitable for charging electric vehicles with ventilation, mechanical ventilation shall include permanently installed supply and exhaust equipment located to intake from inside the building and vent outdoors.

    (a) True
    (b) False

39. Weather-resistant receptacles _____ where replacements are made at receptacle outlets that are required to be so protected elsewhere in the *Code*.

    (a) shall be provided
    (b) are not required
    (c) are optional
    (d) are not allowed

40. The disconnecting means for the controller and motor shall open all ungrounded supply conductors.

    (a) True
    (b) False

41. A minimum of 70 percent of all recreational vehicle sites with electrical supply shall be equipped with a _____,125V receptacle.

    (a) 15A
    (b) 20A
    (c) 30A
    (d) 50A

42. Each vented cell of a battery, as it relates to storage batteries, shall be equipped with _____ that is(are) designed to prevent destruction of the cell due to ignition of gases within the cell by an external spark or flame under normal operating conditions.

    (a) pressure relief
    (b) a flame arrester
    (c) fluid level indicators
    (d) none of these

43. Where flexibility is required, the following wiring methods are permitted in a Class II, Division 2 location _____.

    (a) dusttight flexible connectors
    (b) liquidtight flexible metal conduit with listed fittings
    (c) flexible cords listed for extra-hard usage with listed dusttight cord connectors
    (d) any of these

44. Type MC cable shall not be _____ unless the metallic sheath or armor is resistant to the conditions, or is protected by material resistant to the conditions.

    (a) used for direct burial in the earth
    (b) embedded in concrete
    (c) exposed to cinder fill
    (d) all of these

45. When FMC or LFMC is used as permitted in Class I, Division 2 locations, it shall include an equipment bonding jumper of the wire type in compliance with 250.102.

    (a) True
    (b) False

46. An opening in an outlet box where one or more receptacles have been installed is called "_____."

    (a) a device
    (b) equipment
    (c) a receptacle
    (d) a receptacle outlet

47. Electric vehicle supply equipment intended for connection to _____, 2-pole, 3-wire grounding-type receptacle outlets rated 125V, single phase, 15A and 20A can be cord-and-plug-connected to the premises wiring system.

    (a) nonlocking
    (b) accessible
    (c) readily accessible
    (d) any of these

48. Type TC cable can be used _____.

    (a) for power and lighting circuits
    (b) in cable trays
    (c) in Class 1 control circuits
    (d) all of these

49. Surface nonmetallic raceways shall be permitted _____.

    (a) in dry locations
    (b) where concealed
    (c) in hoistways
    (d) all of these

50. A flexible cord conductor intended to be used as a(n) _____ conductor shall have a continuous identifying marker readily distinguishing it from the other conductor or conductors. One means of identification is a braid finished to show a continuous green color or a green color with one or more yellow stripes on one conductor.

    (a) ungrounded
    (b) equipment grounding
    (c) service
    (d) high-leg

51. Portable lighting equipment must be _____ for use in a Class I, Division 2 location, unless the luminaire is mounted on movable stands and connected by a flexible cord.

    (a) identified
    (b) approved
    (c) marked
    (d) listed

52. Where Type NM cables pass through cut or drilled slots or holes in metal members, the cable shall be protected by _____ which are installed in the opening prior to the installation of the cable and which securely cover all metal edges.

    (a) listed bushings
    (b) listed grommets
    (c) plates
    (d) a or b

53. Fittings used for connecting Type MC cable to boxes, cabinets, or other equipment shall _____.

    (a) be nonmetallic only
    (b) be listed and identified for such use
    (c) be listed and identified as weatherproof
    (d) include anti-shorting bushings

54. The overall covering of Type UF cable is _____.

    (a) flame retardant
    (b) moisture, fungus, and corrosion resistant
    (c) suitable for direct burial in the earth
    (d) all of these

55. All areas designated as hazardous (classified) shall be properly _____ and shall be available to those authorized to design, install, inspect, maintain, or operate electrical equipment at these locations.

    (a) cleaned
    (b) documented
    (c) maintained
    (d) all of these

56. A snap switch with integral nonmetallic enclosure complying with 300.15(E) is required to be connected to an equipment grounding conductor.

    (a) True
    (b) False

57. When armored cable is run parallel to the sides of rafters, studs, or floor joists in an accessible attic, the cable shall be protected with running boards.

    (a) True
    (b) False

58. A box or conduit body shall not be required where cables enter or exit from conduit or tubing that is used to provide cable support or protection against physical damage.

    (a) True
    (b) False

59. A Class III, Division _____ location is where easily ignitible fibers/flyings are stored or handled but not manufactured.

    (a) 1
    (b) 2
    (c) 3
    (d) all of these

60. A buried iron or steel plate used as a grounding electrode shall expose not less than _____ of surface area to exterior soil.

    (a) 2 sq ft
    (b) 4 sq ft
    (c) 9 sq ft
    (d) 10 sq ft

61. The maximum size of conductors in Type UF cable shall be _____ AWG copper.

    (a) 14
    (b) 10
    (c) 1/0
    (d) 4/0

62. All 15A and 20A, 125V receptacles installed in machine rooms and machinery spaces for elevators, escalators, moving walks, and lifts shall have GFCI protection by a _____.

    (a) GFCI receptacle
    (b) GFCI circuit breaker
    (c) a or b
    (d) none of these

63. Type MI cable conductors shall be made of _____, nickel, or nickel-coated copper with a resistance corresponding to standard AWG and kcmil sizes.

    (a) solid copper
    (b) solid or stranded copper
    (c) stranded copper
    (d) solid copper or aluminum

64. The grounding electrode used for grounding strike termination devices of a lightning protection system can be used as a grounding electrode system for the buildings or structures.

    (a) True
    (b) False

65. Metal enclosures for switches or circuit breakers shall be connected to the circuit _____.

    (a) grounded conductor
    (b) grounding conductor
    (c) equipment grounding conductor
    (d) any of these

66. A conduit seal fitting shall be installed in each conduit run leaving a Class I, Division 2 location and it is not required to be _____.

    (a) listed
    (b) installed
    (c) explosionproof
    (d) accessible

67. A listed expansion/deflection fitting or other approved means must be used where a raceway crosses a _____ intended for expansion, contraction or deflection used in buildings, bridges, parking garages, or other structures.

    (a) junction box
    (b) structural joint
    (c) cable tray
    (d) unistrut hanger

68. For grounded systems, electrical equipment and electrically conductive material likely to become energized, shall be installed in a manner that creates a low-impedance circuit capable of safely carrying the maximum ground-fault current likely to be imposed on it from where a ground fault may occur to the _____.

    (a) ground
    (b) earth
    (c) electrical supply source
    (d) none of these

69. When a single equipment grounding conductor is used for multiple circuits in the same raceway, cable, or cable tray, the single equipment grounding conductor shall be sized according to the _____.

    (a) combined rating of all the overcurrent devices
    (b) largest overcurrent device of the multiple circuits
    (c) combined rating of all the loads
    (d) any of these

70. In critical care areas of health care facilities, each patient bed location shall be provided with a minimum of _____ receptacles.

    (a) 10
    (b) 12
    (c) 14
    (d) 16

71. The disconnecting means for a torque motor shall have an ampere rating of at least _____ percent of the motor nameplate current.

    (a) 100
    (b) 115
    (c) 125
    (d) 175

72. On a three-phase, 4-wire, delta-connected service where the midpoint of one phase winding is grounded, the service conductor having the higher phase voltage-to-ground shall be durably and permanently marked by an outer finish that is _____ in color, or by other effective means, at each termination or junction point.

    (a) orange
    (b) red
    (c) blue
    (d) any of these

73. Circuit breakers rated at _____ amperes or less and _____ volts or less shall have the ampere rating molded, stamped, etched, or similarly marked into their handles or escutcheon areas.

    (a) 100, 1,000
    (b) 600, 6,000
    (c) 1,000, 6,000
    (d) 6,000, 1,000

74. Agricultural buildings where excessive dust and dust with water may accumulate, including all areas of _____ confinement systems where litter dust or feed dust may accumulate shall comply with Article 547.

    (a) poultry
    (b) livestock
    (c) fish
    (d) all of these

75. Listed liquidtight flexible metal conduit (LFMC) is acceptable as an equipment grounding conductor when it terminates in listed fittings and is protected by an overcurrent device rated 60A or less for trade sizes ⅜ through ½.

    (a) True
    (b) False

76. Type NM cable shall be permitted in agricultural buildings.

    (a) True
    (b) False

77. Where there is more than one driving machine in an elevator machine room, the disconnecting means shall be numbered to correspond to the identifying number of the _____.

    (a) driving machine they control
    (b) circuit feeding it
    (c) panel from which it is fed
    (d) all of these

78. _____ equipment excludes dust and doesn't permit arcs, sparks, or heat inside the enclosure to ignite accumulations or atmospheric suspensions of a specified dust on or in the vicinity outside of the enclosure.

    (a) Dust-ignitionproof
    (b) Dusttight
    (c) a or b
    (d) a and b

79. Each vented cell of a battery, as it relates to storage batteries, shall be equipped with _____ that is(are) designed to prevent destruction of the cell due to ignition of gases within the cell by an external spark or flame under normal operating conditions.

    (a) pressure relief
    (b) a flame arrester
    (c) fluid level indicators
    (d) none of these

80. Overhead service conductors shall have a minimum of _____ ft vertical clearance from final grade over residential property and driveways, as well as over commercial areas not subject to truck traffic where the voltage is limited to 300 volts-to-ground.

    (a) 10
    (b) 12
    (c) 15
    (d) 18

81. Independent support wires used for the support of electrical raceways and cables within nonfire-rated assemblies shall be distinguishable from the suspended-ceiling framing support wires.

    (a) True
    (b) False

82. Wiring methods and materials permitted in Class I, Division 1 locations include _____.

    (a) threaded rigid metal or threaded steel IMC
    (b) flexible fittings listed for Class I, Division 1 locations
    (c) boxes approved for Class I, Division 1 locations
    (d) all of these

83. Bends in FMC shall be made so that the conduit is not damaged and the internal diameter of the conduit is _____.

    (a) larger than ⅜ in.
    (b) not effectively reduced
    (c) increased
    (d) larger than 1 in.

84. Ground-fault protection of equipment shall not be required at a feeder disconnect if ground-fault protection of equipment is provided on the _____ side of the feeder and on the load side of any transformer supplying the feeder.

    (a) load
    (b) supply
    (c) service
    (d) none of these

85. Temporary wiring methods shall be acceptable only if _____, based on the conditions of use and any special requirements of the temporary installation.

    (a) listed
    (b) identified
    (c) approved
    (d) any of these

86. Alternating-current circuits of less than 50V shall be grounded if supplied by a transformer whose supply system exceeds 150 volts-to-ground.

    (a) True
    (b) False

87. In Class I, Division 1 locations, all utilization equipment must be _____ for use in a Class I, Division 1 location.

    (a) identified
    (b) approved
    (c) marked
    (d) listed

88. The bottom of sign and outline lighting system equipment shall be at least _____ ft above areas accessible to vehicles unless protected from physical damage.

    (a) 12
    (b) 14
    (c) 16
    (d) 18

89. Luminaires made of insulating material that are directly wired or attached to outlets supplied by a wiring method that does not provide a ready means for grounding attachment to an equipment grounding conductor shall be made of insulating material and shall have no exposed conductive parts.

    (a) True
    (b) False

90. The number of conductors permitted in LFNC shall not exceed the percentage fill specified in _____.

    (a) Chapter 9, Table 1
    (b) Table 250.66
    (c) Table 310.15(B)(16)
    (d) 240.6

91. For listed explosionproof equipment, factory-threaded NPT entries shall be made up with at least _____ threads fully engaged.

    (a) 4
    (b) 4½
    (c) 5
    (d) 6

92. Tap conductors not over 25 ft shall be permitted, providing the _____.

    (a) ampacity of the tap conductors is not less than one-third the rating of the overcurrent device protecting the feeder conductors being tapped
    (b) tap conductors terminate in a single circuit breaker or set of fuses that limit the load to the ampacity of the tap conductors
    (c) tap conductors are suitably protected from physical damage
    (d) all of these

93. At circuses and carnivals, all equipment to be grounded shall be connected to a(n) _____ conductor of a type recognized by 250.118.

    (a) equipment grounding
    (b) grounded
    (c) grounding electrode
    (d) ungrounded

94. All 15A and 20A, 125V, single-phase general-purpose receptacles installed _____ of agricultural buildings shall be GFCI protected.

    (a) in areas having an equipotential plane
    (b) outdoors
    (c) in dirt confinement areas for livestock
    (d) any of these

95. The connection of the system bonding jumper for a separately derived system shall be made _____ on the separately derived system from the source to the first system disconnecting means or overcurrent device.

    (a) in at least two locations
    (b) in every location that the grounded conductor is present
    (c) at any single point
    (d) none of these

96. Flexible cords in Class I hazardous (classified) locations must _____.

    (a) be listed as extra-hard usage
    (b) contain an equipment grounding conductor
    (c) be supported by clamps or other suitable means to avoid tension on the terminals
    (d) all of these

97. Receptacle outlets for mobile and manufactured homes are not allowed to be installed _____.

    (a) within or directly over a bathtub or shower space
    (b) in a face-up position in any countertop
    (c) underneath the skirting of the home
    (d) a or b

98. Stockrooms and similar areas adjacent to classified locations of aircraft hangars, but effectively isolated and adequately ventilated, shall be designated as _____ locations.

    (a) Class I, Division 2
    (b) Class II, Division 1
    (c) Class II, Division 2
    (d) unclassified

99. The minimum size conductor for operating control and signaling circuits in an elevator shall be _____.

    (a) 20 AWG
    (b) 16 AWG
    (c) 14 AWG
    (d) 12 AWG

100. When necessary to employ flexible connections in a Class I, Division 1 location, such as at motor terminals, flexible fittings listed for the location or flexible cord in accordance with 501.140, are permitted if terminated with cord connectors listed for the location.

    (a) True
    (b) False

Please use the 2014 *Code* book to answer the following questions.

1. A disconnecting means shall be provided in the supply circuit for each arc welder not equipped with _____, and the identity shall be marked in accordance with 110.22(A).

   (a) a governor
   (b) a shunt-trip device
   (c) an integral disconnect
   (d) GFCI protection

2. Each resistance welder shall have an overcurrent device rated or set at not more than _____ percent of the rated primary current of the welder.

   (a) 80
   (b) 100
   (c) 125
   (d) 300

3. Conductors that supply one or more resistance welders shall be protected by an overcurrent device rated or set at not more than _____ percent of the conductor ampacity.

   (a) 80
   (b) 100
   (c) 125
   (d) 300

4. Audio distribution cable not terminated at equipment and not identified for future use with a tag is considered abandoned.

   (a) True
   (b) False

5. Audio cables installed exposed on the surface of ceilings and sidewalls shall be supported in such a manner that they will not be damaged by normal building use. Cables shall be secured by _____ designed and installed so as not to damage the cable.

   (a) straps
   (b) staples
   (c) cable ties
   (d) any of these

6. Audio cables identified for future use shall be marked with a tag of sufficient durability to withstand _____.

   (a) moisture
   (b) humidity
   (c) the environment involved
   (d) none of these

7. The number of conductors in a raceway for permanent audio system installations shall not be limited by the percentage fill specified in Chapter 9, Table 1.

   (a) True
   (b) False

8. Loudspeakers of permanent audio systems which are installed in fire resistance-rated partitions, walls, or ceilings shall be listed for the purpose or installed in an enclosure or recess that _____.

    (a) maintains the fire-resistance rating
    (b) is no more than 4 in. deep
    (c) is no more than 6 ft 6 in. high
    (d) all of these

9. For information technology equipment, supply circuits and interconnecting cables not terminated to equipment and not identified for future use with a tag are considered to be _____.

    (a) abandoned
    (b) unused
    (c) future use
    (d) none of these

10. Electrical circuits and equipment must be installed in such a way that the spread of fire or products of combustion won't be substantially increased. Openings into or through fire-rated walls, floors, and ceilings for electrical equipment must be firestopped using methods approved by the authority having jurisdiction to maintain the fire-resistance rating of the fire-rated assembly. This rule is in Section 300.21, but it also applies to information technology equipment rooms.

    (a) True
    (b) False

11. Where supply cords of listed information technology equipment are installed under a raised floor, they shall not be longer than _____ ft.

    (a) 10
    (b) 12
    (c) 15
    (d) 16

12. General purpose Type CL2, CM, or CATV cables are permitted within the raised floor area of an information technology equipment room.

    (a) True
    (b) False

13. The accessible portion of abandoned interconnecting cables under an information technology room raised floor shall be removed, unless the cables are contained within a _____.

    (a) raceway
    (b) panelboard
    (c) a and b
    (d) none of these

14. Installed supply circuits and interconnecting cables identified for future use in information technology equipment rooms must be marked with a tag of sufficient durability to withstand the environment involved which must include _____.

    (a) date cable was identified for future use
    (b) date of expected use
    (c) intended future use of the cable
    (d) all of these

15. The remote disconnect means for the control of electronic equipment power and HVAC systems shall be grouped and identified. A single means to control both shall be permitted.

    (a) True
    (b) False

16. Exposed noncurrent-carrying metal parts of an information technology system shall be _____.

    (a) bonded to an equipment grounding conductor
    (b) double insulated
    (c) GFCI protected
    (d) a or b

17. The voltage drop on technical power systems for sensitive electronic equipment shall not exceed _____ percent for branch circuits.

    (a) 1.50
    (b) 2
    (c) 2.50
    (d) 2.80

18. An electrically driven or controlled machine with one or more motors which is used primarily to transport and distribute water for agricultural purposes, and is not hand portable is called a(n) "____."

    (a) irrigation machine
    (b) electric water distribution system
    (c) center pivot irrigation machine
    (d) automatic water distribution system

19. Permanently installed swimming pools include those constructed in the ground or partially in the ground, and all others capable of holding water in a depth greater than ____ in.

    (a) 36
    (b) 42
    (c) 48
    (d) 54

20. A wet-niche luminaire is intended to be installed in a ____.

    (a) transformer
    (b) forming shell
    (c) hydromassage bathtub
    (d) all of these

21. Insulated overhead service conductors that are cabled together with a bare messenger and operate at not over 750 volts-to-ground shall maintain a ____ clearance in any direction to the water level of swimming pools, fountains, and similar installations.

    (a) 14 ft
    (b) 16 ft
    (c) 20 ft
    (d) 22½ ft

22. Overhead conductors for communications systems such as ____ shall be located no less than 10 ft above swimming and wading pools, diving structures, and observation stands, towers, or platforms.

    (a) communications
    (b) radio
    (c) television coaxial cable
    (d) all of these

23. All electric pool water heaters shall have the heating elements subdivided into loads not exceeding ____.

    (a) 20A
    (b) 35A
    (c) 48A
    (d) 60A

24. Underground PVC conduit shall be not less than ____ ft from the inside wall of the pool, unless prevented by space limitations.

    (a) 5
    (b) 8
    (c) 10
    (d) 25

25. Electric swimming pool equipment can be installed in pits where drainage prevents water accumulation during abnormal operation.

    (a) True
    (b) False

26. Outlets supplying pool pump motors connected to single-phase 120V through 240V branch circuits, whether by receptacle or by direct connection, shall be provided with ____ protection for personnel.

    (a) AFCI
    (b) GFCI
    (c) a or b
    (d) a and b

27. Single grounding type, GFCI-protected receptacles that provide power for pump motors related to the circulation and sanitation system of permanently installed pools shall be located at least ____ ft from the inside walls of the pool.

    (a) 3
    (b) 5
    (c) 6
    (d) 12

28. All 15A and 20A, 125V receptacles located within _____ ft of the inside walls of a pool shall be GFCI protected.

    (a) 8
    (b) 10
    (c) 15
    (d) 20

29. Switching devices shall be at least _____ ft horizontally from the inside walls of a pool unless the switch is listed as being acceptable for use within 5 ft.

    (a) 3
    (b) 5
    (c) 10
    (d) 12

30. When PVC conduit extends from the pool light forming shell to a pool junction box, an 8 AWG _____ bonding jumper shall be installed in the raceway.

    (a) solid bare
    (b) solid insulated
    (c) stranded insulated
    (d) b or c

31. EMT is permitted to contain branch-circuit wiring for underwater pool luminaires where the EMT is installed on or within a building.

    (a) True
    (b) False

32. A pool light junction box connected to a conduit that extends directly to a forming shell shall be _____ for this use.

    (a) listed
    (b) identified
    (c) marked
    (d) a and b

33. The junction box connected to a conduit that extends to the forming shell of the luminaire that operates at over 15V shall be located not less than _____ in. above the ground level or pool deck.

    (a) 4
    (b) 6
    (c) 8
    (d) 12

34. The enclosure for a transformer or ground-fault circuit interrupter connected to a conduit that extends directly to a pool light forming shell shall be _____ for this purpose.

    (a) labeled
    (b) listed
    (c) approved
    (d) a and b

35. The feeder to a swimming pool panelboard at a separate building or structure can be supplied with any Chapter 3 wiring method provided the feeder has a separate insulated copper equipment grounding conductor.

    (a) True
    (b) False

36. An 8 AWG or larger solid copper equipotential bonding conductor shall be extended to service equipment to eliminate voltage gradients in the pool area.

    (a) True
    (b) False

37. Which of the following shall be bonded?

    (a) Metal parts of electrical equipment associated with the pool water circulating system.
    (b) Pool structural metal.
    (c) Metal fittings within or attached to the pool.
    (d) all of these

38. Metal conduit and metal piping within _____ horizontally of the inside walls of the pool shall be bonded unless separated by a permanent barrier.

    (a) 4 ft
    (b) 5 ft
    (c) 8 ft
    (d) 10 ft

39. Radiant heating cables embedded in or below a pool deck shall _____.

    (a) not be installed within 5 ft horizontally from the inside walls of the pool
    (b) be mounted at least 12 ft vertically above the pool deck
    (c) not be permitted
    (d) none of these

40. All 15A and 20A, 125V receptacles located within _____ ft of the inside walls of a storable pool, storable spa, or storable hot tub shall be GFCI protected.

    (a) 8
    (b) 10
    (c) 15
    (d) 20

41. Electric equipment, including power-supply cords, used with storable pools shall be _____.

    (a) AFCI protected
    (b) GFCI protected
    (c) a or b
    (d) none of these

42. The equipotential bonding requirements for perimeter surfaces contained in 680.26(B)(2) don't apply to a listed self-contained spa or hot tub installed above a finished floor.

    (a) True
    (b) False

43. At least one 15A or 20A, 125V receptacle on a general-purpose branch circuit shall be located a minimum of _____ and a maximum of 10 ft from the inside wall of a spa or hot tub installed indoors.

    (a) 18 in.
    (b) 2 ft
    (c) 6 ft
    (d) 7 ft 6 in.

44. Switches shall be located at least _____, measured horizontally, from the inside walls of an indoor spa or hot tub.

    (a) 4 ft
    (b) 5 ft
    (c) 7 ft 6 in.
    (d) 12 ft

45. Metal parts associated with an indoor spa or hot tub shall be bonded by _____.

    (a) the interconnection of threaded metal piping and fittings
    (b) metal-to-metal mounting on a common frame or base
    (c) a solid copper bonding jumper not smaller than 8 AWG
    (d) any of these

46. The outlet(s) that supplies a _____ shall be GFCI protected except as otherwise provided in 680.44.

    (a) self-contained spa or hot tub
    (b) packaged spa or hot tub equipment assembly
    (c) field-assembled spa or hot tub with a heater load of 50A or less
    (d) all of these

47. Luminaires installed in fountains shall be _____.

    (a) installed with the top of the luminaire lens below the normal water level
    (b) listed for above-water use
    (c) have the lens guarded or be listed for use without a guard
    (d) any of these

48. A portable electric sign shall not be placed in or within _____ ft from the inside walls of a fountain.

    (a) 5
    (b) 10
    (c) 15
    (d) 20

49. GFCI protection shall be required for all 125V receptacles not exceeding 30A and located within 6 ft measured _____ from the inside walls of a hydromassage bathtub.

    (a) vertically
    (b) horizontally
    (c) across
    (d) none of these

50. Hydromassage bathtubs and their associated electrical components shall be on an individual branch circuit(s) and protected by a(n) _____ GFCI.

    (a) exposed
    (b) accessible
    (c) readily accessible
    (d) concealed

51. Both metal piping systems and all grounded metal parts in contact with the circulating water of a hydromassage bathtub shall be bonded together using a(n) _____ solid copper bonding jumper not smaller than 8 AWG.

    (a) insulated
    (b) covered
    (c) bare
    (d) any of these

52. The provisions of Article 690 apply to _____ systems, including inverter(s), array circuit(s), and controller(s) for such systems.

    (a) solar photoconductive
    (b) solar PV
    (c) solar photogenic
    (d) solar photosynthesis

53. A mechanically integrated assembly of PV modules or panels with a support structure and foundation, tracker, and other components, as required, to form a dc power-producing unit, is known as a(n) _____.

    (a) pulse width modulator
    (b) array
    (c) capacitive supply bank
    (d) alternating-current photovoltaic module

54. A PV array that has two outputs, each having opposite polarity to a common reference point is known as a _____.

    (a) bipolar photovoltaic array
    (b) polar photovoltaic array
    (c) a or b
    (d) neither a or b

55. For PV systems, a piece of equipment that regulates the charging process of a battery by diverting power from energy storage to direct-current or alternating-current loads or to an interconnected utility service is known as a(n) _____.

    (a) alternating charge controller
    (b) diversion charge controller
    (c) direct charge controller
    (d) alternating charge regulator

56. Other than an energy storage subsystem of a solar PV system, such as a battery, a(n) _____ system operates in parallel with and may deliver power to an electrical production and distribution network.

    (a) hybrid
    (b) inverted
    (c) interactive
    (d) internal

57. For PV systems, the conductors between the inverter and an alternating-current panelboard for stand-alone systems, or the conductors between the inverter and the service equipment or another electric power production source, such as a utility, for an electrical production and distribution network, are part of the _____.

    (a) bipolar photovoltaic array
    (b) monopole subarray
    (c) emergency standby power
    (d) inverter output circuit

58. A(n) _____ is a complete, environmentally protected unit consisting of solar cells, and other components, exclusive of tracker, designed to generate direct-current power when exposed to sunlight.

    (a) interface
    (b) battery
    (c) module
    (d) cell bank

59. The circuit conductors between the inverter or direct-current utilization equipment and the PV source circuit(s) are part of the _____.

    (a) photovoltaic output circuit
    (b) photovoltaic input circuit
    (c) inverter input circuit
    (d) inverter output circuit

60. A stand-alone PV system supplies power in conjunction with and to supplement an electrical production and distribution network.

    (a) True
    (b) False

61. Where multiple utility-interactive inverters are remotely located from each other, a directory must be provided at each dc PV system disconnecting means, each ac disconnecting means, and at the main service disconnecting means showing the location of all ac and dc PV system disconnecting means in the building/structure.

    (a) True
    (b) False

62. A ground-fault protection device or system required for PV systems shall be capable of _____.

    (a) interrupting the flow of fault current
    (b) detecting a ground-fault current
    (c) provide an indication of the fault
    (d) all of the above

63. A warning label on the utility-interactive inverter or applied by the _____ must be on the PV utility-interactive inverter stating the following: WARNING ELECTRIC SHOCK HAZARD—IF A GROUND FAULT IS INDICATED, NORMALLY GROUNDED CONDUCTORS MAY BE UNGROUNDED AND ENERGIZED

    (a) homeowner
    (b) inspector
    (c) installer
    (d) power company

64. For PV systems, one source for lowest-expected ambient temperature is the "Extreme Annual Mean Minimum Design Dry Bulb Temperature" found in the ASHRAE Handbook Fundamentals.

    (a) True
    (b) False

65. For PV systems, in one- and two-family dwellings, live parts over 150V to ground must not be accessible to an _____ while energized.

    (a) inspector
    (b) electrician
    (c) unqualified person
    (d) all of these

66. The PV maximum output circuit current is equal to the sum of parallel PV source circuit maximum currents as calculated in _____.

    (a) 690.8(A)(1)
    (b) 690.8(A)(2)
    (c) 690.8(A)(3)
    (d) none of these

67. Overcurrent devices for PV systems shall be rated to carry not less than _____ percent of the maximum currents calculated in 690.8(A).

    (a) 80
    (b) 100
    (c) 125
    (d) 250

68. Fuses or circuit breakers for PV dc circuits must be _____ for use in dc circuits and shall have the appropriate voltage, current, and interrupt ratings.

    (a) identified
    (b) approved
    (c) recognized
    (d) listed

69. A disconnecting means is required to open ungrounded dc circuit conductors of the PV system.

    (a) True
    (b) False

70. For PV systems, means must be provided to disconnect equipment, such as batteries, inverters, charge controllers, and the like, from all ungrounded conductors of all sources.

    (a) True
    (b) False

71. Non-load-break-rated disconnecting means for PV output circuits must be marked "Do not open under load."

    (a) True
    (b) False

72. The PV disconnecting means shall be externally operable without exposing the operator to contact with live parts and shall indicate whether in the open or closed position.

    (a) True
    (b) False

73. PV source circuits and PV output circuits are not permitted to be contained in the same raceway, cable tray, cable, outlet box, junction box, or similar fitting, with non-PV systems unless the two systems are separated by a partition.

    (a) True
    (b) False

74. PV system conductors shall be identified by separate color coding, marking tape, tagging, or other approved means.

    (a) True
    (b) False

75. PV source circuits shall be identified at all points of termination, connection, and splices.

    (a) True
    (b) False

76. The requirement for grouping PV source and output circuits is not required if the circuit enters from a cable or raceway unique to the circuit that makes the grouping obvious.

    (a) True
    (b) False

77. Where dc PV source or output circuits are run inside a building or structure, they must be contained in _____.

    (a) metal raceways
    (b) Type MC cables
    (c) metal enclosures
    (d) any of these

78. Listed fittings and connectors that are intended to be concealed at the time of on-site assembly are permitted for on-site interconnection of PV modules or other array components.

    (a) True
    (b) False

79. The connectors permitted by Article 690 shall _____.

    (a) be polarized
    (b) guard against inadvertent contact with live parts by persons
    (c) require a tool for opening if the circuit operates at over 30V nominal maximum dc or 30V ac
    (d) all of these

80. Junction, pull, and outlet boxes can be located behind PV modules that are secured by removable fasteners.

    (a) True
    (b) False

81. A(n) _____ must be installed between a photovoltaic array and other equipment.

    (a) grounded conductor
    (b) main bonding jumper
    (c) equipment grounding conductor
    (d) system bonding jumper

82. Devices and systems used for mounting PV modules that also provide grounding of the module frames must be _____ for the purpose of grounding PV modules.

    (a) listed
    (b) labeled
    (c) identified
    (d) a and b

83. Devices _____ for bonding the metallic frames of PV modules shall be permitted to bond the exposed metallic frames of PV modules to the metallic frames of adjacent PV modules.

    (a) listed
    (b) labeled
    (c) identified
    (d) a and c

84. All conductors of a circuit, including the equipment grounding conductor, must be installed in the same raceway or cable, or otherwise run with the PV array circuit conductors when they leave the vicinity of the PV array.

    (a) True
    (b) False

85. Where no overcurrent protection is provided for the PV circuit, an assumed overcurrent device rated at the PV maximum circuit current must be used to size the equipment grounding conductor in accordance with _____.

    (a) 250.122
    (b) 250.66
    (c) Table 250.122
    (d) Table 250.66

86. Where exposed and subject to physical damage, PV array equipment grounding conductors smaller than 4 AWG must be protected by raceway or cable armor.

    (a) True
    (b) False

87. PV systems having no direct connection between the dc grounded conductor and ac grounded conductor shall have a(n) _____ grounding system which shall be bonded to the ac grounding system.

    (a) ac
    (b) dc
    (c) separately derived
    (d) none of these

88. PV systems with dc modules having no direct connection between the dc grounded conductor and ac grounded conductor must be bonded to the ac grounding system by a(n) _____.

    (a) separate dc grounding electrode bonded to the ac grounding electrode system with a bonding jumper
    (b) dc grounding electrode conductor sized to 250.166 run from the marked dc grounding electrode connection point to the ac grounding electrode
    (c) unspliced, or irreversibly spliced, combined grounding conductor run from the marked dc grounding electrode connection point along with the ac circuit conductors to the grounding busbar in the associated ac equipment
    (d) any of these

89. Where the removal of equipment opens the bonding connection between the _____ and exposed conducting surfaces in the PV source or output circuit equipment, a bonding jumper shall be installed while the equipment is removed.

    (a) equipment grounding conductor
    (b) grounded conductor
    (c) grounding electrode conductor
    (d) ungrounded conductor

90. Where the removal of the utility-interactive inverter or other equipment disconnects the bonding connection between the grounding electrode conductor and the PV source and/or PV output circuit grounded conductor, a _____ shall be installed to maintain the system grounding while the inverter or other equipment is removed.

    (a) grounding electrode conductor
    (b) fuse
    (c) bonding jumper
    (d) overcurrent device

91. For PV systems, where used for battery interconnections, flexible cables listed for hard-service use and identified as moisture resistant in Article 400, must be a minimum size of _____ AWG.

    (a) 1/0
    (b) 2/0
    (c) 3/0
    (d) 4/0

92. For PV systems, where flexible cables are installed, they are only permitted between the battery terminals to a nearby junction box where they must connect to an approved wiring method, or between batteries and cells within the battery enclosure.

    (a) True
    (b) False

93. For PV systems, where used for battery interconnections, flexible, fine-stranded cables must terminate in terminals, lugs, devices, or connectors that are _____ for fine-stranded conductors.

    (a) identified
    (b) listed
    (c) a or b
    (d) a and b

94. A fuel cell is an electrochemical system that consumes _____ to produce an electric current.

    (a) power
    (b) water
    (c) heat
    (d) fuel

95. The fuel cell system shall be evaluated and _____ for its intended application.

    (a) approved
    (b) identified
    (c) listed
    (d) marked

96. Transformers that supply a fire pump motor shall be sized no less than _____ percent of the sum of the fire pump motor(s) and pressure maintenance pump motors, and 100 percent of associated fire pump accessory equipment.

    (a) 100
    (b) 125
    (c) 250
    (d) 300

97. The primary overcurrent protective device for a transformer supplying a fire pump shall carry the sum of the locked-rotor current of the fire pump motor(s), pressure maintenance pump motor(s), and the full-load current of associated fire pump accessory equipment _____.

    (a) for 15 minutes
    (b) for 45 minutes
    (c) for 3 hours
    (d) indefinitely

98. Fire pump supply conductors on the load side of the final disconnecting means and overcurrent device(s) can be routed through a building(s) using _____.

    (a) 2 in. of concrete encasement
    (b) a listed 2-hour fire-rated assembly dedicated to the fire pump circuit
    (c) a listed electrical circuit protective system with a minimum 2-hour fire rating
    (d) any of these

99. The voltage at the line terminals of a fire pump motor controller shall not drop more than _____ percent below the controller's normal rated voltage under motor-starting conditions.

    (a) 5
    (b) 10
    (c) 15
    (d) 20

100. When a fire pump motor operates at 115 percent of its full-load current rating, the supply voltage at the load terminals of the fire pump controller shall not drop more than _____ percent below the voltage rating of the motor connected to those terminals.

    (a) 5
    (b) 10
    (c) 15
    (d) 20

RANDOM ORDER
[ARTICLES 90–695]

Please use the 2014 *Code* book to answer the following questions.

1. Article _____ contains the wiring requirements for service and repair operations in connection with self-propelled vehicles in which volatile flammable liquids or flammable gases are used for fuel or power.

    (a) 500
    (b) 501
    (c) 511
    (d) 514

2. Where installed in a wet location, all _____ receptacle(s) shall be listed as weather resistant.

    (a) 125V, 30A nonlocking
    (b) 250V, 15A nonlocking
    (c) 125V, 30A locking
    (d) 250V, 15A locking

3. A blocking _____ is used to block reverse current flow into a PV source circuit.

    (a) resistor
    (b) potentiometer
    (c) diode
    (d) all of the above

4. Nonmetallic wireways shall be permitted for _____.

    (a) exposed work
    (b) concealed work
    (c) wet locations if listed for the purpose
    (d) a and c

5. Metal faceplates for switches and receptacles can be connected to the equipment grounding conductor by means of a metal mounting screw(s) securing the faceplate to a grounded outlet box or grounded wiring device in patient care areas.

    (a) True
    (b) False

6. Where flammable liquids having a flash point below 100°F (such as gasoline), or gaseous fuels such as natural gas or hydrogen, will not be transferred in a minor repair garage, such location is considered to be a(n) _____ location, provided the entire floor area has mechanical ventilation providing a minimum of four air changes per hour or one cubic foot per minute of exchanged air for each square foot of floor area.

    (a) Class I, Division 1
    (b) Class I, Division 2
    (c) Class II, Division 1
    (d) unclassified

7. No parts of cord-connected luminaires, chain-, cable-, or cord-suspended luminaires, lighting track, pendants, or paddle fans shall be located within a zone measured 3 ft horizontally and _____ ft vertically from the top of the bathtub rim or shower stall threshold.

    (a) 4
    (b) 6
    (c) 8
    (d) 10

8. A hospital is a building or portion thereof used for the medical, psychiatric, obstetrical, or surgical care, on a 24-hour basis, of _____ or more inpatients.

    (a) two
    (b) three
    (c) four
    (d) five

9. In switchboards and panelboards, load terminals for field wiring shall be so located that it is not necessary to reach across or beyond a(n) _____ ungrounded line bus in order to make connections.

    (a) insulated
    (b) uninsulated
    (c) grounded
    (d) high impedance

10. The 8 AWG solid bonding jumper required for hydromassage bathtubs shall not be required to be extended to any _____.

    (a) remote panelboard
    (b) service equipment
    (c) electrode
    (d) any of these

11. In agricultural building locations where surfaces are periodically washed or sprayed with water, boxes, conduit bodies, and fittings shall be listed for use in wet locations.

    (a) True
    (b) False

12. Fixture wires of 18 AWG or 16 AWG, shall be permitted for the control and operating circuits of X-ray equipment when protected by an overcurrent device not larger than _____.

    (a) 15A
    (b) 20A
    (c) 25A
    (d) 30A

13. Article 600 covers the installation of conductors, equipment, and field wiring for _____.

    (a) electric signs
    (b) outline lighting
    (c) neon tubing
    (d) all of these

14. TPT and TST cords shall be permitted in lengths not exceeding _____ ft when attached directly to a portable appliance rated 50W or less.

    (a) 8
    (b) 10
    (c) 15
    (d) 20

15. Electrical equipment and wiring methods in or on portable structures for carnival or circuses shall have mechanical protection where subject to _____.

    (a) public access
    (b) physical damage
    (c) exposure to the weather
    (d) operator access

16. X-ray equipment mounted on a permanent base equipped with wheels for moving while completely assembled describes "_____."

    (a) portable
    (b) mobile
    (c) movable
    (d) room

17. Each motor fuel dispensing device shall be provided with a means to remove all external voltage sources, including power, communications, data, video circuits, and feedback, during periods of maintenance and service of the fuel dispensing equipment.

    (a) True
    (b) False

18. A switching device with a marked OFF position shall completely disconnect all _____ conductors of the load it controls.

    (a) grounded
    (b) ungrounded
    (c) grounding
    (d) all of these

19. A nursing home is an area used for the housing and nursing care, on a 24-hour basis, of _____ or more persons who, because of mental or physical incapacity, might be unable to provide for their own needs and safety without the assistance of another person.

    (a) two
    (b) three
    (c) four
    (d) five

20. All _____, 125V receptacle outlets that are not part of the permanent wiring of the building or structure and are used by personnel for temporary power shall be GFCI protected.

    (a) 15A
    (b) 20A
    (c) 30A
    (d) all of these

21. A 125V receptacle shall be installed a minimum of 6 ft and a maximum of 20 ft from the inside wall of a permanently installed pool.

    (a) True
    (b) False

22. The power supply to contact conductors of a crane in Class III locations shall _____.

    (a) be electrically isolated from all other systems
    (b) be equipped with an acceptable ground detector
    (c) give an alarm in the case of a ground fault
    (d) all of these

23. Grounding-type GFCI-protected receptacles of the single type for motors related to the circulation and sanitation system of a pool can be located not less than _____ from the inside walls of the pool.

    (a) 3 ft
    (b) 6 ft
    (c) 8 ft
    (d) 12 ft

24. The maximum rating or setting of an inverse time breaker used as the motor branch-circuit short-circuit and ground-fault protective device for a single-phase motor is _____ percent of the full-load current given in Table 430.248.

    (a) 125
    (b) 175
    (c) 250
    (d) 300

25. Metal boxes shall be _____ in accordance with Article 250.

    (a) grounded
    (b) bonded
    (c) a and b
    (d) none of these

26. The distribution point is an electrical supply point from which _____ to agricultural buildings or structures under single management are supplied.

    (a) service drops or service conductors
    (b) feeders or branch circuits
    (c) a or b
    (d) none of these

27. Where raceways are installed in wet locations above grade, the interior of these raceways shall be considered a _____ location.

    (a) wet
    (b) dry
    (c) damp
    (d) corrosive

28. Conductors supplying several motors shall not be sized smaller than _____ percent of the full-load current rating of the highest rated motor, plus the sum of the full-load current ratings of all other motors in the group, plus the ampacity or other loads.

    (a) 80
    (b) 100
    (c) 125
    (d) 150

29. Vegetation shall not be used to support overhead conductor spans of _____ for temporary installations.

    (a) branch circuits
    (b) feeders
    (c) a or b
    (d) none of these

30. For stand-alone PV systems, circuit breakers that are marked "Line" and "Load" can be backfed.

    (a) True
    (b) False

31. A switchboard or panelboard containing a 4-wire, _____ system where the midpoint of one phase winding is grounded, shall be legibly and permanently field-marked to caution that one phase has a higher voltage-to-ground.

    (a) wye-connected
    (b) delta-connected
    (c) solidly grounded
    (d) ungrounded

32. The conductors of PV output circuits and inverter input and output circuits shall be identified at all points of termination, connection, and splices.

    (a) True
    (b) False

33. In Class III locations, switches, circuit breakers, motor controllers, and fuses, including pushbuttons, relays, and similar devices, shall be provided with _____.

    (a) Class I enclosures
    (b) general duty enclosures
    (c) dusttight enclosures
    (d) seals at each enclosure

34. Each doorway leading into a transformer vault from the building interior shall be provided with a tight-fitting door having a minimum fire rating of _____ hours.

    (a) 2
    (b) 3
    (c) 4
    (d) 6

35. In spas or hot tubs, a clearly labeled emergency shutoff or control switch shall be _____, not less than 5 ft away, and within sight of the spa or hot tub.

    (a) accessible
    (b) readily accessible
    (c) available
    (d) none of these

36. Where equipment grounding is required for an installation of HDPE, a separate equipment grounding conductor shall be _____.

    (a) an insulated copper conductor
    (b) installed within the conduit
    (c) a stranded bare copper conductor
    (d) a solid bare copper conductor

37. Nonmetallic surface extensions shall be secured in place by approved means at intervals not exceeding _____ in.

    (a) 6
    (b) 8
    (c) 10
    (d) 16

38. Recognized as suitable for the specific purpose, function, use, environment, and application is the definition of "_____."

    (a) labeled
    (b) identified (as applied to equipment)
    (c) listed
    (d) approved

39. Each elevator shall have a means for disconnecting all ungrounded main power-supply conductors for each unit _____.

    (a) excluding the emergency power system
    (b) including the emergency or standby power system
    (c) excluding the emergency power system if it is automatic
    (d) and the power supply may not be an emergency power system

40. Metal gas piping shall be considered bonded by the equipment grounding conductor for the circuit that is likely to energize the piping.

    (a) True
    (b) False

41. In Division 1 or Division 2 locations where the boxes, fittings, or enclosures are required to be explosionproof, if a flexible cord is used it must terminate with a cord connector or attachment plug listed for the location, or a listed cord connector installed with a seal that is listed for the location. In Division 2 locations where explosionproof equipment is not required, the cord shall terminate _____.

    (a) with a listed cord connector
    (b) with a listed attachment plug
    (c) in a splice of any manner
    (d) a or b

42. Thermal insulation shall not be installed above a recessed luminaire or within _____ in. of the recessed luminarie's enclosure, wiring compartment, ballast, transformer, LED driver, or power supply unless it is identified as a Type IC luminaire.

    (a) ½
    (b) 3
    (c) 6
    (d) 12

43. Motors, generators, or other rotating electrical machinery identified for Class I, Division 2 locations can be used in Class I, Division 1 locations.

    (a) True
    (b) False

44. The ampacity of Type UF cable shall be that of _____ conductors in accordance with 310.15.

    (a) 60°C
    (b) 75°C
    (c) 90°C
    (d) 105°C

45. Phase converters shall be permitted to be used for fire pump service.

    (a) True
    (b) False

46. Buildings/structures containing both utility service and a PV system must have a permanent _____ placed at the service disconnecting means and the PV system disconnecting means identifying the location of the other system if they are not located at the same location.

    (a) plaque
    (b) directory
    (c) a and b
    (d) a or b

47. If more than one luminaire is installed on a branch circuit that isn't of the multiwire type, a disconnecting means isn't required for every luminaire when the light switch for the space ensures that some of the luminaires in the space will still provide illumination.

    (a) True
    (b) False

48. For circuits rated 100A or less, when the equipment terminals are listed for use with 75°C conductors, the ____ column of Table 310.15(B)(16) shall be used to determine the ampacity of THHN conductors.

    (a) 30°C
    (b) 60°C
    (c) 75°C
    (d) 90°C

49. Type SE cable can be used for interior wiring as long as it complies with the installation requirements of Part II of Article 334, excluding 334.80.

    (a) True
    (b) False

50. In industrial establishments where conditions of maintenance and supervision ensure that only qualified persons service the installation, flexible cords and cables can be installed in aboveground raceways that are no longer than ____ ft, to protect the flexible cord or cable from physical damage.

    (a) 25
    (b) 50
    (c) 100
    (d) 150

51. Type USE cable is not permitted for ____ wiring.

    (a) underground
    (b) interior
    (c) a or b
    (d) a and b

52. The number of conductors permitted in ENT shall not exceed the percentage fill specified in ____.

    (a) Chapter 9, Table 1
    (b) Table 250.66
    (c) Table 310.15(B)(16)
    (d) 240.6

53. A ____ shall be located in sight from the motor location and the driven machinery location.

    (a) controller
    (b) protection device
    (c) disconnecting means
    (d) all of these

54. Single-pole breakers utilizing identified handle ties are not permitted to be used for the required disconnecting means for motor fuel dispensing equipment.

    (a) True
    (b) False

55. Flexible cords for fixed or stationary pool equipment shall ____.

    (a) not exceed 3 ft
    (b) have a copper equipment grounding conductor not smaller than 12 AWG
    (c) terminate in a grounding-type attachment plug
    (d) all of these

56. Equipment shall be identified not only for the class of hazardous (classified) location, but also for the explosive, combustible, or ignitible properties of the specific ____ present.

    (a) gas or vapor
    (b) dust
    (c) fibers/flyings
    (d) any of these

57. Metal equipment racks and enclosures for permanent audio system installations shall be grounded.

    (a) True
    (b) False

58. The cross-sectional area of the conductors or optical fiber tubes permitted in a sealing fitting shall not exceed ____ percent of the cross-sectional area of RMC of the same trade size.

    (a) 25
    (b) 50
    (c) 100
    (d) 125

59. For installations consisting of not more than two 2-wire branch circuits, the building disconnecting means shall have a rating of not less than _____.

(a) 15A
(b) 20A
(c) 25A
(d) 30A

60. Which of the following statements about Type MI cable is correct?

(a) It may be used in any hazardous (classified) location where permitted by other articles of the *Code*.
(b) It shall not be permitted for branch circuits.
(c) It shall be securely supported at intervals not exceeding 10 ft.
(d) none of these

61. Dry-type transformers installed indoors rated over _____ shall be installed in a vault.

(a) 1,000V
(b) 20,000V
(c) 35,000V
(d) 50,000V

62. Field-installed skeleton tubing lighting is not required to be _____ where installed in conformance with the *Code*.

(a) listed
(b) identified for the purpose
(c) marked
(d) none of these

63. Two or more grounding electrodes bonded together are considered a single grounding electrode system.

(a) True
(b) False

64. A(n) _____ shall be located at the point of entry to an elevator machine room.

(a) directory
(b) lighting switch
(c) control circuit disconnecting means
(d) emergency exit map

65. When replacing receptacles in locations that would require GFCI protection under the current *NEC*, _____ receptacles shall be installed.

(a) dedicated
(b) isolated ground
(c) GFCI-protected
(d) grounding

66. The _____ is the basic PV device that generates electricity when exposed to light.

(a) solar battery
(b) solar cell
(c) solar atom
(d) solar ray

67. Listed cord sets or adapters that incorporate listed GFCI protection can be used to meet the GFCI requirement with portable generators manufactured prior to _____.

(a) January 1, 2005
(b) January 1, 2011
(c) January 1, 2014
(d) January 1, 2015

68. The ampacity adjustment factors of 310.15(B)(3)(a) shall not apply to conductors installed in surface metal raceways where the _____.

(a) cross-sectional area exceeds 4 sq in.
(b) current-carrying conductors do not exceed 30 in number
(c) total cross-sectional area of all conductors does not exceed 20 percent of the interior cross-sectional area of the raceway
(d) all of these

69. When determining the number of current-carrying conductors, a grounding or bonding conductor shall not be counted when applying the provisions of 310.15(B)(3)(a).

(a) True
(b) False

70. In motor fuel dispensing facilities, all metal raceways, the metal armor or metallic sheath on cables, and all noncurrent-carrying metal parts of fixed and portable electrical equipment _____ shall be grounded and bonded.

    (a) operating at under 600V
    (b) regardless of voltage
    (c) over 300V
    (d) under 50V

71. When supplying a room air conditioner rated 120V, the length of a flexible supply cord shall not exceed _____ ft.

    (a) 4
    (b) 6
    (c) 8
    (d) 10

72. An automotive-type vehicle for on-road use, such as _____ primarily powered by an electric motor is known as an electric vehicle.

    (a) passenger automobiles
    (b) buses, trucks, vans
    (c) neighborhood electric vehicles, and electric motorcycles
    (d) all of these

73. When service-entrance conductors exceed 1,100 kcmil for copper, the required grounded conductor for the service shall be sized not less than _____ percent of the circular mil area of the largest set of ungrounded service-entrance conductor(s).

    (a) 9
    (b) 11
    (c) 12½
    (d) 15

74. Parking garages used for parking or storage can be considered as an unclassified location.

    (a) True
    (b) False

75. Provisions appropriate to the battery technology shall be made for sufficient diffusion and ventilation of the gases from a storage battery to prevent the accumulation of a(n) _____ mixture.

    (a) corrosive
    (b) explosive
    (c) toxic
    (d) all of these

76. Resistance-type heating elements in electric space-heating equipment shall be protected at not more than _____.

    (a) 24A
    (b) 36A
    (c) 48A
    (d) 60A

77. An attachment plug and receptacle can serve as the disconnecting means for cord-connected _____.

    (a) room air conditioners
    (b) household refrigerators and freezers
    (c) drinking water coolers and beverage dispensers
    (d) all of these

78. Power distribution blocks shall be permitted in pull and junction boxes over 100 cubic inches when _____.

    (a) they are listed as a power distribution block.
    (b) they are installed in a box not smaller than required by the installation instructions of the power distribution block.
    (c) the junction box is sized so that the wire-bending space requirements of 312.6 can be met.
    (d) all of these

79. Where multiple services or separately derived systems supply portable structures of carnival, circuses, or fairs, all structures separated by less than _____ ft shall be bonded together at the portable structures.

    (a) 6
    (b) 8
    (c) 10
    (d) 12

80. NUCC larger than _____ shall not be used.

    (a) trade size 1
    (b) trade size 2
    (c) trade size 3
    (d) trade size 4

81. For PV systems, where all terminals of a disconnecting means may be energized when the switch is in the open position, a warning sign must be placed on or adjacent to the disconnecting means. The sign shall be similar to: WARNING ELECTRIC SHOCK HAZARD. DO NOT TOUCH TERMINALS. TERMINALS ON BOTH THE LINE AND LOAD SIDES MAY BE ENERGIZED IN THE OPEN POSITION.

    (a) True
    (b) False

82. When a building is supplied with a(n) _____ fire sprinkler system, ENT shall be permitted to be used within walls, floors, and ceilings, exposed or concealed, in buildings exceeding three floors above grade.

    (a) listed
    (b) identified
    (c) NFPA 13-2013
    (d) none of these

83. In Class III locations, portable lighting equipment shall be equipped with handles and protected with substantial guards. Lampholders shall be of the unswitched type with no provision for _____.

    (a) receiving attachment plugs
    (b) grounding connections
    (c) lamp installation
    (d) hooks or hangers

84. A conductor used for open wiring on insulators that penetrates a wall, floor, or other framing member shall be carried through a _____.

    (a) separate sleeve or tube
    (b) weatherproof tube
    (c) tube of absorbent material
    (d) grounded metallic tube

85. A separate _____ shall supply the elevator hoistway pit lighting and receptacle(s). The required lighting shall not be connected to the load side of a ground-fault circuit interrupter.

    (a) feeder
    (b) subpanel
    (c) emergency system
    (d) branch circuit

86. _____ are among the wiring methods permitted within a Class I, Division 2 location.

    (a) Enclosed gasketed busways and enclosed gasketed wireways
    (b) PLTC and Type PLTC-ER cable and ITC and ITC-ER cable terminated with listed fittings
    (c) Types MC, MV, OFNP, OFCP, OFC, or TC cables including installation in cable tray systems and terminated with listed fittings
    (d) all of these

87. For grounded systems, electrical equipment and other electrically conductive material likely to become energized, shall be installed in a manner that creates a _____ from any point on the wiring system where a ground fault may occur to the electrical supply source.

    (a) circuit facilitating the operation of the overcurrent device
    (b) low-impedance circuit
    (c) circuit capable of safely carrying the ground-fault current likely to be imposed on it
    (d) all of these

88. Power to fire pump motors must be supplied by a reliable source of power that has the capacity to carry the _____.

    (a) sum of locked-rotor current of the fire pump motor(s)
    (b) locked-rotor current of the pressure maintenance pump motors
    (c) full-load current of any associated fire pump equipment
    (d) all of these

89. The ampacity of supply branch-circuit conductors and the overcurrent protective devices for X-ray equipment shall not be less than _____.

    (a) 50 percent of the momentary rating
    (b) 100 percent of the long-time rating
    (c) the larger of a or b
    (d) the smaller of a or b

90. Luminaires and ceiling fans located over or within 5 ft, measured horizontally, from the inside walls of an indoor spa or hot tub shall have a mounting height of not less than _____ above the maximum water level when GFCI protected.

    (a) 4.70 ft
    (b) 5 ft
    (c) 7 ft 6 in.
    (d) 12 ft

91. The allowable ampacity of flexible cords and cables is found in _____.

    (a) Table 310.15(B)(16)
    (b) Tables 400.5(A)(1) and (2)
    (c) Chapter 9, Table 1
    (d) Table 430.52

92. Ground-fault protection of equipment shall _____ for fire pumps.

    (a) not be permitted
    (b) be provided
    (c) be permitted
    (d) be listed

93. Except as specifically modified by Article 590, all other *Code* requirements for permanent wiring apply to temporary wiring installations.

    (a) True
    (b) False

94. A motor _____ device that can restart a motor automatically after overload tripping shall not be installed if automatic restarting of the motor can result in injury to persons.

    (a) short-circuit
    (b) ground-fault
    (c) overcurrent
    (d) overload

95. A 120V section of lighting track that is continuously loaded shall not exceed 12 ft in length, in accordance with 220.43(B).

    (a) True
    (b) False

96. An arc welder shall have overcurrent protection rated or set at not more than _____ percent of the rated primary current of the welder.

    (a) 100
    (b) 125
    (c) 150
    (d) 200

97. The ampacity of capacitor circuit conductors shall not be less than _____ percent of the rated current of the capacitor.

    (a) 100
    (b) 115
    (c) 125
    (d) 135

98. A _____ subarray has two conductors in the output circuit, one positive (+) and one negative (-). Two of these subarrays are used to form a bipolar photovoltaic array.

    (a) bipolar
    (b) monopole
    (c) double-pole
    (d) module

99. In a health care facility, receptacles and attachment plugs in a hazardous (classified) location within an anesthetizing area shall be listed for use in Class I, Group _____ locations.

    (a) A
    (b) B
    (c) C
    (d) D

100. Conductors and cables of intrinsically safe circuits run in other than raceway or cable tray systems shall be separated by at least _____ in. and secured from conductors and cables of any nonintrinsically safe circuits.

    (a) 2
    (b) 6
    (c) 12
    (d) 18

STRAIGHT ORDER
[ARTICLE 700–CHAPTER 9]

Please use the 2014 *Code* book to answer the following questions.

1. An emergency system shall have adequate capacity and rating for _____ to be operated simultaneously.

   (a) 80% of the loads
   (b) all loads
   (c) 125% of the load
   (d) none of these

2. A portable or temporary alternate source _____ whenever the emergency generator for emergency systems is out of service for major maintenance or repair.

   (a) shall not be required
   (b) is recommended
   (c) shall be available
   (d) shall be avoided

3. Emergency systems transfer equipment, including transfer switches, shall be _____.

   (a) automatic
   (b) identified for emergency use
   (c) approved by the authority having jurisdiction
   (d) all of these

4. An emergency transfer switch for emergency systems shall supply _____.

   (a) emergency loads
   (b) computer equipment
   (c) UPS equipment
   (d) all of these

5. In locations containing an emergency system, a sign shall be placed at the service-entrance equipment indicating the type and location of on-site emergency power sources.

   (a) True
   (b) False

6. Wiring from an emergency source or emergency source distribution overcurrent protection to emergency loads shall be kept independent of all other wiring and equipment except in _____.

   (a) transfer equipment enclosures
   (b) exit or emergency luminaires supplied from two sources
   (c) listed load control relays supplying emergency or exit luminaires, or a common junction box, attached to exit or emergency luminaires supplied from two sources
   (d) all of these

7. Wiring from an emergency source can emergency or other loads, provided the conductors _____.

   (a) terminate in separate vertical sections of a switchboard
   (b) terminate in the same vertical section of a switchboard
   (c) terminate in a junction box identified for emergency use
   (d) are identified as emergency conductors

8. Emergency systems circuit wiring shall be designed and located to minimize the hazards that might cause failure because of _____.

   (a) flooding
   (b) fire
   (c) icing
   (d) all of these

9. In the event of failure of the normal supply to the building/structure, emergency power shall be available within _____ seconds.

   (a) 5
   (b) 10
   (c) 30
   (d) 60

10. If a generator for emergency system power located outdoors is equipped with a readily accessible disconnecting means in accordance with 445.18, and the disconnecting means is located within sight (within 50 ft) of the building/structure, an additional disconnecting means isn't required on or at the building/structure for the generator feeder conductors that serve or pass through the building/structure.

    (a) True
    (b) False

11. Unit equipment for emergency systems shall be on the same branch circuit that serves the normal lighting in the area and connected _____ any local switches.

    (a) with
    (b) ahead of
    (c) after
    (d) downstream of

12. In emergency systems, only appliances and lamps required for emergency use, shall be supplied by _____.

    (a) emergency circuits
    (b) multiwire branch circuits
    (c) HID-rated circuit breakers
    (d) a and b

13. Where batteries are used for _____ of prime movers of legally required standby systems, the authority having jurisdiction shall require periodic maintenance.

    (a) control
    (b) starting or ignition
    (c) a and b
    (d) none of these

14. A written record shall be kept of required tests and maintenance on legally required standby systems.

    (a) True
    (b) False

15. Testing legally required standby system lighting and power systems during maximum anticipated load conditions shall be avoided so as not to tax the standby system unnecessarily.

    (a) True
    (b) False

16. A legally required standby system shall have adequate capacity and rating for _____ that are expected to operate simultaneously on the standby system.

    (a) all of the loads
    (b) 80% of the loads
    (c) 125% of the loads
    (d) none of these

17. A sign shall be placed at the service equipment indicating the _____ of on-site legally required standby power sources.

    (a) type
    (b) location
    (c) manufacturer
    (d) a and b

18. Individual unit equipment for legally required standby illumination shall be permanently fixed in place. Flexible cord-and-plug connection shall be permitted, provided the cord does not exceed _____ in length.

    (a) 12 in.
    (b) 18 in.
    (c) 3 ft
    (d) 6 ft

19. Article 702 applies to _____ optional standby systems used for backup power to public or private facilities or property where life safety does not depend on the performance of the system.

    (a) permanently installed
    (b) portable
    (c) a and b
    (d) none of these

20. Optional standby systems are typically installed to provide an alternate source of power for _____.

    (a) data processing and communication systems
    (b) emergency systems for health care facilities
    (c) emergency systems for hospitals
    (d) none of these

21. A transfer switch shall be required for all fixed or portable optional standby power systems for buildings or structures at which an electric utility is either the normal or standby source, unless permitted by an exception.

    (a) True
    (b) False

22. For optional standby systems, the temporary connection of a portable generator without transfer equipment shall be permitted where conditions of maintenance and supervision ensure that only qualified persons will service the installation, and where the normal supply is physically isolated by _____.

    (a) a lockable disconnecting means
    (b) the disconnection of the normal supply conductors
    (c) an extended power outage
    (d) a or b

23. For interconnected electric power production sources, the generating source and all distribution equipment associated with it that generates electricity from a source other than a utility supplied service is called _____.

    (a) a service drop
    (b) power production equipment
    (c) the service point
    (d) utilization equipment

24. For interconnected electric power production sources, an electric power production source is permitted to be connected to the supply side of the service disconnecting means.

    (a) True
    (b) False

25. For interconnected electric power production sources, the sum of the ratings of all overcurrent devices connected to power production sources are permitted to exceed the rating of the service.

    (a) True
    (b) False

26. In accordance with Article 705, where two sources, one a utility and the other an inverter, are located at opposite ends of a busbar that contains loads, a permanent warning label must be applied to the panelboard to warn others that the inverter output connection circuit breaker must not be relocated.

    (a) True
    (b) False

27. For interconnected electric power production sources, panelboards containing ac inverter circuit breakers must be field marked to indicate the presence of multiple ac power sources.

    (a) True
    (b) False

28. For interconnected electric power production sources, _____, unless otherwise marked, are suitable for backfeeding.

    (a) circuit breakers
    (b) PV system overcurrent devices
    (c) utility-interactive inverters
    (d) fused disconnects

29. Critical operations power systems are those systems so classed by municipal, state, federal, or other codes by any governmental agency having jurisdiction or by facility engineering documentation establishing the necessity for such a system.

    (a) True
    (b) False

30. Article 720 covers the installation requirements for circuits and equipment operating at less than _____.

    (a) 20V
    (b) 30V
    (c) 40V
    (d) 50V

31. Due to its power limitations, a Class 2 circuit is considered safe from a fire initiation standpoint and provides acceptable protection from electric shock.

    (a) True
    (b) False

32. Since Class 3 control circuits permit higher allowable levels of voltage and current than Class 2 control circuits, additional _____ are specified to provide protection against the electric shock hazard.

    (a) circuits
    (b) safeguards
    (c) conditions
    (d) requirements

33. If remote-control, signaling, and power-limited circuits are installed in a raceway that is subjected to different temperatures, and where condensation is known to be a problem, the raceway must be filled with a material approved by the authority having jurisdiction that will prevent the circulation of warm air to a colder section of the raceway. An explosionproof seal _____.

    (a) is required for this purpose
    (b) has been proven effective for this purpose
    (c) isn't required for this purpose
    (d) is the only method of doing this

34. Accessible portions of abandoned Class 2 and Class 3 cables shall be removed.

    (a) True
    (b) False

35. Overcurrent devices for Class 1 circuits shall be located at the point where the conductor to be protected _____.

    (a) terminates to the load
    (b) is spliced to any other conductor
    (c) receives its supply
    (d) none of these

36. The power source for a Class 2 circuit shall be _____.

    (a) a listed Class 2 transformer
    (b) a listed Class 2 power supply
    (c) other listed equipment marked to identify the Class 2 power source
    (d) any of these

37. Cables and conductors of Class 2 and Class 3 circuits _____ be placed with conductors of electric light, power, Class 1, nonpower-limited fire alarm circuits, and medium power network-powered broadband communications circuits.

    (a) shall be permitted to
    (b) shall not
    (c) shall
    (d) none of these

38. Conductors of Class 2 and Class 3 circuits shall not be placed in any enclosure, raceway, cable, or similar fittings with conductors of Class 1 or electric light or power conductors, unless _____.

    (a) insulated for the maximum voltage present
    (b) totally comprised of aluminum conductors
    (c) separated by a barrier
    (d) all of these

39. Raceways shall not be used as a means of support for Class 2 or Class 3 cables.

    (a) True
    (b) False

40. Class 2 and Class 3 riser cables listed as suitable for use in a vertical run in a shaft, or from floor to floor shall be Type(s) _____.

    (a) CL2P and CL3P
    (b) CL2R and CL3R
    (c) CL2 and CL3
    (d) PLTC

41. Overcurrent protection for Type ITC cable shall not exceed _____ for 20 AWG and larger conductors.

    (a) 3A
    (b) 5A
    (c) 10A
    (d) 15A

42. Fire alarm systems include _____.

    (a) fire detection and alarm notification
    (b) guard's tour
    (c) sprinkler waterflow
    (d) all of these

43. Fire alarm cables that are not terminated at equipment and not identified for future use with a tag are considered abandoned.

    (a) True
    (b) False

44. If fire alarm conductors are installed in a raceway that is subjected to different temperatures, and where condensation is known to be a problem, the raceway must be filled with a material approved by the authority having jurisdiction that will prevent the circulation of warm air to a colder section of the raceway. An explosionproof seal _____.

    (a) is required for this purpose
    (b) has been proven effective for this purpose
    (c) isn't required for this purpose
    (d) is the only method of doing this

45. Exposed fire alarm circuit cables shall be supported by the building structure using straps, staples, hangers, cable ties or similar fittings designed and installed so as not to damage the cable.

    (a) True
    (b) False

46. Accessible portions of abandoned fire alarm cable shall be removed.

    (a) True
    (b) False

47. Fire alarm cables identified for future use shall be marked with a tag of sufficient durability to withstand _____.

    (a) moisture
    (b) humidity
    (c) the environment involved
    (d) none of these

48. The power source for a nonpower-limited fire alarm circuit shall not be supplied through a(n) _____.

    (a) ground-fault circuit interrupter
    (b) arc-fault circuit interrupter
    (c) inverse time circuit breaker
    (d) a or b

49. The number of nonpower-limited fire alarm conductors in a raceway shall not be required to comply with the fill requirements contained in 300.17.

    (a) True
    (b) False

50. Fire alarm equipment supplying power-limited fire alarm circuits shall be durably marked where plainly visible to indicate each circuit that is _____.

    (a) supplied by a nonpower-limited fire alarm circuit
    (b) a power-limited fire alarm circuit
    (c) a fire alarm circuit
    (d) none of these

51. Cables and conductors of two or more power-limited fire alarm circuits can be installed in the same cable, enclosure, cable tray, raceway, or cable routing assembly.

    (a) True
    (b) False

52. Audio system circuits using Class 2 or Class 3 wiring methods shall not be installed in the same cable, raceway, or cable routing assembly with _____.

    (a) other audio system circuits
    (b) power-limited fire alarm conductors or cables
    (c) a or b
    (d) none of these

53. Cables used in power-limited fire alarm systems shall have an insulation rating of not less than _____.

    (a) 100V
    (b) 300V
    (c) 600V
    (d) 1,000V

54. Optical fiber cables not terminated at equipment, and not identified for future use with a tag are considered abandoned.

    (a) True
    (b) False

55. Composite optical fiber cables contain optical fibers and _____.

    (a) strength members
    (b) vapor barriers
    (c) current-carrying electrical conductors
    (d) none of these

56. Nonconductive optical fiber cable is a factory assembly of one or more optical fibers with an overall covering and containing no electrically conductive materials.

    (a) True
    (b) False

57. Nonconductive optical fiber cable contains no metallic members and no other _____ materials.

    (a) electrically conductive
    (b) inductive
    (c) synthetic
    (d) insulating

58. An optical fiber cable is a factory assembly or field assembly of one or more optical fibers having a(n) _____ covering.

    (a) conductive
    (b) nonconductive
    (c) overall
    (d) metallic

59. Exposed optical fiber cables shall be supported by the building structure using hardware including straps, staples, cable ties, hangers, or similar fittings designed and installed so as not to damage the cable.

    (a) True
    (b) False

60. Accepted industry practices for optical fiber installations are described in _____.

    (a) ANSI/NECA/BICSI 568, *Standard for Installing Commercial Building Telecommunications Cabling*
    (b) ANSI/NECA/FOA 301, *Standard for Installing and Testing Fiber Optic Cables*
    (c) other ANSI-approved installation standards
    (d) all of these

61. Where exposed to contact with electric light or power conductors, the noncurrent-carrying metallic members of optical fiber cables entering buildings shall be _____.

    (a) grounded as specified in 770.100 as close to the point of entrance as practicable
    (b) interrupted as close to the point of entrance as practicable by an insulating joint or equivalent device
    (c) a or b
    (d) a and b

62. When optical fiber cable is installed in a Chapter 3 raceway, the raceway shall be installed in accordance with Chapter 3 requirements.

    (a) True
    (b) False

63. Conductive optical fiber cables can occupy the same cable tray, raceway, box, enclosure, or cable routing assembly with conductors for electric light, power, and Class 1 circuits.

    (a) True
    (b) False

64. Optical fiber cables shall not be _____ to the exterior of any conduit or raceway as a means of support.

    (a) strapped
    (b) taped
    (c) attached
    (d) all of these

65. Types _____ nonconductive and conductive general-purpose optical fiber cables shall be listed as being suitable for general-purpose use, with the exception of risers and plenums, and shall also be listed as being resistant to the spread of fire.

    (a) OFNP and OFCP
    (b) OFNR and OFCR
    (c) OFNG and OFCG
    (d) OFN and OFC

66. Types _____ nonconductive and conductive optical fiber cables shall be listed as being suitable for general-purpose use, with the exception of risers, plenums, and other spaces used for environmental air, and shall also be listed as being resistant to the spread of fire.

    (a) OFNP and OFCP
    (b) OFNR and OFCR
    (c) OFNG and OFCG
    (d) OFN and OFC

67. The point of entrance of a communications circuit is the point _____ at which the communications cable emerges from an external wall, from a concrete floor slab, from RMC, or from IMC.

    (a) outside a building
    (b) within a building
    (c) on the building
    (d) none of these

68. Equipment intended to be permanently electrically connected to a communications network shall be listed.

    (a) True
    (b) False

69. Communications cables installed _____ on the surface of ceilings and walls shall be supported by the building structure in such a manner that the cable will not be damaged by normal building use.

    (a) exposed
    (b) concealed
    (c) hidden
    (d) a and b

70. Accessible portions of abandoned communications cable shall be removed.

    (a) True
    (b) False

71. Openings around penetrations of communications cables, communications raceways, and cable routing assemblies through fire-resistant–rated walls, partitions, floors, or ceilings shall be _____ using approved methods to maintain the fire-resistance rating.

    (a) closed
    (b) opened
    (c) draft stopped
    (d) firestopped

72. Outside plant communications cables shall not be required to be listed where the length of the cable within the building, measured from its point of entrance, does not exceed _____ ft and the cable enters the building from the outside and is terminated in an enclosure or on a listed primary protector.

    (a) 25
    (b) 30
    (c) 50
    (d) 100

73. For buildings with grounding means but without an intersystem bonding termination, the grounding conductor for communications circuits shall terminate to the nearest _____.

    (a) building or structure grounding electrode system
    (b) interior metal water piping system, within 5 ft from its point of entrance
    (c) service equipment enclosure
    (d) any of these

74. Communications wires, communications cables, communications raceways, and cable routing assemblies installed in buildings shall be listed except for up to 50 ft past the point of entry as allowed by 800.48.

    (a) True
    (b) False

75. Communications wires and cables shall be separated by at least 2 in. from conductors of _____ circuits, unless permitted otherwise.

    (a) power
    (b) lighting
    (c) Class 1
    (d) all of these

76. Article _____ contains the installation requirements for the wiring of television and radio receiving equipment, such as digital satellite receiving equipment for television signals and amateur/citizen band radio equipment antennas.

    (a) 680
    (b) 700
    (c) 810
    (d) 840

77. Outdoor antennas and lead-in conductors shall be securely supported and the lead-in conductors shall be securely attached to the antenna, but they shall not be attached to the electric service mast.

    (a) True
    (b) False

78. A receiving station outdoor wire-strung antenna conductor with a span of 75 ft shall be at least _____ AWG if a copper-clad steel conductor is used.

    (a) 17
    (b) 14
    (c) 12
    (d) 10

79. The bonding conductor or grounding electrode conductor for an antenna mast or antenna discharge unit shall be run to the grounding electrode in as straight a line as practicable.

    (a) True
    (b) False

80. An open span length of 200 ft for antenna conductors of hard-drawn copper located at an amateur transmitting and receiving station requires a minimum conductor size of _____ AWG.

    (a) 14
    (b) 12
    (c) 10
    (d) 8

81. CATV cable not terminated at equipment other than a coaxial cable connector and not identified for future use with a tag is considered abandoned.

    (a) True
    (b) False

82. Coaxial cable is a cylindrical assembly composed of a conductor centered inside a metallic tube or shield, separated by a(n) _____ material and usually covered by an insulating jacket.

    (a) insulating
    (b) conductive
    (c) isolating
    (d) dielectric

83. The point of entrance of a CATV coaxial cable is the point _____ at which the coaxial cable emerges from an external wall, from a concrete floor slab, from rigid metal conduit (RMC). or from intermediate metal conduit (IMC).

    (a) outside a building
    (b) within a building
    (c) on the building
    (d) none of these

84. Overhead coaxial cables for a CATV system shall be separated by at least _____ from lightning conductors, where practicable.

    (a) 3 in.
    (b) 6 in.
    (c) 2 ft
    (d) 6 ft

85. Community antenna television and radio system coaxial cables shall not be required to be listed and marked where the length of the cable within the building, measured from its point of entrance, does not exceed _____ ft, the cable enters the building from the outside and the cable is terminated at a grounding block.

    (a) 25
    (b) 30
    (c) 50
    (d) 100

86. The outer conductive shield of a CATV coaxial cable entering a building shall be grounded as close to the point of entrance as practicable.

    (a) True
    (b) False

87. The conductor used to ground the outer cover of a CATV coaxial cable shall be permitted to be _____.

    (a) insulated
    (b) 14 AWG minimum
    (c) bare
    (d) all of these

88. In one- and two-family dwellings, the grounding electrode conductor for CATV shall be as short as practicable, not to exceed _____ in length.

    (a) 5 ft
    (b) 8 ft
    (c) 10 ft
    (d) 20 ft

89. Bonding conductors and grounding electrode conductors shall be _____ where exposed to physical damage.

    (a) electrically
    (b) arc-fault
    (c) protected
    (d) none of these

90. A bonding jumper not smaller than _____ copper or equivalent shall be connected between the CATV system's grounding electrode and the power grounding electrode system at the building or structure served where separate electrodes are used.

    (a) 12 AWG
    (b) 8 AWG
    (c) 6 AWG
    (d) 4 AWG

91. Raceway fill limitations of 300.17 apply to coaxial cables installed in a raceway.

    (a) True
    (b) False

92. CATV coaxial cable can be placed in a raceway, compartment, outlet box, or junction box with the conductors of light or power circuits, or Class 1 circuits when _____.

    (a) installed in rigid metal conduit
    (b) separated by a permanent barrier
    (c) insulated
    (d) none of these

93. Coaxial cables used for CATV systems shall not be strapped, taped, or attached by any means to the exterior of any _____ as a means of support.

    (a) conduit
    (b) raceway
    (c) raceway-type mast intended for overhead spans of such cables
    (d) a or b

94. CATVP cables are community antenna television coaxial cables that must be listed for installation in ducts, plenums and other spaces used for environmental air and shall also be listed as having adequate fire-resistant and low smoke-producing characteristics.

    (a) True
    (b) False

95. Type _____ coaxial cables for community antenna television systems shall be listed as suitable for being installed in vertical runs in a shaft, with fire-resistant characteristics capable of preventing the carrying of fire from floor to floor.

    (a) CATV
    (b) CATVX
    (c) CATVR
    (d) any of these

96. Network-powered broadband communications cable not terminated at equipment other than a connector, and not identified for future use with a tag, is considered abandoned.

    (a) True
    (b) False

97. Exposed network-powered broadband communications cables shall be secured to structural components by hardware including straps, staples, cable ties, hangers, or similar fittings designed and installed so as not to damage the cable.

    (a) True
    (b) False

98. In network-powered broadband communications systems, all separate electrodes shall be bonded together using a minimum _____ AWG copper bonding jumper.

    (a) 10
    (b) 8
    (c) 6
    (d) 4

99. The permitted raceway fill for two conductors is _____ percent.

    (a) 30
    (b) 31
    (c) 40
    (d) 53

100. For the purposes of conduit fill, a multiconductor cable, optical fiber cable, or flexible cord of two or more conductors is considered _____ conductor(s).

    (a) one
    (b) two
    (c) three
    (d) four

RANDOM ORDER
[ARTICLE 90–CHAPTER 9]

Please use the 2014 *Code* book to answer the following questions.

1. In an FMC installation, _____ connectors shall not be concealed.

   (a) straight
   (b) angle
   (c) grounding-type
   (d) none of these

2. Metal piping systems associated with a fountain shall be bonded to the equipment grounding conductor of the _____.

   (a) branch circuit supplying the fountain
   (b) bonding grid
   (c) equipotential plane
   (d) grounding electrode system

3. Service-drop conductors shall have _____.

   (a) sufficient ampacity to carry the load
   (b) adequate mechanical strength
   (c) a or b
   (d) a and b

4. Exposed audio cables shall be secured by _____ or similar fittings designed and installed so as not to damage the cable.

   (a) straps
   (b) staples
   (c) hangers
   (d) any of these

5. Motor control circuit conductors that extend beyond the motor control equipment enclosure shall have short-circuit and ground-fault protection sized not greater than _____ percent of value specified in Table 310.15(B)(16) for 60°C conductors.

   (a) 100
   (b) 150
   (c) 300
   (d) 400

6. For one- and two-family dwellings, the maximum voltage for PV source or PV circuits is _____.

   (a) 24V
   (b) 48V
   (c) 250V
   (d) 600V

7. Emergency systems are generally installed where artificial illumination is required for safe exiting and for panic control in buildings occupied by large numbers of persons, such as _____ and similar institutions.

   (a) hotels
   (b) theaters and sports arenas
   (c) health care facilities
   (d) all of these

8. Attachment plugs and receptacles in Class I locations of aircraft hangars shall be _____.

   (a) identified for use in Class I locations
   (b) designed so that they cannot be energized while the connections are being made or broken
   (c) a or b
   (d) none of these

9. In one- and two-family and multifamily dwellings, the bonding conductor or grounding electrode conductor for network-powered broadband communications systems shall be as short as practicable, not to exceed _____ ft in length.

   (a) 5
   (b) 6
   (c) 10
   (d) 20

10. Which of the following is not standard size fuses or inverse time circuit breakers?

    (a) 45A
    (b) 70A
    (c) 75A
    (d) 80A

11. Each circuit leading to or through motor fuel dispensing equipment shall be provided with a clearly identified and readily accessible switch or other approved means, located remote from the dispensing devices, to disconnect all conductors of the circuit including the grounded conductor.

    (a) True
    (b) False

12. Type OFNG, OFN, OFCG, and OFC optical fiber cables can be installed in vertical riser runs when _____.

    (a) encased in a metal raceway
    (b) having firestops at each floor
    (c) a or b
    (d) none of these

13. Communications grounding electrodes must be bonded to the power grounding electrode system at the building or structure served using a minimum _____ AWG copper bonding jumper.

    (a) 10
    (b) 8
    (c) 6
    (d) 4

14. No wiring of any type shall be installed in ducts used to transport _____.

    (a) dust
    (b) flammable vapors
    (c) loose stock
    (d) all of these

15. A device that, when electrically coupled to an electric vehicle inlet, establishes an electrical connection to the electric vehicle for the purpose of power transfer and information exchange is known as an "electric vehicle _____."

    (a) coupler
    (b) connector
    (c) inlet
    (d) any of these

16. Feeder conductors to a mobile home shall consist of a _____.

    (a) listed cord
    (b) permanently installed feeder consisting of four color-coded, insulated conductors
    (c) a or b
    (d) none of these

17. Type IC recessed luminaires are permitted to make contact with combustible material at _____.

    (a) recessed parts
    (b) points of support
    (c) portions passing through or finishing off the opening in the building structure
    (d) all of these

18. Feeder conductors supplying fire pump motors and accessory equipment shall be sized no less than _____ percent of the sum of the fire pump motor(s) and pressure maintenance motor(s) full-load currents, plus 100 percent of the ampere rating of the fire pump accessory equipment.

    (a) 100
    (b) 125
    (c) 250
    (d) 600

19. Conductors of intrinsically safe circuits shall be separated at least _____ in. from conductors of any nonintrinsically safe circuits within the same enclosures.

    (a) 2
    (b) 6
    (c) 12
    (d) 18

20. If the motor control circuit transformer is located in the controller enclosure, the transformer shall be connected to the _____ side of the control circuit disconnecting means.

    (a) line
    (b) load
    (c) adjacent
    (d) none of these

21. Each run of nonmetallic extension shall terminate in a fitting that covers the _____.

    (a) device
    (b) box
    (c) end of the extension
    (d) end of the assembly

22. An overcurrent device shall be provided in each ungrounded conductor for each capacitor bank. The rating or setting of the overcurrent device shall be _____.

    (a) as low as practicable
    (b) not to exceed 20A
    (c) not to exceed 40A
    (d) not to exceed 100A

23. Service equipment for floating docks or marinas shall be located _____ the floating structure.

    (a) adjacent to
    (b) on
    (c) in
    (d) any of these

24. The power source for a nonpower-limited fire alarm circuit shall not operate at more than _____.

    (a) 120V
    (b) 300V
    (c) 600V
    (d) 20A

25. Enclosures and fittings installed in areas of agricultural buildings where excessive dust may be present shall be designed to minimize the entrance of dust and shall have no openings through which dust can enter the enclosure.

    (a) True
    (b) False

26. Electronic organs or other electronic musical instruments are included in the scope of Article 640.

    (a) True
    (b) False

27. A hoistway is any _____ in which an elevator or dumbwaiter is designed to operate.

    (a) hatchway or well hole
    (b) vertical opening or space
    (c) shaftway
    (d) all of these

28. Torque requirements for motor control circuit device terminals shall be a minimum of _____ lb-in. (unless otherwise identified) for screw-type pressure terminals used for 14 AWG and smaller copper conductors.

    (a) 7
    (b) 9
    (c) 10
    (d) 15

29. The cut ends of HDPE conduit shall be _____ to avoid rough edges.

    (a) filed on the inside
    (b) trimmed inside and outside
    (c) cut only with a hacksaw
    (d) all of these

30. Where it is unlikely that two or more noncoincident loads will be in use simultaneously, only the _____ the loads used at one time is required to be used in computing the total load to a feeder.

    (a) smaller of
    (b) largest of
    (c) difference between
    (d) none of these

31. Audio system equipment supplied by branch-circuit power shall not be located within _____ horizontally of the inside wall of a pool, spa, hot tub, fountain, or tidal high-water mark.

    (a) 18 in.
    (b) 2 ft
    (c) 5 ft
    (d) 10 ft

32. A fixed storage-type water heater having a capacity of _____ gallons or less shall be considered a continuous load for the purposes of sizing branch circuits.

    (a) 60
    (b) 75
    (c) 90
    (d) 120

33. Underground service conductors are the underground conductors between the service point and the first point of connection to the service-entrance conductors in a terminal box, meter, or other enclosure, _____ the building wall.

    (a) inside
    (b) outside
    (c) above
    (d) a or b

34. The solid 8 AWG copper conductor used for bonding hydromassage bathtubs must have sufficient length to terminate on a _____, and must terminate to the equipment grounding conductor of the motor circuit when a double-insulated circulating pump motor is used.

    (a) replacement non-double insulated pump motor
    (b) replacement double-insulated pump motor
    (c) grounding electrode
    (d) b or c

35. Luminaires located within the actual outside dimension of a bathtub and shower shall be marked for damp locations, or marked for wet locations where they are _____.

    (a) below 7 ft in height
    (b) below 6 ft 7 in. in height
    (c) subject to shower spray
    (d) not GFCI protected

36. Where motors are provided with terminal housings, the housings shall be of _____ and of substantial construction.

    (a) steel
    (b) iron
    (c) metal
    (d) copper

37. The disconnecting means for air-conditioning and refrigerating equipment shall be _____ from the air-conditioning or refrigerating equipment.

    (a) readily accessible
    (b) within sight
    (c) a or b
    (d) a and b

38. It is frequently possible to locate much of the equipment in less hazardous or unclassified locations and thus reduce the amount of special equipment required.

    (a) True
    (b) False

39. Nominal battery voltage is typically _____.

    (a) 2V per cell for lead-acid systems
    (b) 1.20V for per cell for alkali systems
    (c) 3.60 to 3.80V per cell for Li-ion systems
    (d) all of these

40. The *NEC* specifies wiring methods for manufactured buildings.

    (a) True
    (b) False

41. An equipotential plane is an area where wire mesh or other conductive elements are embedded in or placed under concrete, bonded to _____.

    (a) all metal structures
    (b) fixed nonelectrical equipment that may become energized
    (c) the electrical grounding system
    (d) all of these

42. Audible and visual signal devices shall be provided on optional standby systems to indicate _____, where practicable.

    (a) derangement of the optional standby source
    (b) that the optional standby source is carrying load
    (c) that the battery charger is not functioning
    (d) a and b

43. The swimming pool structure, including the structural reinforcing steel of the pool shell and deck, except reinforcing steel encapsulated with a nonconductive compound shall be bonded.

    (a) True
    (b) False

44. In Class III locations, _____ used as, or in conjunction with, control equipment for motors, generators, and appliances shall be provided with dusttight enclosures complying with the temperature limitations in 503.5.

    (a) transformers
    (b) impedance coils
    (c) resistors
    (d) all of these

45. For stand-alone PV systems, the ac current output from a stand-alone inverter(s) can be _____ than the calculated load connected to the disconnect, but not less than the largest single utilization equipment connected to the system.

    (a) less
    (b) more
    (c) greater
    (d) any of these

46. Receptacles on construction sites shall not be installed on the _____ as temporary lighting.

    (a) same branch circuit
    (b) the same feeders
    (c) a or b
    (d) none of these

47. Conduits or raceways through which moisture may contact live parts shall be _____ at either or both ends.

    (a) sealed
    (b) plugged
    (c) bushed
    (d) a or b

48. Network-powered broadband communications system cables shall be separated at least 2 in. from conductors of _____ circuits.

    (a) power
    (b) electric light
    (c) Class 1
    (d) all of these

49. Office furnishings that are secured to building surfaces shall be permanently connected to the building electrical system by a Chapter 3 wiring method.

    (a) True
    (b) False

50. When replacing a nongrounding-type receptacle where attachment to an equipment grounding conductor does not exist in the receptacle enclosure, the receptacle can use a _____.

    (a) nongrounding-type receptacle
    (b) grounding receptacle
    (c) GFCI-type receptacle
    (d) a or c

51. Electrical materials, devices, fittings, and associated equipment of electric vehicle equipment shall be _____.

    (a) listed
    (b) labeled
    (c) identified
    (d) all of these

52. The _____ shall conduct or witness a test of the complete emergency system upon installation and periodically afterward.

    (a) electrical engineer
    (b) authority having jurisdiction
    (c) qualified person
    (d) manufacturer's representative

53. Receptacles rated 30A or less, 125V located within 10 ft of the inside walls of an indoor spa or hot tub, shall be _____.

    (a) GFCI protected
    (b) AFCI protected
    (c) a or b
    (d) none of these

54. The minimum size parallel conductors permitted for elevator lighting shall be _____, provided the combined ampacity is equivalent to at least that of a 14 AWG conductor.

    (a) 20 AWG
    (b) 16 AWG
    (c) 14 AWG
    (d) 1/0 AWG

55. For temporary installations, cable assemblies, flexible cords, and flexible cables shall be supported by _____ or similar fittings so as not to damage the wiring.

    (a) staples
    (b) cable ties
    (c) straps
    (d) any of these

56. Emergency lighting systems shall be designed and installed so that the failure of any individual lighting element, such as the burning out of a lamp, will not leave in total darkness any space that requires emergency illumination.

    (a) True
    (b) False

57. PV systems are permitted to supply a building or other structure in addition to any other _____ supply system(s).

    (a) electrical
    (b) telephone
    (c) plumbing
    (d) none of these

58. The disconnecting means for motor circuits rated 1,000 volts, nominal, or less shall have an ampere rating not less than _____ percent of the full-load current rating of the motor.

    (a) 80
    (b) 100
    (c) 115
    (d) 125

59. Limiting the length of the primary protector grounding conductors for community antenna television and radio systems reduces voltages that may develop between the building's _____ and communications systems during lightning events.

    (a) power
    (b) fire alarm
    (c) lighting
    (d) lightning protection

60. If the building or structure served has an intersystem bonding termination, the bonding conductor for an antenna mast shall be connected to the intersystem bonding termination.

    (a) True
    (b) False

61. A portable or mobile electric sign in a wet or damp location shall have listed GFCI protection provided by the manufacturer _____.

    (a) located on the sign
    (b) located in the power-supply cord within 12 in. of the attachment plug
    (c) as an integral part of the attachment plug of the supply cord
    (d) b or c

62. Single-conductor Type USE-2 and single conductor cable _____ as PV wire can be run exposed at outdoor locations for PV source circuits for PV module interconnections within the PV array.

    (a) approved
    (b) listed or labeled
    (c) listed and labeled
    (d) none of these

63. Temporary electrical power and lighting shall be permitted during emergencies and for _____.

    (a) tests
    (b) experiments
    (c) developmental work
    (d) all of these

64. Temporary wiring in exhibition halls for display booths in assembly occupancies is permitted to be in accordance with Article 590, except _____.

    (a) GFCI-protection requirements of Article 590 are not required
    (b) flexible cords and cables approved for hard or extra-hard usage cords can be laid on floors where protected from contact with the general public
    (c) GFCI protection must be provided where required by the *NEC* except for the Article 590 requirements
    (d) all of these

65. Conductors, including splices and taps, shall not fill a strut-type channel raceway to more than _____ percent of its area at that point.

    (a) 25
    (b) 75
    (c) 80
    (d) 125

66. Accessible portions of abandoned network-powered broadband cable shall be removed.

    (a) True
    (b) False

67. Type NM cable shall closely follow the surface of the building finish or running boards when run exposed.

    (a) True
    (b) False

68. A common dc grounding electrode conductor of a PV system is permitted to serve multiple inverters with the size of the common grounding electrode and the tap conductors in accordance with 250.166. The tap conductors must be connected to the common grounding electrode conductor in such a manner that the common grounding electrode conductor remains _____.

    (a) without a splice or joint
    (b) inside inverter enclosures
    (c) inside a raceway
    (d) supported on insulators

69. Communications cables not terminated at both ends with a connector or other equipment and not identified for future use with a tag are considered abandoned.

    (a) True
    (b) False

70. The markings required on signs and outline lighting systems in 600.4(a) and listing labels are required to be visible after installation, as well as during servicing.

    (a) True
    (b) False

71. Nonpower-limited fire alarm circuit conductors are permitted to be in the same cable, enclosure, or raceway with power-supply circuits where connected to the same equipment.

    (a) True
    (b) False

72. Power-limited fire alarm cables installed within buildings shall be _____ as being resistant to the spread of fire.

    (a) marked FR
    (b) listed
    (c) identified
    (d) color-coded

73. A circuit breaker with a _____ rating, such as 120/240V or 277/480V can be used on a solidly grounded circuit where the nominal voltage of any conductor to ground does not exceed the lower of the two values, and the nominal voltage between any two conductors does not exceed the higher value.

    (a) straight
    (b) slash
    (c) high
    (d) low

74. Insulated conductors used within a switchboard shall be _____.

    (a) listed
    (b) flame retardant
    (c) rated for the highest voltage it may contact
    (d) all of these

75. Exposed CATV cables shall be secured by hardware such as straps, staples, cable ties, hangers, or similar fittings designed and installed so as not to damage the cables.

    (a) True
    (b) False

76. Snap switches are considered to be part of the effective ground-fault current path when _____.

    (a) the switch is connected to the intersystem bonding termination
    (b) the switch is mounted with metal screws to a metal box or a metal cover that's connected to an equipment grounding conductor
    (c) an equipment grounding conductor or equipment bonding jumper is connected to the equipment grounding termination of the snap switch
    (d) b or c

77. Indoor antenna and lead-in conductors for radio and television receiving equipment shall be separated by at least _____ from conductors of any electric light, power, or Class 1 circuit conductors, unless otherwise permitted.

    (a) 2 in.
    (b) 12 in.
    (c) 18 in.
    (d) 6 ft

78. Type NM cable can be installed above a Class I location in a commercial garage.

    (a) True
    (b) False

79. The purpose of special separately derived systems for sensitive electronic equipment is to reduce objectionable noise in sensitive electronic equipment in _____ locations.

    (a) commercial
    (b) industrial
    (c) a or b
    (d) institutional

80. Switchboards shall be placed so as to reduce to a minimum the probability of communicating _____ to adjacent combustible materials.

    (a) sparks
    (b) backfed
    (c) fire
    (d) all of these

81. Flexible cords are not permitted in Class I locations.

    (a) True
    (b) False

82. Where the air conditioner disconnecting means is not within sight from the equipment, the disconnecting means must be _____.

    (a) guarded
    (b) exposed
    (c) lockable
    (d) elevated

83. Surface-mounted fluorescent or LED luminaires are permitted within the closet storage space if identified for this use.

    (a) True
    (b) False

84. When installed under metal-corrugated sheet roof decking, cables, raceways, and enclosures are permitted in concealed locations of metal-corrugated sheet decking type roofing if they are at least 2 in. away from a structural support member.

    (a) True
    (b) False

85. A disconnecting switch is permitted to open the grounded dc conductor of a PV system when the switch is _____.

    (a) used only for PV array maintenance
    (b) accessible only by qualified persons
    (c) rated for the maximum dc voltage and current, including ground-fault conditions
    (d) all of these

86. Where Type MI cable terminates, a(n) _____ shall be installed immediately after stripping to prevent the entrance of moisture into the insulation.

    (a) bushing
    (b) connector
    (c) flexible fitting
    (d) end seal fitting

87. Connection of conductors to terminal parts shall ensure a thoroughly good connection without damaging the conductors and shall be made by means of _____.

    (a) solder lugs
    (b) pressure connectors
    (c) splices to flexible leads
    (d) any of these

88. The ungrounded PV system dc disconnect must be placed at a readily accessible location _____ of a building or structure to disconnect the ungrounded PV system dc circuit conductors.

    (a) outside
    (b) inside, nearest the point of entrance
    (c) anywhere inside
    (d) a or b

89. Cable splices or terminations in power-limited fire alarm systems shall be made in listed _____ or utilization equipment.

    (a) fittings
    (b) boxes or enclosures
    (c) fire alarm devices
    (d) any of these

90. Branch-circuit wiring on the supply side of enclosures and junction boxes for underwater luminaires shall be installed in _____.

    (a) RMC or IMC
    (b) LFNC and PVC conduit
    (c) any wiring method
    (d) a or b

91. For Class I locations where 501.140(A)(5) is applied, flexible cords shall be _____ from the power source to the temporary portable assembly and from the temporary portable assembly to the utilization equipment.

    (a) permitted to be spliced
    (b) of continuous length
    (c) installed in a metal raceway
    (d) spliced only using listed splicing kits

92. Conductors supplying one or more air-conditioner motor-compressor(s) shall have an ampacity not less than the sum of the rated-load or branch-circuit selection current ratings, whichever is larger, of all the air-conditioner motor-compressors plus the full-load currents of any other motor(s), plus _____ percent of the highest motor or motor-compressor rating in the group.

    (a) 25
    (b) 50
    (c) 80
    (d) 100

93. A _____ shall be provided to disconnect each resistance welder and its control equipment from the supply circuit.

    (a) switch
    (b) circuit breaker
    (c) magnetic starter
    (d) a or b

94. When practicable, audible and visual signal devices for an emergency system shall be provided to indicate _____.

    (a) that the battery is carrying load
    (b) derangement of the emergency source
    (c) that the battery charger is not functioning
    (d) all of these

95. Electrical equipment enclosures at marinas must be securely and substantially supported by structural members, independent of any raceway connected to them.

    (a) True
    (b) False

96. Legally required standby system equipment shall be suitable for _____ at its terminals.

    (a) the maximum available fault current
    (b) the maximum overload current only
    (c) the minimum fault current
    (d) a one-hour rating

97. Nonlocking 15A and 20A, 125V and 250V receptacles installed in damp locations shall be listed as _____.

    (a) raintight
    (b) watertight
    (c) weatherproof
    (d) weather resistant

98. In a Class III location, pendant luminaires suspended by stems longer than _____ ft shall be provided with a fitting or flexible connector identified for the location, or shall be provided with effective bracing.

    (a) 1
    (b) 2
    (c) 3
    (d) 4

99. Network-powered broadband communications cables installed _____ on the surface of ceilings and walls shall be supported by the structural components of the building in such a manner that the network-powered broadband communications cables will not be damaged by normal building use.

    (a) exposed
    (b) concealed
    (c) hidden
    (d) a and b

100. When a raceway is used for the support or protection of cables for remote-control, signaling, and power-limited circuits, a bushing to reduce the potential for abrasion must be placed at the location the cables enter the raceway.

    (a) True
    (b) False

NEC PRACTICE EXAMS

There are five Practice Exams in random order to help you evaluate your exam-taking skills. The questions in the Practice Exams don't follow the chapters of the *Code* book; they're organized in a random manner, and include Article 90 through Chapter 9. You might find them harder to answer but as you work through them your *Code* skills will improve.

Mike Holt's NEC Exam Practice Questions, based on the 2014 NEC

RANDOM ORDER
[ARTICLE 90–CHAPTER 9]

Please use the 2014 *Code* book to answer the following questions.

1. For cord-and-plug-connected appliances, a(n) _____ plug and receptacle is permitted to serve as the disconnecting means.

   (a) labeled
   (b) accessible
   (c) metal enclosed
   (d) none of these

2. 15A and 20A, 125V receptacles located in patient bed locations of general care or critical care areas of health care facilities, other than those covered by 210.8(B)(1), aren't required to be GFCI protected.

   (a) True
   (b) False

3. The primary overcurrent protection for a transformer rated 1,000V, nominal, or less, with no secondary protection and having a primary current rating of over 9A must be set at not more than _____ percent.

   (a) 125
   (b) 167
   (c) 200
   (d) 300

4. The _____ pool bonding conductor shall be connected to the equipotential bonding grid either by exothermic welding or by pressure connectors in accordance with 250.8.

   (a) 8 AWG
   (b) insulated or bare
   (c) copper
   (d) all of these

5. Equipment supplying Class 2 or Class 3 circuits shall be durably marked where plainly visible to indicate _____.

   (a) each circuit that is a Class 2 or Class 3 circuit
   (b) the circuit VA rating
   (c) the size of conductors serving each circuit
   (d) all of these

6. All switchboards and panelboards supplied by a feeder(s) in _____ shall be marked to indicate each device or equipment where the power supply originates.

   (a) other than one- or two-family dwellings
   (b) all dwelling units
   (c) all nondwelling units
   (d) b and c

7. Soft-drawn or medium-drawn copper lead-in conductors for receiving antenna systems shall be permitted where the maximum span between points of support is less than _____ ft.

    (a) 10
    (b) 20
    (c) 30
    (d) 35

8. The disconnecting means for a building supplied by a feeder shall plainly indicate whether it is in the _____ position.

    (a) open or closed
    (b) correct
    (c) up or down
    (d) none of these

9. When a building is supplied with a fire sprinkler system, ENT can be installed above any suspended ceiling.

    (a) True
    (b) False

10. In a multiple-occupancy building where electric service and electrical maintenance are provided by the building management under continuous building management supervision, the service disconnecting means can be accessible to authorized _____ only.

    (a) inspectors
    (b) tenants
    (c) management personnel
    (d) qualified persons

11. Openings around penetrations of CATV coaxial cables and communications raceways through fire-resistant–rated walls, partitions, floors, or ceilings shall be _____ using approved methods to maintain the fire-resistance rating.

    (a) closed
    (b) opened
    (c) draft stopped
    (d) firestopped

12. Exposed metal conductive parts of luminaires shall be _____.

    (a) connected to an equipment grounding conductor
    (b) painted
    (c) removed
    (d) a and b

13. Short-circuit and ground-fault protection for an individual air-conditioner motor-compressor shall not exceed _____ percent of the motor-compressor rated-load current or branch-circuit selection current, whichever is greater.

    (a) 80
    (b) 125
    (c) 175
    (d) 250

14. Alternating-current general-use snap switches are permitted to control _____.

    (a) resistive and inductive loads that do not exceed the ampere and voltage rating of the switch
    (b) tungsten-filament lamp loads that do not exceed the ampere rating of the switch at 120V
    (c) motor loads that do not exceed 80 percent of the ampere and voltage rating of the switch
    (d) all of these

15. Where overhead communications cables enter buildings, they shall _____.

    (a) be located below the electric light or power conductors, where practicable
    (b) not be attached to a cross-arm that carries electric light or power conductors
    (c) have a vertical clearance of not less than 8 ft from all points of roofs above which they pass
    (d) all of these

16. Optical fibers shall be permitted within the same composite cable as electric light, power, and Class 1 circuits operating at 1,00V, or less where the functions of the optical fibers and the electrical conductors are associated.

    (a) True
    (b) False

17. Overhead network-powered broadband communications systems conductors shall be located no less than _____ ft from the water's edge of swimming and wading pools, or the base of diving structures.

    (a) 10
    (b) 12
    (c) 18
    (d) 25

18. A separate branch circuit shall supply elevator machine room/machinery space lighting and receptacle(s). The required lighting shall not be connected to the load side of a(n) _____.

    (a) local subpanel
    (b) SWD-type circuit breaker
    (c) HID-type circuit breaker
    (d) GFCI

19. Where run vertically, nonmetallic wireways shall be securely supported at intervals not exceeding _____ ft, unless listed otherwise, with no more than one joint between supports.

    (a) 4
    (b) 6
    (c) 8
    (d) 10

20. In a dwelling unit, each wall space _____ or wider requires a receptacle.

    (a) 2 ft
    (b) 3 ft
    (c) 4 ft
    (d) 5 ft

21. The voltage drop on technical power systems for sensitive electronic equipment shall not exceed _____ percent for feeder and branch-circuit conductors combined.

    (a) 1.50
    (b) 2
    (c) 2.50
    (d) 3

22. Type CMX communications cables can be installed in _____.

    (a) one- or two-family dwellings
    (b) multifamily dwellings in nonconcealed spaces
    (c) a or b
    (d) none of these

23. Where a generator for an optional standby system is installed outdoors and equipped with a readily accessible disconnecting means located _____, an additional disconnecting means is not required where ungrounded conductors serve or pass through the building or structure.

    (a) inside the building or structure
    (b) within sight of the building or structure
    (c) inside the generator enclosure
    (d) a or c

24. Conductors larger than that for which the wireway is designed can be installed in any wireway.

    (a) True
    (b) False

25. Article 760 covers the requirements for the installation of wiring and equipment of _____.

    (a) communications systems
    (b) antennas
    (c) fire alarm systems
    (d) fiber optics

26. Overcurrent devices for nonpower-limited fire alarm circuits shall be located at the point where the conductor to be protected _____.

    (a) terminates at the load
    (b) is spliced to any other conductor
    (c) receives its supply
    (d) none of these

27. Neon tubing which is readily accessible to pedestrians shall be protected from physical damage, other than _____.

    (a) Class I, Division 1 locations
    (b) listed dry-location portable signs
    (c) fixed equipment
    (d) wet-location portable signs

28. The distribution point is also known as the _____.

    (a) center yard pole
    (b) meter pole
    (c) common distribution point
    (d) all of these

29. A sealing fitting shall be permitted to be installed within _____ of either side of the boundary where a conduit leaves a Class I, Division 1 location.

    (a) 5 ft
    (b) 6 ft
    (c) 8 ft
    (d) 10 ft

30. All raceway and cable wiring methods included in this *Code*, other wiring systems and fittings specifically listed for use on PV arrays, and wiring as part of a listed system shall be permitted.

    (a) True
    (b) False

31. Motor overload protection shall not be shunted or cut out during the starting period if the motor is _____.

    (a) not automatically started
    (b) automatically started
    (c) manually started
    (d) none of these

32. Where flexibility _____, liquidtight flexible metal conduit shall be permitted to be used as an equipment grounding conductor when installed in accordance with 250.118(6).

    (a) is required after installation
    (b) is not required after installation
    (c) either a or d
    (d) is optional

33. Overhead feeder conductors to a building shall have a vertical clearance of final spans above, or within _____ measured horizontally from platforms, projections, or surfaces from which they might be reached.

    (a) 3 ft
    (b) 6 ft
    (c) 8 ft
    (d) 10 ft

34. The source interconnection of one or more inverters installed in one system shall be made at a dedicated circuit breaker or fusible disconnecting means.

    (a) True
    (b) False

35. A device or utilization equipment wider than a single 2 in. device box shall have _____ volume allowances provided for each gang required for mounting.

    (a) single
    (b) double
    (c) triple
    (d) none of these

36. Where combination surface nonmetallic raceways are used for both signaling conductors and lighting and power circuits, the different systems shall be run in separate compartments identified by _____ of the interior finish.

    (a) stamping
    (b) imprinting
    (c) color coding
    (d) any of these

37. Portable carnival or circus structures shall be maintained not less than _____ ft in any direction from overhead conductors operating at 600 volts or less.

    (a) 7½
    (b) 10
    (c) 12½
    (d) 15

38. Article 647 covers the installation and wiring of separately derived systems that operate at _____ volts-to-ground and _____ volts line-to-line for sensitive electronic equipment.

    (a) 30, 60
    (b) 60, 120
    (c) 120, 120
    (d) 120, 240

39. Wiring methods permitted in the ceiling areas used for environmental air include _____.

    (a) electrical metallic tubing
    (b) FMC of any length
    (c) RMC without an overall nonmetallic covering
    (d) all of these

40. Electric vehicle supply equipment _____ as suitable for charging electric vehicles indoors without ventilation is permitted indoors.

    (a) listed
    (b) labeled
    (c) identified
    (d) all of these

41. In commercial garages, GFCI protection for personnel shall be provided on all 15A and 20A, 125V receptacles installed where _____ is(are) to be used.

    (a) electrical diagnostic equipment
    (b) electrical hand tools
    (c) portable lighting equipment
    (d) any of these

42. Where an internal-combustion engine is used as the prime mover for an emergency system, an on-site fuel supply shall be provided for not less than _____ hours of full-demand operation of the system.

    (a) 2
    (b) 3
    (c) 4
    (d) 5

43. Access to electrical equipment shall not be denied by an accumulation of CATV coaxial cables that _____ removal of suspended-ceiling panels.

    (a) prevents
    (b) hinders
    (c) blocks
    (d) require

44. Currents of PV systems are to be considered _____.

    (a) safe
    (b) continuous
    (c) noncontiguous
    (d) inverted

45. _____ conductors shall not be used for more than one branch circuit, one multiwire branch circuit, or more than one set of ungrounded feeder conductors except as allowed elsewhere in the *Code*.

    (a) Equipment grounding
    (b) Neutral
    (c) Grounding electrode
    (d) Bonding

46. Power-limited fire alarm cable used in a _____ location shall be listed for use in _____ locations or have a moisture-impervious metal sheath.

    (a) dry
    (b) damp
    (c) wet
    (d) hazardous

47. Overload devices are intended to protect motors, motor control apparatus, and motor branch-circuit conductors against _____.

    (a) excessive heating due to motor overloads
    (b) excessive heating due to failure to start
    (c) short circuits and ground faults
    (d) a and b

48. A _____ rated in amperes shall be permitted as a controller for all motors.

    (a) branch-circuit inverse time circuit breaker
    (b) molded case switch
    (c) a and b
    (d) none of these

49. Running threads shall not be used on IMC for connection at couplings.

    (a) True
    (b) False

50. For interconnected electric power production sources, the circuit conductors from the inverter output terminals that supply ac power to the utility powered electric system is known as the utility-interactive inverter output circuit.

    (a) True
    (b) False

51. For interconnected electric power production sources, utility-interactive inverters must be _____ for interconnection service.

    (a) listed
    (b) labeled
    (c) identified
    (d) a and c

52. The power source for a power-limited fire alarm circuit can be supplied through a ground-fault circuit interrupter or an arc-fault circuit interrupter.

    (a) True
    (b) False

53. Service-entrance and overhead service conductors shall be arranged so that _____ will not enter the service raceway or equipment.

    (a) dust
    (b) vapor
    (c) water
    (d) none of these

54. Exposed communications cables shall be secured by hardware including straps, staples, cable ties, hangers, or similar fittings designed and installed so as not to damage the cable.

    (a) True
    (b) False

55. A vented alkaline-type battery, as it relates to storage batteries, operating at not over 250V shall be installed with not more than _____ cells in the series circuit of any one tray.

    (a) 10
    (b) 12
    (c) 18
    (d) 20

56. All unused openings in equipment for hazardous (classified) locations must be closed with listed _____ close-up plugs.

    (a) nonmetallic
    (b) metal
    (c) composition
    (d) a or b

57. Agricultural buildings where corrosive atmospheres exist include areas where the following conditions exist:

    (a) poultry and animal excrement
    (b) corrosive particles which may combine with water
    (c) areas of periodic washing with water and cleansing agents
    (d) all of these

58. Separate information technology equipment units can be interconnected by means of listed cables and cable assemblies. Where exposed to physical damage, the installation shall be protected.

    (a) True
    (b) False

59. Branch-circuit conductors within _____ in. of a ballast shall have an insulation temperature rating not lower than 90°C (194°F).

    (a) 1
    (b) 3
    (c) 6
    (d) 8

60. For stand-alone PV systems, energy storage or backup power supplies are required.

    (a) True
    (b) False

61. Each lead-in conductor from an outdoor antenna shall be provided with a listed antenna discharge unit, unless enclosed in a continuous metallic shield that is either grounded or protected by an antenna discharge unit.

    (a) True
    (b) False

62. Electric utilities may include entities that install, operate, and maintain ____.

    (a) communications systems (telephone, CATV, Internet, satellite, or data services)
    (b) electric supply systems (generation, transmission, or distribution systems)
    (c) local area network wiring on the premises
    (d) a or b

63. The essential electrical systems in a health care facility shall be supplied from ____.

    (a) a normal source generally supplying the entire electrical system
    (b) one or more alternate sources for use when the normal source is interrupted
    (c) a or b
    (d) a and b

64. A horsepower-rated ____ having a horsepower rating not less than the motor rating shall be permitted to serve as the disconnecting means.

    (a) attachment plug and receptacle
    (b) flanged surface inlet and cord connector
    (c) automatic controller
    (d) a or b

65. Overcurrent devices for emergency power systems ____ all supply-side overcurrent devices.

    (a) shall be selectively coordinated with
    (b) can be selectively coordinated with
    (c) shall be the same amperage as
    (d) shall be a higher amperage than

66. Photovoltaic wiring methods containing ____ must be terminated only with terminals, lugs, devices, or connectors that are identified and listed for such use.

    (a) flexible, fine-stranded cables
    (b) solid conductors
    (c) flexible raceways
    (d) all of these

67. Where electric vehicle supply equipment is located indoors, it shall be located for direct electrical coupling of the EV connector to the electric vehicle.

    (a) True
    (b) False

68. Luminaires installed in Class II, Division 2 locations shall be protected from physical damage by a suitable ____.

    (a) warning label
    (b) pendant
    (c) guard or by location
    (d) all of these

69. FMC shall not be installed ____.

    (a) in wet locations
    (b) embedded in poured concrete
    (c) where subject to physical damage
    (d) all of these

70. Cord connectors for carnivals, circuses, and fairs can be laid on the ground when the connectors are ____ for a wet location.

    (a) listed
    (b) labeled
    (c) approved
    (d) identified

71. A ____ is the location of an inpatient sleeping bed, or the bed or procedure table used in a critical care area.

    (a) patient bed location
    (b) patient care area
    (c) a or b
    (d) none of these

72. ENT is composed of a material resistant to moisture and chemical atmospheres, and is ____.

    (a) flexible
    (b) flame retardant
    (c) fireproof
    (d) flammable

73. The maintenance disconnecting means required for swimming pool equipment shall be _____ and at least 5 ft from the water's edge, unless separated by a permanently installed barrier.

    (a) readily accessible
    (b) within sight of its equipment
    (c) capable of being locked in the open position
    (d) a and b

74. Communications plenum cable shall be _____ as being suitable for use in other spaces used for environmental air.

    (a) marked
    (b) identified
    (c) approved
    (d) listed

75. Fire alarm circuits shall be identified at all terminal and junction locations in a manner that helps prevent unintentional signals on fire alarm system circuits during _____ of other systems.

    (a) installation
    (b) testing and servicing
    (c) renovations
    (d) all of these

76. Type UF cable can be used in commercial garages.

    (a) True
    (b) False

77. A meter disconnect switch located ahead of service equipment must have a short-circuit current rating equal to or greater than the available short-circuit current and be capable of interrupting the load served.

    (a) True
    (b) False

78. Equipment such as _____ shall be considered appliances, and the provisions of Article 422 apply in addition to Article 440.

    (a) room air conditioners
    (b) household refrigerators and freezers
    (c) drinking water coolers and beverage dispensers
    (d) all of these

79. Complete raceway systems of underground PVC can be located less than 5 ft from the inside wall of a pool when space limitations are encountered and shall be buried not less than _____ in. if not covered with concrete.

    (a) 6
    (b) 10
    (c) 12
    (d) 18

80. In health care facilities, installations of communications and signaling systems in other-than-patient-care areas must be in accordance with Chapter 7 and Chapter 8 as applicable.

    (a) True
    (b) False

81. Signaling, alarm, remote-control, and communications system circuits containing contacts installed in Class II, Division 2 locations shall be in enclosures that are _____ or otherwise identified for the location.

    (a) dust-ignitionproof
    (b) dusttight
    (c) dustproof
    (d) explosionproof

82. Power-supply conductors and Class 1 circuit conductors can occupy the same cable, enclosure, or raceway _____.

    (a) only where both are functionally associated with the equipment powered
    (b) where the circuits involved are not a mixture of ac and dc
    (c) under no circumstances
    (d) none of these

83. A disconnecting means that serves a hermetic refrigerant motor-compressor shall have an ampere rating of at least _____ percent of the nameplate rated-load current or branch-circuit selection current, whichever is greater.

    (a) 80
    (b) 100
    (c) 115
    (d) 125

84. Cord-and-plug-connected vending machines manufactured or remanufactured on or after January 1, 2005 shall include a ground-fault circuit interrupter identified for portable use as an integral part of the attachment plug or in the power-supply cord within 12 in. of the attachment plug. Older vending machines not incorporating integral GFCI protection shall be _____.

    (a) remanufactured
    (b) disabled
    (c) connected to a GFCI-protected outlet
    (d) connected to an AFCI-protected circuit

85. When EMT is installed in wet locations, all supports, bolts, straps, and screws shall be _____.

    (a) of corrosion-resistant materials
    (b) protected against corrosion
    (c) a or b
    (d) of nonmetallic materials only

86. The mobile home park secondary electrical distribution system to mobile home lots shall be _____.

    (a) 120/208V, single-phase
    (b) 120/240V single-phase
    (c) a or b
    (d) none of these

87. Rigid metal conduit and IMC shall not be required to be threaded when used in Class II, Division 2 locations.

    (a) True
    (b) False

88. The continuity of the equipment grounding conductor system used to reduce electrical shock hazards at carnivals, circuses, fairs, and similar events shall be verified each time that portable electrical equipment is connected.

    (a) True
    (b) False

89. The walls and roofs of transformer vaults shall be constructed of materials that have approved structural strength for the conditions with a minimum fire-resistance rating of _____ hours.

    (a) 2
    (b) 3
    (c) 4
    (d) 6

90. Optical fiber riser cables listed as suitable for use in a vertical run in a shaft or from floor to floor include Types _____.

    (a) OFNP and OFCP
    (b) OFNR and OFCR
    (c) OFNG and OFCG
    (d) OFN and OFC

91. Receptacles incorporating an isolated grounding conductor connection intended for the reduction of electrical noise shall be identified by _____ on the face of the receptacle.

    (a) an orange triangle
    (b) a green triangle
    (c) the color orange
    (d) the engraved word ISOLATED

92. A permanent label must be applied by the installer at the PV dc power source disconnect indicating the _____.

    (a) rated maximum power-point current and voltage
    (b) maximum system voltage and circuit current
    (c) maximum rated output current of the charge controller (if installed)
    (d) all of these

93. Wiring for an amusement ride, attraction, tent, or similar structure at a carnival, circus, or fair shall not be supported by any other ride or structure unless specifically designed for the purpose.

    (a) True
    (b) False

94. In aircraft hangars, equipment less than _____ ft above wings and engine enclosures of aircraft and that may produce arcs, sparks, or particles of hot metal shall be of the totally enclosed type or constructed so as to prevent the escape of sparks or hot metal particles.

    (a) 2
    (b) 3
    (c) 10
    (d) 20

95. Type MC cable shall be secured at intervals not exceeding _____ ft.

    (a) 3
    (b) 4
    (c) 6
    (d) 8

96. Receptacles rated other than 125V, single-phase, 15A, 20A, and 30A for temporary installations shall be protected by a _____.

    (a) GFCI device
    (b) written assured equipment grounding conductor program
    (c) AFCI device
    (d) a or b

97. When an overload device sized in accordance with 430.32(A)(1) and (B)(1) is not sufficient to start the motor, higher size sensing elements shall be permitted if the trip current does not exceed _____ percent of the motor nameplate full-load current rating, when the motor is marked with a service factor of 1.12.

    (a) 100
    (b) 110
    (c) 120
    (d) 130

98. Class 2 cables identified for future use shall be marked with a tag of sufficient durability to withstand _____.

    (a) moisture
    (b) humidity
    (c) the environment involved
    (d) none of these

99. A motor for general use shall be marked with a time rating of _____.

    (a) continuous
    (b) 5 or 15 minutes
    (c) 30 or 60 minutes
    (d) any of these

100. An alternating-current photovoltaic module is designed to generate ac power when exposed to _____.

    (a) electromagnetic induction
    (b) heat
    (c) sunlight
    (d) hysteresis

Please use the 2014 *Code* book to answer the following questions.

1. Article 690 requirements pertaining to dc PV source circuits do not apply to ac PV modules since ac PV modules have no dc output. The PV source circuit, conductors and inverters are considered as internal wiring of an ac module.

   (a) True
   (b) False

2. Mechanical elements used to terminate a grounding electrode conductor to a grounding electrode shall be accessible.

   (a) True
   (b) False

3. The conductors contained within Type ITC cable shall be rated 300V, and not smaller than _____ AWG nor larger than _____ AWG.

   (a) 22, 12
   (b) 18, 10
   (c) 16, 8
   (d) 14, 1/0

4. On a three-phase, 4-wire, wye circuit, where the major portion of the load consists of nonlinear loads, the neutral conductor shall be counted when applying 310.15(B)(3)(a) adjustment factors.

   (a) True
   (b) False

5. Legally required standby system wiring can occupy the same raceways, cables, boxes, and cabinets with other general-purpose wiring.

   (a) True
   (b) False

6. The branch-circuit protective device can serve as the controller for a stationary motor rated at _____ or less that is normally left running and cannot be damaged by overload or failure to start.

   (a) ⅛ hp
   (b) ¼ hp
   (c) ⅜ hp
   (d) ½ hp

7. All cables installed in agricultural buildings shall be secured within _____ in. of each cabinet, box, or fitting.

   (a) 8
   (b) 12
   (c) 18
   (d) 24

8. Coaxial cables can be installed in any Chapter 3 raceway in accordance with the requirements of Chapter 3.

   (a) True
   (b) False

9. A minimum of 20 percent of all recreational vehicle sites with electrical supply shall be equipped with a _____,125/250V receptacle.

   (a) 15A
   (b) 20A
   (c) 30A
   (d) 50A

10. Joints between HDPE conduit shall be made using _____.

   (a) expansion fittings
   (b) an approved method
   (c) a listed method
   (d) none of these

11. Type ITC cable is used for instrumentation and control circuits operating at _____.

   (a) 150V or less and 5A or less
   (b) 300V or less and 0.50A or less
   (c) 480V or less and 10A or less
   (d) over 600V

12. Cut ends of ENT shall be trimmed inside and _____ to remove rough edges.

   (a) outside
   (b) tapered
   (c) filed
   (d) beveled

13. Circuits and equipment operating at less than 50V shall have receptacles that are rated at not less than _____.

   (a) 10A
   (b) 15A
   (c) 20A
   (d) 30A

14. Access to electrical equipment shall not be denied by an accumulation of remote-control, signaling, or power-limited wire and cables that prevent removal of panels, including suspended-ceiling panels.

   (a) True
   (b) False

15. A permanently mounted luminaire in a commercial garage, located over lanes on which vehicles are commonly driven, shall be located not less than _____ ft above floor level.

   (a) 10
   (b) 12
   (c) 14
   (d) 16

16. Type FCC cable consists of _____ copper conductors placed edge-to-edge, separated and enclosed within an insulating assembly.

   (a) three or more square
   (b) two or more round
   (c) two or more flat
   (d) three or more flat

17. The grounding electrode conductor for an antenna mast shall be _____ protected where subject to physical damage.

   (a) electrically
   (b) mechanically
   (c) arc-fault
   (d) none of these

18. Manufactured wiring systems constructed with Type MC cable shall be supported and secured at intervals not exceeding _____ ft.

   (a) 3
   (b) 4
   (c) 6
   (d) 8

19. Where the conductors of more than one PV system occupy the same junction box or raceway with removable cover(s), the ac and dc conductors of each system shall be grouped separately by cable ties or similar means at least once, and then shall be grouped at intervals not to exceed _____.

   (a) 6 in.
   (b) 12 in.
   (c) 36 in.
   (d) 6 ft

20. _____ is a listed thin-wall, metallic tubing of circular cross section used for the installation and physical protection of electrical conductors when joined together with listed fittings.

    (a) LFNC
    (b) EMT
    (c) NUCC
    (d) RTRC

21. Prewired raceway assemblies shall be used only where specifically permitted in the *NEC* for the applicable wiring method.

    (a) True
    (b) False

22. Grounding electrode conductors of the wire type shall be _____.

    (a) solid
    (b) stranded
    (c) insulated or bare
    (d) any of these

23. A mobile home that is factory-equipped with gas or oil-fired central heating equipment and cooking appliances can be provided with a listed mobile home power-supply cord rated _____.

    (a) 30A
    (b) 35A
    (c) 40A
    (d) 50A

24. The purpose of the equipotential plane in agricultural buildings or adjacent areas is to minimize differences in voltage within the plane, as well as between planes, grounded equipment, and the earth.

    (a) True
    (b) False

25. The terminal of a wiring device for the connection of the equipment grounding conductor shall be identified by a green-colored, _____.

    (a) not readily removable terminal screw with a hexagonal head
    (b) hexagonal, not readily removable terminal nut
    (c) pressure wire connector
    (d) any of these

26. A run of IMC shall not contain more than the equivalent of _____ quarter bend(s) between pull points such as conduit bodies and boxes.

    (a) one
    (b) two
    (c) three
    (d) four

27. When a fire pump is supplied by an individual source, the _____ shall be rated to carry indefinitely the sum of the locked-rotor current of the largest fire pump motor and pressure maintenance pump motor(s) and the full-load current of all of the other motors and associated fire pump accessory equipment.

    (a) overcurrent protective device(s)
    (b) pump motor conductors
    (c) a and b
    (d) none of these

28. For switchboards that are not totally enclosed, a space of _____ or more shall be provided between the top of the switchboard and any combustible ceiling.

    (a) 12 in.
    (b) 18 in.
    (c) 2 ft
    (d) 3 ft

29. Electrical equipment used in hazardous (classified) locations that is designed for use in the ambient temperature range between _____ requires no ambient temperature marking. For equipment rated for a temperature range other than _____, the marking must specify the range of ambient temperatures in degrees Celsius.

    (a) -10°C and +20°C
    (b) -10°C and +30°C
    (c) -25°C and +40°C
    (d) -40°C and +40°C

30. Nonmetallic wireways can pass transversely through a wall _____.

    (a) if the length through the wall is unbroken
    (b) if the wall is not of fire-rated construction
    (c) in hazardous (classified) locations
    (d) if the wall is of fire-rated construction

31. The working clearance for a panelboard in a recreational vehicle shall be not less than _____.

    (a) 24 in. wide
    (b) 30 in. deep
    (c) 30 in. wide
    (d) a and b

32. GFCI protection is not permitted at carnivals, circuses, and fairs for _____.

    (a) portable structures
    (b) egress lighting
    (c) a and b
    (d) none of these

33. Each run of cable tray shall be _____ before the installation of cables.

    (a) tested for 25 ohms resistance
    (b) insulated
    (c) completed
    (d) all of these

34. CATV coaxial cables installed _____ on the surface of ceilings and walls shall be supported by the building structure in such a manner that the cables will not be damaged by normal building use.

    (a) exposed
    (b) concealed
    (c) hidden
    (d) a and b

35. In one- and two-family dwellings where it is not practicable to achieve an overall maximum bonding conductor or equipment grounding conductor length of _____ for CATV, a separate grounding electrode as specified in 250.52(A)(5), (A)(6), or (A)(7) shall be used.

    (a) 5 ft
    (b) 8 ft
    (c) 10 ft
    (d) 20 ft

36. Live parts of PV storage battery systems for dwellings shall be _____ to prevent accidental contact by persons or objects regardless of voltage.

    (a) isolated
    (b) grounded
    (c) insulated
    (d) guarded

37. Luminaires that require adjustment or aiming after installation can be cord-connected without an attachment plug, provided the exposed cord is of the hard-usage type and is not longer than that required for maximum adjustment.

    (a) True
    (b) False

38. Receptacles, cord connectors, and attachment plugs shall be constructed so that the receptacles or cord connectors do not accept an attachment plug with a different _____ or current rating than that for which the device is intended.

    (a) voltage rating
    (b) ampere interrupting capacity (AIC)
    (c) temperature rating
    (d) all of these

39. A luminaire intended for installation in the floor or wall of a pool, spa, or fountain in a niche that's sealed against the entry of water is called a "_____."

    (a) wet-niche luminaire
    (b) dry-niche luminaire
    (c) submersible luminaire
    (d) none of these

40. The voltage between conductors in a surface metal raceway shall not exceed _____ unless the metal has a thickness of not less than 0.040 in. nominal.

    (a) 150V
    (b) 300V
    (c) 600V
    (d) 1,000V

41. Faulted circuits required to have ground-fault protection in a photovoltaic system shall be isolated by automatically disconnecting the _____, or the inverter charge controller fed by the faulted circuits shall automatically stop supplying power to output circuits.

    (a) ungrounded conductors
    (b) grounded conductors
    (c) equipment grounding conductors
    (d) all of these

42. In installations where the communications cable enters a building, the metallic sheath members of the cable shall be _____ as close as practicable to the point of entrance.

    (a) grounded as specified in 800.100
    (b) interrupted by an insulating joint or equivalent device
    (c) a or b
    (d) a and b

43. Raceways permitted as a wiring method in Class II, Division 2 locations include _____.

    (a) RMC and IMC
    (b) EMT
    (c) ENT
    (d) a and b

44. Automatic transfer switches on legally required standby systems shall be electrically operated and _____ held.

    (a) electrically
    (b) mechanically
    (c) gravity
    (d) any of these

45. Ground rod electrodes shall be installed so that at least _____ of the length is in contact with the soil.

    (a) 5 ft
    (b) 8 ft
    (c) one-half
    (d) 80 percent

46. Conductors smaller than 1/0 AWG can be connected in parallel to supply control power, provided _____.

    (a) they are all contained within the same raceway or cable
    (b) each parallel conductor has an ampacity sufficient to carry the entire load
    (c) the circuit overcurrent device rating does not exceed the ampacity of any individual parallel conductor
    (d) all of these

47. The branch-circuit overcurrent devices for legally required standby systems shall be accessible only to _____.

    (a) the authority having jurisdiction
    (b) authorized persons
    (c) the general public
    (d) qualified persons

48. For interconnected electric power production sources, the output of a utility-interactive inverter can be connected to the load side of the service disconnecting means at any distribution equipment on the premises.

    (a) True
    (b) False

49. Audio system circuits using Class 2 or Class 3 wiring methods are not permitted in the same cable, raceway, or cable routing assembly with _____.

    (a) other audio system circuits
    (b) Class 2 conductors or cables
    (c) Class 3 conductors or cables
    (d) b or c

50. Class 2 and Class 3 circuits installed _____ on the surface of ceilings and walls shall be supported by the building structure in such a manner that the cable will not be damaged by normal building use.

    (a) exposed
    (b) concealed
    (c) hidden
    (d) a and b

51. Transfer equipment for legally required standby systems, including automatic transfer switches, shall be _____.

    (a) automatic
    (b) identified for standby use
    (c) approved by the authority having jurisdiction
    (d) all of these

52. Access to electrical equipment shall not be denied by an accumulation of communications _____ that prevents the removal of suspended-ceiling panels.

    (a) wires
    (b) cables
    (c) ductwork
    (d) a and b

53. For nonpower-limited fire alarm circuits, an 18 AWG conductor shall be considered protected if the overcurrent device protecting the circuit is not over _____.

    (a) 7A
    (b) 10A
    (c) 15A
    (d) 20A

54. The inside diameter of trade size 1 IMC is _____ in.

    (a) 0.314
    (b) 0.826
    (c) 1.000
    (d) 1.105

55. Each generator shall be provided with a _____ listing the manufacturer's name, the rated frequency, power factor, number of phases (if of alternating current), and its rating in kilowatts or kilovolt-amperes.

    (a) list
    (b) faceplate
    (c) nameplate
    (d) sticker

56. Legally required standby systems that are tested upon installation and found to be acceptable to the authority having jurisdiction shall not be required to undergo any future tests unless the equipment is modified.

    (a) True
    (b) False

57. Receptacles or their cover plates, supplied from the essential electrical system in nursing homes shall have a distinctive color or marking so as to be readily identifiable.

    (a) True
    (b) False

58. Power-limited fire alarm cables can be supported by strapping, taping, or attaching to the exterior of a conduit or raceway.

    (a) True
    (b) False

59. For temporary power outlets existing or installed as permanent wiring, GFCI protection can be incorporated into a listed _____.

    (a) circuit breaker
    (b) receptacle
    (c) cord set
    (d) any of these

60. Antenna discharge units shall be located outside the building only.

    (a) True
    (b) False

61. Communications circuits are circuits that extend _____ and outside wiring for fire alarms and burglar alarms from the communications utility to the customer's communications equipment up to and including equipment such as a telephone, fax machine, or answering machine.

    (a) voice
    (b) audio and video
    (c) interactive services
    (d) all of these

62. A communications circuit that is in such a position that, in case of failure of supports or _____, contact with another circuit may result, and is considered to be exposed to accidental contact.

    (a) insulation
    (b) shield
    (c) fittings
    (d) grounding conductor

63. Which of the following types of luminaires can be installed in a clothes closet?

    (a) A surface or recessed incandescent luminaire with completely enclosed light source.
    (b) A surface or recessed fluorescent luminaire.
    (c) A surface-mounted or recessed LED luminaire with a completely enclosed light source.
    (d) all of these

64. Remote-control circuits to safety-control equipment shall be classified as _____ if the failure of the equipment to operate introduces a direct fire or life hazard.

    (a) Class 1
    (b) Class 2
    (c) Class 3
    (d) Class I, Division 1

65. For ungrounded systems, noncurrent-carrying conductive materials enclosing electrical conductors or equipment, or forming part of such equipment, shall be connected together and to the supply system equipment in a manner that creates a low-impedance path for ground-fault current that is capable of carrying _____.

    (a) the maximum branch-circuit current
    (b) at least twice the maximum ground-fault current
    (c) the maximum fault current likely to be imposed on it
    (d) the equivalent to the main service rating

66. Antenna conductors for amateur transmitting stations attached to buildings shall be firmly mounted at least _____ in. clear of the surface of the building on nonabsorbent insulating supports.

    (a) 1
    (b) 2
    (c) 3
    (d) 4

67. A device that, when interrupting currents in its current-limiting range, reduces the current flowing in the faulted circuit to a magnitude substantially less than that obtainable in the same circuit if the device were replaced with a solid conductor having comparable impedance, is a(n) _____ protective device.

    (a) short-circuit
    (b) overload
    (c) ground-fault
    (d) current-limiting overcurrent

68. Luminaires installed in a fountain shall _____.

    (a) be capable of being removed from the water for relamping or normal maintenance
    (b) not be permanently embedded into the fountain structure
    (c) a and b
    (d) a or b

69. The conductors between the inverter and the battery in a stand-alone system or the conductors between the inverter and the PV output circuits for an electrical production and distribution network are part of the _____.

    (a) branch circuit
    (b) feeder
    (c) inverter input circuit
    (d) inverter output circuit

70. For interconnected electric power production sources, a permanent _____, denoting all electric power sources on or in the premises, must be installed at each service equipment location and all interconnected electric power production sources.

    (a) label
    (b) plaque
    (c) directory
    (d) b or c

71. The ungrounded and grounded conductors of each _____ shall be grouped by wire ties or similar means at the panelboard or other point of origination.

    (a) branch circuit
    (b) multiwire branch circuit
    (c) feeder circuit
    (d) service-entrance conductor

72. Single-throw knife switches shall be installed so that gravity will tend to close the switch.

    (a) True
    (b) False

73. When a raceway is used for the support or protection of cables for fire alarm circuits, a bushing to reduce the potential for abrasion must be placed at the location the cables enter the raceway.

    (a) True
    (b) False

74. Materials such as straps, bolts, and so forth., associated with the installation of RMC in wet locations shall be _____.

    (a) weatherproof
    (b) weathertight
    (c) corrosion resistant
    (d) none of these

75. Listed flexible metal conduit or listed liquidtight flexible metal conduit for secondary circuit conductors for neon tubing can be used as a bonding means if the total accumulative length of the conduit does not exceed _____.

    (a) 3 ft
    (b) 10 ft
    (c) 50 ft
    (d) 100 ft

76. The location of PV source and output conductors embedded in built-up, laminate, or membrane roofing materials in areas not covered by PV modules and associated equipment must be clearly marked.

    (a) True
    (b) False

77. Emergency power systems are those systems legally required and classed as emergency by a governmental agency having jurisdiction. These systems are intended to automatically supply illumination and/or power essential for _____.

    (a) community activity
    (b) safety to human life
    (c) public recreation
    (d) police and emergency services exclusively

78. Type NM cables shall not be used in one- and two-family dwellings exceeding three floors above grade.

    (a) True
    (b) False

79. Service-entrance cables mounted in contact with a building shall be supported at intervals not exceeding _____.

    (a) 24 in.
    (b) 30 in.
    (c) 3 ft
    (d) 4 ft

80. For interconnected electric power production sources, installation of one or more electrical power production sources operating in parallel with a primary source(s) of electricity must be installed only by _____.

    (a) qualified persons
    (b) a utility company
    (c) the authority having jurisdiction
    (d) b or c

81. A disconnecting means shall be provided in each ungrounded conductor for each capacitor bank, and shall _____.

    (a) open all ungrounded conductors simultaneously
    (b) be permitted to disconnect the capacitor from the line as a regular operating procedure
    (c) be rated no less than 135 percent of the rated current of the capacitor
    (d) all of these

82. Receptacles or their cover plates, supplied from the essential electrical system in hospitals shall have a distinctive color or marking so as to be readily identifiable.

    (a) True
    (b) False

83. Switches and circuit breakers used as switches shall be installed so that they may be operated from a readily accessible place.

    (a) True
    (b) False

84. Class 1, 2, and 3 circuits installed through fire-resistant-rated walls, partitions, floors, or ceilings must be firestopped to limit the possible spread of fire or products of combustion.

    (a) True
    (b) False

85. Equipment grounding conductors for PV circuits having overcurrent protection must be sized in accordance with _____.

    (a) 250.122
    (b) 250.66
    (c) Table 250.122
    (d) Table 250.66

86. Where network-powered broadband communications system aerial cables are installed outside and entering buildings, they shall _____.

    (a) be located below the electric light or power conductors, where practicable
    (b) not be attached to a cross-arm that carries electric light or power conductors
    (c) have a vertical clearance of not less than 8 ft from all points of roofs above which they pass
    (d) all of these

87. The emergency controls for unattended self-service motor fuel dispensing facilities shall be located more than _____ ft but less than _____ ft from motor fuel dispensers.

    (a) 10, 25
    (b) 20, 50
    (c) 20, 100
    (d) 50, 100

88. Each commercial occupancy accessible to pedestrians shall have at least one outside sign outlet in an accessible location at each entrance supplied by a branch circuit rated at least _____.

    (a) 15A
    (b) 20A
    (c) 30A
    (d) 40A

89. In Class II, Division 2 locations, flexible cord can serve as the supporting means for a pendant luminaire.

    (a) True
    (b) False

90. _____ conductor cables 4 AWG and marked for use in cable trays shall be permitted for equipment grounding within a raised floor of an information technology equipment room.

    (a) Green
    (b) Insulated
    (c) Single
    (d) all of these

91. _____ identified for use on lighting track shall be designed specifically for the track on which they are to be installed.

    (a) Fittings
    (b) Receptacles
    (c) Devices
    (d) all of these

92. Article _____ covers the installation of electric power production sources operating in parallel with a primary source(s) of electricity.

    (a) 700
    (b) 701
    (c) 702
    (d) 705

93. Article 440 applies to electric motor-driven air-conditioning and refrigerating equipment that has a hermetic refrigerant motor-compressor.

    (a) True
    (b) False

94. In dwelling units, all nonlocking type 125V, 15A and 20A receptacles installed _____ shall be listed as tamper resistant.

    (a) in bedrooms
    (b) outdoors, at grade level
    (c) above counter tops
    (d) in all areas specified in 210.52, except as covered by exceptions

95. When installing shield cables and twisted-pair cables in conduit in a Class I, Division 1 hazardous (classified) location, the removal of shielding material or the separation of the twisted pairs of shielded cables and twisted pair cables isn't required within the conduit seal fitting.

    (a) True
    (b) False

96. Optical fiber cables installed _____ on the surface of ceilings and walls shall be supported by the building structure in such a manner that the cable will not be damaged by normal building use.

    (a) exposed
    (b) concealed
    (c) hidden
    (d) a and b

97. The maximum PV inverter output circuit current is equal to the _____ output current rating.

    (a) average
    (b) peak
    (c) continuous
    (d) intermittent

98. A nonmetallic _____ is a flame-retardant raceway with removable covers for housing and protecting electric conductors and cable, and in which conductors are placed after the raceway has been installed as a complete system.

    (a) cable
    (b) raceway
    (c) wireway
    (d) none of these

99. The sum of the cross-sectional areas of all contained conductors at any cross section of a nonmetallic wireway shall not exceed _____ percent of the interior cross-sectional area of the nonmetallic wireway.

    (a) 20
    (b) 30
    (c) 40
    (d) 50

100. Bends in Type ITC cable shall be made _____.

    (a) so as not to exceed 45 degrees
    (b) so as not to damage the cable
    (c) not less than five times the diameter of the cable
    (d) using listed bending tools

RANDOM ORDER
[ARTICLE 90–CHAPTER 9]

Please use the 2014 *Code* book to answer the following questions.

1. Unless overload protection is provided by other approved means, the minimum number of overload units required for a three-phase ac motor is _____.

    (a) one
    (b) two
    (c) three
    (d) any of these

2. The rules of _____, as applicable, shall apply to air-conditioning and refrigerating equipment that does not incorporate a hermetic refrigerant motor-compressor.

    (a) Article 422
    (b) Article 424
    (c) Article 430
    (d) any of these

3. The continuous current-carrying capacity of a 1½ sq in. copper busbar mounted in an unventilated sheet metal auxiliary gutter is _____.

    (a) 500A
    (b) 650A
    (c) 750A
    (d) 1,500A

4. Reliable sources of power for a fire pump are considered to include a(n) _____.

    (a) separate service or a connection located ahead of but not within the service disconnecting means
    (b) on-site power supply, such as a generator, located and protected to minimize damage by fire
    (c) dedicated feeder derived from a service connection
    (d) all of these

5. Listed spa and hot tub packaged units installed indoors, rated 20A or less, can be cord-and-plug-connected.

    (a) True
    (b) False

6. The ampacity of the supply conductors to an individual electric arc welder shall not be less than the effective current value on the rating plate.

    (a) True
    (b) False

7. Raceways enclosing cables and conductors for fire alarm systems must be large enough to permit the _____ of conductors without damaging conductor insulation as limited by 300.17.

    (a) installation
    (b) removal
    (c) splicing
    (d) a and b

8. Bends in PVC conduit shall be made only _____.

   (a) by hand forming the bend
   (b) with bending equipment identified for the purpose
   (c) with a truck exhaust pipe
   (d) by use of an open flame torch

9. In dwellings, battery cells for PV systems must be connected so as to operate at _____, nominal, or less.

   (a) 20V
   (b) 30V
   (c) 40V
   (d) 50V

10. A written record shall be kept of required tests and maintenance on emergency systems.

    (a) True
    (b) False

11. The circuit that extends voice, audio, video, interactive services, telegraph (except radio), and outside wiring for fire alarm and burglar alarm from the communications utility to the customer's communications equipment up to and including equipment such as a telephone, fax machine or answering machine defines a "_____ circuit."

    (a) limited-energy
    (b) remote-signaling
    (c) power-limited
    (d) communications

12. Unlisted conductive and nonconductive outside plant optical fiber cables shall be permitted to be installed in locations other than risers, ducts used for environmental air, plenums used for environmental air, and other spaces used for environmental air, where the length of the cable within the building, measured from its point of entrance, does not exceed _____ ft and the cable enters the building from the outside and is terminated in an enclosure.

    (a) 25
    (b) 50
    (c) 75
    (d) 100

13. The fire alarm circuit disconnecting means for a power-limited fire alarm system must _____.

    (a) have red identification
    (b) be accessible only to qualified personnel
    (c) be identified as "FIRE ALARM CIRCUIT"
    (d) all of these

14. Receptacles that provide shore power for boats shall be rated not less than _____.

    (a) 15A
    (b) 20A
    (c) 30A
    (d) 60A

15. Fifteen and 20A, single-phase, 125V receptacles used for other than shore power in marinas but not installed in marine power outlets shall be provided with _____.

    (a) lockouts
    (b) GFCI protection
    (c) warning labels
    (d) all of these

16. Enclosures for switches or overcurrent devices are allowed to have conductors feeding through where the wiring space at any cross section is not filled to more than _____ percent of the cross-sectional area of the space.

    (a) 20
    (b) 30
    (c) 40
    (d) 60

17. Bends in Type MI cable shall be made so that the cable will not be _____.

    (a) damaged
    (b) shortened
    (c) a and b
    (d) none of these

18. Where the main bonding jumper is installed from the grounded conductor terminal bar to the equipment grounding terminal bar in service equipment, the _____ conductor is permitted to be connected to the equipment grounding terminal bar.

    (a) grounding
    (b) grounded
    (c) grounding electrode
    (d) none of these

19. Power distribution blocks installed in metal wireways on the line side of the service equipment shall be listed for the purpose.

    (a) True
    (b) False

20. In installations where optical fiber cable is terminated on the outside of the building and is exposed to contact with electrical conductors, the metallic sheath members of the cable shall be _____ in accordance with 770.100, or interrupted by an insulating joint or equivalent device.

    (a) bonded
    (b) connected
    (c) grounded
    (d) isolated

21. The smallest size fixture wire permitted by the *NEC* is _____ AWG.

    (a) 22
    (b) 20
    (c) 18
    (d) 16

22. The provisions of Article _____ apply to stationary storage battery installations.

    (a) 450
    (b) 460
    (c) 470
    (d) 480

23. Branch circuits that supply lighting units that have ballasts, autotransformers, or LED drivers shall have the calculated load based on _____ of the units, not to the total wattage of the lamps.

    (a) 50 percent of the rating
    (b) 80 percent of the rating
    (c) the total ampere rating
    (d) 150 percent of the rating

24. The PV system disconnecting means must be _____ to identify it as a photovoltaic system disconnect.

    (a) listed
    (b) approved
    (c) permanently marked
    (d) temporarily marked

25. Underground service conductors shall have _____.

    (a) adequate mechanical strength
    (b) sufficient ampacity for the loads calculated
    (c) a and b
    (d) none of these

26. Article 501 covers the requirements for electrical and electronic equipment and wiring for all voltages in Class I locations where fire or explosion hazards may exist due to flammable _____.

    (a) gases
    (b) vapors
    (c) liquids
    (d) any of these

27. Type UF cable can be used for service conductors.

    (a) True
    (b) False

28. Ground-fault protection of equipment shall be provided for solidly grounded wye electrical systems of more than 150 volts-to-ground, but not exceeding 1,000V phase-to-phase for each individual device used as a building or structure main disconnecting means rated _____ or more, unless specifically exempted.

    (a) 1,000A
    (b) 1,500A
    (c) 2,000A
    (d) 2,500A

29. A _____ provides protection against electric shock of personnel for electric vehicles.

    (a) GFCI device
    (b) GFP device
    (c) AFCI device
    (d) personnel protection system

30. A(n) _____ disconnecting means is required within sight of the storage battery for all ungrounded battery system conductors operating at over 50V nominal.

    (a) accessible
    (b) readily accessible
    (c) safety
    (d) all of these

31. Personnel doors for transformer vaults shall _____ and be equipped with panic bars, pressure plates, or other devices that are normally latched but open under simple pressure.

    (a) be clearly identified
    (b) swing out
    (c) a and b
    (d) a or b

32. When electric-discharge and LED luminaires that are designed not to be supported solely by the outlet box are surface mounted over a concealed outlet box, the luminaire shall provide access to the wiring within the outlet box by means of suitable openings in the back of the luminaire.

    (a) True
    (b) False

33. When calculating raceway conductor fill, equipment grounding conductors shall _____.

    (a) not be required to be counted
    (b) have the actual dimensions used
    (c) not be counted if in a nipple
    (d) not be counted if for a wye three-phase balanced load

34. An electric-discharge or LED luminaire or listed assembly can be cord connected if located _____ the outlet, the cord is visible for its entire length outside the luminaire, and the cord is not subject to strain or physical damage.

    (a) within
    (b) directly below
    (c) directly above
    (d) adjacent to

35. The total marked rating of a cord-and-plug-connected room air conditioner, connected to the same branch circuit which supplies lighting units, other appliances, or general-use receptacles, shall not exceed _____ percent of the branch-circuit rating.

    (a) 40
    (b) 50
    (c) 70
    (d) 80

36. EMT shall not be threaded.

    (a) True
    (b) False

37. Where the conductors of more than one PV system occupy the same junction box, raceway, or equipment, the conductors of each system shall be identified at all termination, connection, and splice points.

    (a) True
    (b) False

38. The _____ conductor terminals of a junction box (pool deck box), transformer enclosure, or other enclosure in the supply circuit to a wet-niche luminaire shall be connected to the equipment grounding terminal of the panelboard.

    (a) equipment grounding
    (b) grounded
    (c) grounding electrode
    (d) ungrounded

39. Luminaires shall be wired so that the _____ of each lampholder is connected to the same luminaire or circuit conductor or terminal.

    (a) stem
    (b) arm
    (c) supplemental protection
    (d) screw shell

40. CATV coaxial cable can deliver power to equipment that is directly associated with the radio frequency distribution system if the voltage is not over _____ and if the current supply is from a transformer or other power-limiting device.

    (a) 60V
    (b) 120V
    (c) 180V
    (d) 270V

41. Where ventilation marking is not required, the electric vehicle supply equipment shall be clearly field marked, that "ventilation is not required."

    (a) True
    (b) False

42. HDPE conduit shall not be subjected to ambient temperatures in excess of _____, unless listed otherwise.

    (a) 50°C
    (b) 60°C
    (c) 75°C
    (d) 90°C

43. Article _____ covers the installation of coaxial cables for distributing radio frequency signals typically employed in community antenna television (CATV) systems.

    (a) 300
    (b) 430
    (c) 800
    (d) 820

44. Monopole subarrays in a bipolar PV system shall be physically _____ where the sum of the PV system voltages, without consideration of polarity, of the two monopole subarrays exceeds the rating of the conductors and connected equipment.

    (a) separated
    (b) connected
    (c) joined
    (d) together

45. Surface-mounted luminaires _____ located over or within 5 ft, measured horizontally, from the inside walls of an indoor spa or hot tub can be installed at less than 7 ft 6 in. above the maximum water level when GFCI protected.

    (a) with a glass or plastic globe
    (b) with a nonmetallic body or a metallic body isolated from contact
    (c) suitable for use in a damp location
    (d) all of these

46. Nonlocking type 15A and 20A, 125V receptacles in a dwelling unit shall be listed as tamper resistant except _____.

    (a) receptacles located more than 5½ ft above the floor
    (b) receptacles that are part of a luminaire or appliance
    (c) a receptacle located within dedicated space for an appliance that, in normal use, is not easily moved from one place to another
    (d) all of these

47. Examples of assembly occupancies include _____.

    (a) restaurants
    (b) conference rooms
    (c) pool rooms
    (d) all of these

48. Luminaires designed for end-to-end assembly, or luminaires connected together by _____, can contain a 2-wire branch circuit, or one multiwire branch circuit, supplying the connected luminaires. One additional 2-wire branch circuit separately supplying one or more of the connected luminaires is permitted.

    (a) rigid metal conduit
    (b) recognized wiring methods
    (c) flexible wiring methods
    (d) EMT

49. The direct-current system grounding connection must be made at any _____ point(s) on the PV output circuit.

    (a) single
    (b) two
    (c) three
    (d) four

50. Intrinsically safe and associated apparatus are permitted to be installed in _____.

    (a) any hazardous (classified) location for which they have been identified
    (b) Class I locations
    (c) Class II locations
    (d) Class III locations

51. _____, 125V and 250V receptacles installed in a wet location shall have an enclosure that is weatherproof whether or not the attachment plug cap is inserted.

    (a) 15A
    (b) 20A
    (c) a and b
    (d) none of these

52. The location of the disconnecting means for an elevator shall be _____ to qualified persons.

    (a) accessible
    (b) readily accessible
    (c) disclosed only
    (d) accessible only with a key

53. Where nails or screws are likely to penetrate nonmetallic-sheathed cable or ENT installed through metal framing members, a steel sleeve, steel plate, or steel clip not less than _____ in thickness shall be used to protect the cable or tubing.

    (a) $\frac{1}{16}$ in.
    (b) $\frac{1}{8}$ in.
    (c) $\frac{1}{2}$ in.
    (d) $\frac{3}{4}$ in.

54. Unbroken lengths of surface metal raceways can be run through dry _____.

    (a) walls
    (b) partitions
    (c) floors
    (d) all of these

55. A storage battery supplying emergency lighting and power for emergency systems shall maintain not less than 87½ percent of normal voltage at total load for a period of at least _____ hour(s).

    (a) 1
    (b) 1½
    (c) 2
    (d) 2½

56. In Class II locations, dust must be prevented from entering the required dust-ignitionproof enclosure through a raceway by which of the following method(s)?

    (a) A permanent effective seal.
    (b) A horizontal raceway not less than 10 ft long.
    (c) A vertical raceway that extends downward for not less than 5 ft.
    (d) any of these

57. An outdoor disconnecting means for a mobile home shall be installed so the bottom of the enclosure is not less than _____ ft above the finished grade or working platform.

    (a) 1
    (b) 2
    (c) 3
    (d) 6

58. Unused openings for circuit breakers and switches in switchboards and panelboards shall be closed using _____ or other approved means that provide protection substantially equivalent to the wall of the enclosure.

    (a) duct seal and tape
    (b) identified closures
    (c) exothermic welding
    (d) sheet metal

59. For an emergency system power generator installed outdoors, where conditions of maintenance and supervision ensure that only qualified persons will monitor and service the installation and where documented safe switching procedures are established and maintained for disconnection, the generator set disconnecting means is not required to be located within sight of the building or structure served.

(a) True
(b) False

60. For PV systems, the circuit(s) between modules and from modules to the common connection point(s) of the direct-current system are known as the _____.

(a) photovoltaic source circuit
(b) photovoltaic array circuit
(c) photovoltaic input circuit
(d) photovoltaic output circuit

61. _____ include photovoltaic cells, devices, modules, or modular materials that are integrated into the outer surface or structure of a building and serve as the outer protective surface of that building.

(a) Protective photovoltaics
(b) Building integrated photovoltaics
(c) Bipolar photovoltaic arrays
(d) Bipolar photoconductive arrays

62. The point of interconnection of the PV system power source to other sources must be marked at an accessible location at the _____ as a power source and with the rated ac output current and nominal operating ac voltage.

(a) disconnecting means
(b) array
(c) inverter
(d) none of these

63. Flexible cords used in Class II, Division 1 or 2 locations shall _____, except as permitted for pendant luminaires .

(a) be listed for hard usage
(b) be listed for extra-hard usage
(c) not be permitted
(d) none of these

64. Complete raceway systems of underground PVC can be located less than 5 ft from the inside wall of a pool when space limitations are encountered and shall be buried not less than _____ in. with at least 4 in. of concrete cover.

(a) 6
(b) 10
(c) 12
(d) 18

65. Indoor transformers of greater than _____ rating shall be installed in a transformer room of fire-resistant construction.

(a) 75 kVA
(b) 87½ kVA
(c) 112½ kVA
(d) 35,000 kVA

66. HDPE conduit can be joined using _____.

(a) heat fusion
(b) electrofusion
(c) mechanical fittings
(d) any of these

67. For installations of resistors and reactors, a thermal barrier shall be required if the space between them and any combustible material is less than _____ in.

(a) 2
(b) 3
(c) 6
(d) 12

68. Ground-fault protection for personnel is required for all temporary wiring used for construction, remodeling, maintenance, repair, or demolition of buildings, structures, or equipment, from power derived from an _____.

(a) electric utility company
(b) on-site-generated power source
(c) a or b
(d) none of these

69. Snap switches, including dimmer and similar control switches, shall be connected to an equipment grounding conductor and shall provide a means to connect metal faceplates to the equipment grounding conductor, whether or not a metal faceplate is installed.

    (a) True
    (b) False

70. The _____ shall conduct or witness a test of the complete legally required standby system upon installation.

    (a) electrical engineer
    (b) authority having jurisdiction
    (c) qualified person
    (d) manufacturer's representative

71. Equipment enclosures on piers must be located so as not to interfere with mooring lines.

    (a) True
    (b) False

72. Flexible conductors used to supply portable stage equipment other than switchboards shall be _____ cords or cables.

    (a) listed
    (b) extra-hard usage
    (c) hard-usage
    (d) a and b

73. The required ampacity for the supply conductors for a resistance welder with a duty cycle of 15 percent and a primary current of 21A is _____.

    (a) 5.67A
    (b) 6.72A
    (c) 8.19A
    (d) 9.45A

74. The connection to a _____ shall be arranged so that removal of either from a PV source circuit does not interrupt a grounded conductor connection to other PV source circuits.

    (a) panelboard or switchboard
    (b) bus or lug
    (c) module or panel
    (d) array or subarray

75. Where communications wires and cables are installed in a Chapter 3 raceway, the raceway shall be installed in accordance with Chapter 3 requirements.

    (a) True
    (b) False

76. At least one wall switch-controlled lighting outlet shall be installed in every habitable room and bathroom of a guest room or guest suite of hotels, motels, and similar occupancies. A receptacle outlet controlled by a wall switch may be used to meet this requirement in other than _____.

    (a) bathrooms
    (b) kitchens
    (c) sleeping areas
    (d) a and b

77. The *NEC* defines a(n) "_____" as one who has skills and knowledge related to the construction and operation of the electrical equipment and installations and has received safety training to recognize and avoid the hazards involved.

    (a) inspector
    (b) master electrician
    (c) journeyman electrician
    (d) qualified person

78. The use of NUCC shall be permitted _____.

    (a) for direct burial underground installations
    (b) to be encased or embedded in concrete
    (c) in cinder fill
    (d) all of these

79. A large single panel, frame, or assembly of panels on which switches, overcurrent and other protective devices, buses, and instruments are mounted is a "_____." They are generally accessible from the rear as well as from the front and are not intended to be installed in cabinets.

    (a) switchboard
    (b) panel box
    (c) switch box
    (d) panelboard

80. Article 645 covers _____ of information technology equipment and systems in an information technology equipment room that meets the requirements of 645.4.

    (a) equipment
    (b) power-supply wiring
    (c) interconnecting wiring
    (d) all of these

81. Luminaires located more than 7½ ft above the floor can be connected to the equipment grounding return path complying with 517.13(A), without being connected to an insulated equipment grounding conductor.

    (a) True
    (b) False

82. The requirements of Article 517 apply to buildings or portions of buildings in which medical, _____, or surgical care are provided.

    (a) psychiatric
    (b) nursing
    (c) obstetrical
    (d) any of these

83. The metal frame of a building shall be considered a grounding electrode where one of the *NEC*-prescribed methods for connection of the metal frame to earth has been met.

    (a) True
    (b) False

84. Switches not required for projectors, flood or other special effect lamps shall not be installed in projection rooms.

    (a) True
    (b) False

85. A system intended to provide protection of equipment from damaging line-to-ground fault currents by opening all ungrounded conductors of the faulted circuit at current levels less than the supply circuit overcurrent device defines the phrase "_____."

    (a) ground-fault protection of equipment
    (b) guarded
    (c) personal protection
    (d) automatic protection

86. Optional standby systems utilizing automatic transfer equipment shall have adequate capacity and rating for the supply of _____.

    (a) all emergency lighting and power loads
    (b) the load, as calculated in Article 220
    (c) 100 percent of the appliance loads and 50 percent of the lighting loads
    (d) 100 percent of the lighting loads and 75 percent of the appliance loads

87. Cables laid in wood notches require protection against nails or screws by using a steel plate at least _____ thick, installed before the building finish is applied.

    (a) ¹⁄₁₆ in.
    (b) ⅛ in.
    (c) ¼ in.
    (d) ½ in.

88. In Class I, Division 1 locations, all apparatus and equipment of signaling, alarm, remote-control, and communications systems _____ shall be identified for Class I, Division 1 locations.

    (a) above 50V
    (b) above 100 volts-to-ground
    (c) regardless of voltage
    (d) except under 24V

89. Overcurrent devices for PV source circuits must be readily accessible.

    (a) True
    (b) False

90. Where overcurrent protection is provided as part of an industrial machine, the machine shall be marked "_____."

    (a) Overcurrent Protection Provided At Machine Supply Terminals
    (b) This Unit Contains Overcurrent Protection
    (c) Fuses Or Circuit Breaker Enclosed
    (d) Overcurrent Protected

91. Class 2 and Class 3 plenum cables listed as suitable for use in ducts, plenums, and other spaces used for environmental air shall be Type _____.

    (a) CL2P and CL3P
    (b) CL2R and CL3R
    (c) CL2 and CL3
    (d) PLTC

92. For interconnected electric power production sources, upon loss of utility source power, an electric power production source must be manually disconnected from all ungrounded conductors of the utility source and must not be reconnected until the utility source has been restored.

    (a) True
    (b) False

93. Lighting systems operating at 30V or less shall not be installed within _____ ft of pools, spas, fountains, or similar locations.

    (a) 5
    (b) 6
    (c) 10
    (d) 20

94. In assembly occupancies, Type NM cable, AC cable, ENT, and PVC conduit can be installed in those portions of the building not required to be of _____ construction by the applicable building code.

    (a) Class I, Division 1
    (b) fire-rated
    (c) occupancy-rated
    (d) aboveground

95. For PV systems, a(n) _____ is a device that changes direct-current input to an alternating-current output.

    (a) diode
    (b) rectifier
    (c) transistor
    (d) inverter

96. Locations in which combustible dust is in the air under normal operating conditions in quantities sufficient to produce explosive or ignitible mixtures are classified as _____.

    (a) Class I, Division 2
    (b) Class II, Division 1
    (c) Class II, Division 2
    (d) Class III, Division 1

97. "Low voltage contact limit" is a voltage not exceeding _____.

    (a) 15V (RMS) for sinusoidal ac or 21.20V peak for nonsinusoidal ac
    (b) 30V for continuous dc
    (c) 12.40V peak for dc that is interrupted at a rate of 10 to 200 Hz
    (d) all of these

98. Battery chargers and the batteries being charged can be located in any area of a commercial garage.

    (a) True
    (b) False

99. Exposed elements of impedance heating systems shall be physically guarded, isolated, or thermally insulated with a _____ jacket to protect against contact by personnel in the area.

    (a) corrosion-resistant
    (b) waterproof
    (c) weatherproof
    (d) flame-retardant

100. Each circuit leading to or through motor fuel dispensing equipment, including all associated power, communications, data, video circuits, and equipment for remote pumping systems, shall be provided with a switch or other approved means to disconnect _____ from the source of supply all conductors of the circuit, including the grounded conductor, if any.

    (a) automatically
    (b) simultaneously
    (c) manually
    (d) individually

RANDOM ORDER
[ARTICLE 90–CHAPTER 9]

Please use the 2014 *Code* book to answer the following questions.

1. Grounded dc PV arrays must be provided with direct-current _____ meeting the requirements of 690.5(a) through (c) to reduce fire hazards.

    (a) arc-fault protection
    (b) rectifier protection
    (c) ground-fault monitors
    (d) ground-fault protection

2. Each strap containing one or more devices shall count as a _____ volume allowance in accordance with Table 314.16(B), based on the largest conductor connected to a device(s) or equipment supported by the strap.

    (a) single
    (b) double
    (c) triple
    (d) none of these

3. When sizing a feeder for the fixed appliance loads in dwelling units, a demand factor of 75 percent of the total nameplate ratings can be applied if there are _____ or more appliances fastened in place on the same feeder.

    (a) two
    (b) three
    (c) four
    (d) five

4. The authority having jurisdiction shall not be allowed to enforce any requirements of Chapter 7 (Special Conditions) or Chapter 8 (Communications Systems).

    (a) True
    (b) False

5. A legally required standby system is intended to automatically supply power to _____ in the event of failure of the normal source.

    (a) those systems classed as emergency systems
    (b) selected loads
    (c) a and b
    (d) none of these

6. Feeders for temporary installations can be cable assemblies or multiconductor cords or cables identified for hard usage or extra-hard usage.

    (a) True
    (b) False

7. When calculations in Article 220 result in a fraction of an ampere that is less than _____, such fractions can be dropped.

    (a) 0.49
    (b) 0.50
    (c) 0.51
    (d) 0.80

8. Optical fiber cables are not required to be listed and marked where the length of the cable within the building, measured from its point of entrance, does not exceed _____ ft and the cable enters the building from the outside and is terminated in an enclosure.

    (a) 25
    (b) 30
    (c) 50
    (d) 100

9. Unless supplemented or modified by Article 690, Chapters 1, 2, 3, and 4 in the *NEC* shall apply. However, if any provisions of Article 690 differ with other articles of the *Code*, Article 690 requirements apply within the scope of Article 690 installations.

    (a) True
    (b) False

10. Listed plenum signaling raceways enclosing _____ cable can be installed in other spaces used for environmental air.

    (a) Type CL2P
    (b) Type CL3P
    (c) a or b
    (d) none of these

11. Bends in LFNC shall _____ between pull points.

    (a) not be made
    (b) not be limited in degrees
    (c) be limited to 360 degrees
    (d) be limited to 180 degrees

12. Receptacles that are located within the patient rooms, bathrooms, playrooms, and activity rooms of designated pediatric units, other than nurseries, shall be listed as _____, or shall employ a listed _____ cover.

    (a) tamper resistant
    (b) isolated
    (c) GFCI-protected
    (d) specification grade

13. A grounding electrode conductor shall be permitted to be run to any convenient grounding electrode available in the grounding electrode system where the other electrode(s), if any, is connected by bonding jumpers in accordance with 250.53(C).

    (a) True
    (b) False

14. For each floor area inside a major repair garage where ventilation is not provided and flammable liquids having a flash point below 100°F are transferred, the entire area up to a level of _____ in. above the floor is considered to be a Class I, Division 2 location.

    (a) 6
    (b) 12
    (c) 18
    (d) 24

15. For PV systems, metallic mounting structures used for grounding purposes must be _____ as equipment grounding conductors or have _____ bonding jumpers or devices connected between the separate metallic sections and be bonded to the grounding system.

    (a) listed/labeled
    (b) labeled/listed
    (c) identified/identified
    (d) a and b

16. Bonding jumpers for service raceways shall be used around impaired connections such as _____.

    (a) oversized concentric knockouts
    (b) oversized eccentric knockouts
    (c) reducing washers
    (d) any of these

17. Flexible cords and flexible cables are permitted for the electrical connection of permanently installed equipment racks of audio systems to facilitate access to equipment.

    (a) True
    (b) False

18. Flexible cords immersed in or exposed to water in a fountain shall be ____.

    (a) extra-hard usage type
    (b) listed with a W suffix
    (c) encased in not less than 2 in. of concrete
    (d) a and b

19. Automatic transfer switches for emergency systems shall be ____.

    (a) electrically operated
    (b) mechanically held
    (c) listed for emergency system use if rated 1,000V ac and below
    (d) all of these

20. ____ connectors shall not be concealed when used in installations of LFMC .

    (a) Straight
    (b) Angle
    (c) Grounding-type
    (d) none of these

21. An impedance heating system that is operating at a(n) ____ greater than 30, but not more than 80, shall be grounded at a designated point(s).

    (a) voltage
    (b) amperage
    (c) wattage
    (d) temperature

22. A ____ is an electrical subset of a photovoltaic array.

    (a) panel
    (b) module
    (c) circuit
    (d) subarray

23. Concrete-encased electrodes of ____ shall not be required to be part of the grounding electrode system where the steel reinforcing bars or rods aren't accessible for use without disturbing the concrete.

    (a) hazardous (classified) locations
    (b) health care facilities
    (c) existing buildings or structures
    (d) agricultural buildings with equipotential planes

24. Type ____ cable is a factory assembly of two or more insulated conductors under a nonmetallic sheath for installation in cable trays or raceways.

    (a) NM
    (b) TC
    (c) SE
    (d) UF

25. Overcurrent protection shall not exceed ____.

    (a) 15A for 14 AWG copper
    (b) 20A for 12 AWG copper
    (c) 30A for 10 AWG copper
    (d) all of these

26. For transformers, other than Class 2 and Class 3, a means is required to disconnect all transformer ungrounded primary conductors. The disconnecting means must be located within sight of the transformer unless the disconnect ____.

    (a) location is field marked on the transformer
    (b) is lockable in accordance with 110.25
    (c) is nonfusible
    (d) a and b

27. Coaxial cables can be installed in listed communications raceways. If coaxial cables are installed in a listed communications nonmetallic raceway, the raceway must be installed in accordance with 362.24 through 362.56, where the requirements applicable to ENT apply.

    (a) True
    (b) False

28. Hydromassage bathtub electrical equipment shall be _____ without damaging the building structure or building finish.

    (a) readily accessible
    (b) accessible
    (c) within sight
    (d) none of these

29. A recessed luminaire not identified for contact with insulation shall have all recessed parts spaced not less than _____ in. from combustible materials, except for points of support.

    (a) ¼
    (b) ½
    (c) 1¼
    (d) 6

30. Underground antenna conductors for radio and television receiving equipment shall be separated at least _____ from any light, power, or Class 1 circuit conductors.

    (a) 12 in.
    (b) 18 in.
    (c) 5 ft
    (d) 6 ft

31. Snap switches shall not be grouped or ganged in enclosures unless the voltage between adjacent devices does not exceed _____.

    (a) 100V
    (b) 200V
    (c) 300V
    (d) 400V

32. Emergency equipment for emergency systems must be designed and located so as to minimize the hazards that might cause complete failure due to _____.

    (a) flooding
    (b) fires
    (c) icing, and vandalism
    (d) all of these

33. Communications circuits and equipment installed in a location that is _____ in accordance with 500.5 shall comply with the applicable requirements of Chapter 5.

    (a) designed
    (b) classified
    (c) located
    (d) approved

34. If a separate grounding electrode is installed for the radio and television equipment, it shall be bonded to the building's electrical power grounding electrode system with a bonding jumper not smaller than _____ AWG.

    (a) 10
    (b) 8
    (c) 6
    (d) 1/0

35. Branch-circuit overcurrent devices in emergency circuits shall be accessible to _____ only.

    (a) the authority having jurisdiction
    (b) authorized persons
    (c) the general public
    (d) qualified persons

36. In straight pulls, the length of the box or conduit body shall not be less than _____ times the trade size of the largest raceway.

    (a) six
    (b) eight
    (c) twelve
    (d) none of these

37. An inverter or an ac module in an interactive PV system must automatically de-energize its output to the connected electrical distribution system upon _____ of voltage and remain de-energized until the electrical distribution system voltage has been restored.

    (a) surge
    (b) spike
    (c) loss
    (d) unbalance

38. Cable trays shall _____.

    (a) include fittings or other suitable means for changes in direction and elevation of runs
    (b) have side rails or equivalent structural members
    (c) be made of corrosion-resistant material or protected from corrosion as required by 300.6
    (d) all of these

39. Type UF cable shall not be used _____.

    (a) in any hazardous (classified) location except as otherwise permitted in this *Code*
    (b) embedded in poured cement, concrete, or aggregate
    (c) where exposed to direct rays of the sun, unless identified as sunlight resistant
    (d) all of these

40. When installed under metal-corrugated sheet roof decking, the rules for spacing from roof decking apply equally to rigid metal conduit and intermediate metal conduit.

    (a) True
    (b) False

41. When conduit nipples having a maximum length not exceeding 24 in. are installed between boxes, the nipple can be filled to 60 percent.

    (a) True
    (b) False

42. A _____ conductor that carries only the unbalanced current from other conductors of the same circuit shall not be required to be counted when applying the provisions of 310.15(B)(3)(a).

    (a) neutral
    (b) ungrounded
    (c) grounding
    (d) none of these

43. By special permission, the authority having jurisdiction may waive specific requirements in this *Code* where it is assured that equivalent objectives can be achieved by establishing and maintaining effective safety.

    (a) True
    (b) False

44. Cable trays shall be supported at intervals in accordance with the installation instructions.

    (a) True
    (b) False

45. Exposed Class 2 and Class 3 cables shall be supported by straps, staples, hangers, or similar fittings designed and installed so as not to damage the cable.

    (a) True
    (b) False

46. In one- and two-family dwellings, the primary protector bonding conductor or grounding electrode conductor for communications systems shall be as short as practicable, not to exceed _____ ft in length.

    (a) 5
    (b) 8
    (c) 10
    (d) 20

47. Accessible portions of abandoned CATV cable shall be removed unless tagged for future use.

    (a) True
    (b) False

48. In anesthetizing locations of health care facilities, low-voltage equipment in frequent contact with the bodies of persons shall _____.

    (a) operate on an electrical potential of 10V or less
    (b) be moisture resistant
    (c) be intrinsically safe or double-insulated
    (d) any of these

49. Openings around penetrations of optical fiber cables and communications raceways through fire-resistant–rated walls, partitions, floors, or ceilings shall be _____ using approved methods to maintain the fire-resistance rating.

    (a) closed
    (b) opened
    (c) draft stopped
    (d) firestopped

50. The electric motor and controller for an electrically operated pool cover shall be _____.

    (a) GFCI protected
    (b) AFCI protected
    (c) a and b
    (d) a or b

51. In Class II, Division 1 locations, receptacles shall be part of the premises wiring and attachment plugs shall be of the type that provides for connection to the _____ of the flexible cord.

    (a) equipment bonding conductor
    (b) equipment grounding conductor
    (c) building grounding electrode system
    (d) any of these

52. Lampholders of the screw-shell type shall be installed for use as lampholders only.

    (a) True
    (b) False

53. All 15A and 20A, 125V receptacles installed in bathrooms of _____ shall have ground-fault circuit-interrupter (GFCI) protection for personnel.

    (a) guest rooms in hotels/motels
    (b) dwelling units
    (c) office buildings
    (d) all of these

54. Cord-and-plug-connected equipment in fountains _____ shall have GFCI protection.

    (a) except pumps
    (b) including power-supply cords
    (c) less than 6 ft high
    (d) except power-supply cords

55. Accessible portions of abandoned optical fiber cable shall be removed.

    (a) True
    (b) False

56. A single array or aggregate of arrays that generates direct-current power at system voltage and current is the photovoltaic _____.

    (a) output source
    (b) source circuit
    (c) power source
    (d) array source

57. Where the box is mounted on the surface, direct metal-to-metal contact between the device yoke and the box shall be permitted to ground the receptacle to the box if at least _____ of the insulating washers of the receptacle is (are) removed.

    (a) one
    (b) two
    (c) three
    (d) none of these

58. The disconnecting means for a shore power connection shall be not more than _____ in. from the receptacle it controls.

    (a) 12
    (b) 24
    (c) 30
    (d) 36

59. Plug-in type backfed circuit breakers for a stand-alone or multimode inverter connected to a stand-alone PV system are not required to be secured in place by an additional fastener that requires other than a pull to release the breaker from the panelboard.

    (a) True
    (b) False

60. The emergency controls for attended self-service motor fuel dispensing facilities shall be located no more than _____ ft from motor fuel dispensers.

    (a) 20
    (b) 50
    (c) 75
    (d) 100

61. Where ungrounded supply conductors are paralleled in two or more raceways or cables, the bonding jumper for each raceway or cable shall be based on the size of the _____ in each raceway or cable.

    (a) overcurrent protection for conductors
    (b) grounded conductors
    (c) ungrounded supply conductors
    (d) sum of all conductors

62. A section sign is a sign or _____, shipped as subassemblies that requires field-installed wiring between the subassemblies to complete the overall sign.

    (a) outline lighting system
    (b) skeleton tubing system
    (c) neon system
    (d) sign body

63. Hazardous (classified) locations shall be classified depending on the properties of the _____ that may be present, and the likelihood that a flammable or combustible concentration or quantity is present.

    (a) flammable liquid-produced vapors
    (b) flammable gases
    (c) combustible dusts
    (d) all of these

64. Disconnecting means must be provided to disconnect a fuse from all sources of supply if energized from both directions and shall be capable of being disconnected independently of fuses in other PV source circuits.

    (a) True
    (b) False

65. Bends in NUCC can be _____ so that the conduit will not be damaged and the internal diameter of the conduit will not be effectively reduced.

    (a) manually made
    (b) made only with approved benders
    (c) made with RMC bending shoes
    (d) made using an open flame torch

66. Cleat-type lampholders located at least _____ ft above the floor can have exposed terminals.

    (a) 3
    (b) 6
    (c) 8
    (d) 10

67. When practicable, a separation of at least _____ ft shall be maintained between communications cables on buildings and lightning conductors.

    (a) 6
    (b) 8
    (c) 10
    (d) 12

68. An electrical production and distribution network, such as a utility and connected load is internal to and controlled by a photovoltaic power system.

    (a) True
    (b) False

69. A spa or hot tub is a hydromassage pool or tub and is not designed to have the contents drained or discharged after each use.

    (a) True
    (b) False

70. Service equipment shall be securely fastened to a solid backing and be installed so as to be protected from the weather, unless of weatherproof construction.

    (a) True
    (b) False

71. When installing auxiliary electrodes, the earth shall not be used as an effective ground-fault current path.

    (a) True
    (b) False

72. Sprinkler piping shall be permitted to share a cable tray with fire alarm conductors, provided the conductors are supplied by a power-limited source.

    (a) True
    (b) False

73. For carnivals and fairs, receptacles of the locking type not accessible from grade level that facilitate quick disconnecting and reconnecting of electrical equipment shall not be required to be provided with GFCI protection.

    (a) True
    (b) False

74. The point of entrance _____ a building of a network-powered broadband communications cable is the point at which the cable emerges from an external wall, from a concrete floor slab, from rigid metal conduit (RMC), or from intermediate metal conduit (IMC).

    (a) outside
    (b) within
    (c) on
    (d) none of these

75. Resistance heating elements of embedded deicing and snow-melting _____ shall not be installed where they bridge expansion joints unless provision is made for expansion and contraction.

    (a) cables
    (b) units
    (c) panels
    (d) all of these

76. Surface-mounted luminaires with a ballast shall have a minimum clearance of _____ in. from combustible low-density cellulose fiberboard, unless the luminaire is marked for surface mounting on combustible low-density cellulose fiberboard.

    (a) ½
    (b) 1
    (c) 1½
    (d) 2

77. A vertical run of 4/0 AWG copper shall be supported at intervals not exceeding _____.

    (a) 40 ft
    (b) 80 ft
    (c) 100 ft
    (d) 120 ft

78. Means to bypass and isolate transfer switch equipment shall not be permitted on legally required standby systems.

    (a) True
    (b) False

79. The bonding conductor or grounding electrode conductor for a radio/television antenna system must be protected where subject to physical damage, and where installed in a metal raceway, both ends of the raceway must be bonded to the _____ conductor.

    (a) contained
    (b) grounded
    (c) ungrounded
    (d) b or c

80. Circuit breakers in Class I, Division 2 locations that are not hermetically sealed or oil-immersed shall be installed in a Class I, Division 1 enclosure.

    (a) True
    (b) False

81. Equipment installed in hazardous (classified) locations shall be marked to show the _____.

    (a) class
    (b) group
    (c) temperature class (T Code) or operating temperature at a 40°C ambient temperature
    (d) all of these

82. For emergency systems, manual switches controlling emergency circuits shall be convenient to authorized persons responsible for their _____.

    (a) maintenance
    (b) actuation
    (c) inspection
    (d) evaluation

83. For interconnected electric power production sources, dedicated ac inverter circuit breakers that are backfed must be secured in place by an additional fastener as required by 408.36(D).

    (a) True
    (b) False

84. A limited care facility is an area used on a(n) _____ basis for the housing of four or more persons who are incapable of self-preservation because of age; physical limitation due to accident or illness; or mental limitations, mental illness, or chemical dependency.

    (a) occasional
    (b) 10-hour or less per day
    (c) 24-hour
    (d) temporary

85. Sealing compound shall be used in Type MI cable termination fittings to _____.

    (a) prevent the passage of gas or vapor
    (b) exclude moisture and other fluids from the cable insulation
    (c) limit a possible explosion
    (d) prevent the escape of powder

86. Communications _____ cables shall be listed as being suitable for use in a vertical run in a shaft, or from floor to floor, and shall also be listed as having fire-resistant characteristics capable of preventing the carrying of fire from floor to floor.

    (a) plenum
    (b) riser
    (c) general-purpose
    (d) none of these

87. Wiring systems for office furnishings shall be identified as suitable for providing power for lighting accessories and utilization equipment used within office furnishings.

    (a) True
    (b) False

88. All equipment intended for use in PV power systems shall be _____ for the PV application.

    (a) identified
    (b) listed
    (c) approved
    (d) a and b

89. Luminaires and ceiling fans located over or within 5 ft, measured horizontally, from the inside walls of an indoor spa or hot tub shall have a mounting height of not less than _____ above the maximum water level when not GFCI protected.

    (a) 4.70 ft
    (b) 5 ft
    (c) 7 ft 6 in.
    (d) 12 ft

90. A motor disconnecting means can be a listed _____.

    (a) molded case circuit breaker
    (b) motor-circuit switch rated in horsepower
    (c) molded case switch
    (d) any of these

91. The radius of the curve of the inner edge of any bend, during or after installation, shall not be less than _____ times the diameter of Type USE or SE cable.

    (a) five
    (b) seven
    (c) 10
    (d) 12

92. The alternate source for legally required standby systems shall not be required to have ground-fault protection of equipment.

    (a) True
    (b) False

93. Indoor antenna lead-in conductors for radio and television receiving equipment can be in the same enclosure with conductors of other wiring systems where separated by an effective permanently installed barrier.

    (a) True
    (b) False

94. For circuits and equipment operating at less than 50V, cables shall be supported by the building structure in such a manner that the cable will not be damaged by normal building use.

    (a) True
    (b) False

95. Optional standby system wiring is permitted to occupy the same raceways, cables, boxes, and cabinets with other general wiring.

    (a) True
    (b) False

96. An intrinsically safe circuit is a circuit in which any spark or thermal effect is incapable of causing ignition of a mixture of flammable or combustible material in air under _____.

    (a) water
    (b) prescribed test conditions
    (c) supervision
    (d) duress

97. Junction boxes connected to conduits that extend directly to forming shells of swimming pool no-niche luminaires shall be provided with a number of grounding terminals that is at least _____ the number of conduit entries.

    (a) one more than
    (b) two more than
    (c) the same as
    (d) none of these

98. Class 2 and Class 3 cable not terminated at equipment and not identified for future use with a tag is considered abandoned.

    (a) True
    (b) False

99. Metal parts of signs and outline lighting systems must be bonded to the transformer or power-supply equipment grounding conductor of the branch circuit or feeder supplying the sign or outline lighting system, with the exception that remote metal parts of a section sign or outline lighting system only supplied by a remote Class 2 power supply are not required to be connected to an equipment grounding conductor.

    (a) True
    (b) False

100. Supplying 120/240V, 3-wire shore power receptacles from a 120/208V, 3-wire supply may cause overheating or malfunctioning of connected equipment.

    (a) True
    (b) False

Please use the 2014 *Code* book to answer the following questions.

1. The alternate source for emergency systems shall have ground-fault protection of equipment.

   (a) True
   (b) False

2. Listed packaged spa or hot tub equipment assemblies, or self-contained spas or hot tubs installed outdoors, are permitted to have flexible connections using _____.

   (a) LFMC or LFNC
   (b) cords not longer than 15 ft, where GFCI protected
   (c) a or b
   (d) none of these

3. Each circuit supplying a sign within or adjacent to a fountain shall _____.

   (a) have GFCI protection
   (b) be capable of being locked in the open position
   (c) operate at less than 15V
   (d) be an intrinsically safe circuit

4. A separate _____ shall be provided for the elevator car lights, receptacle(s), auxiliary lighting power source, and ventilation on each elevator car.

   (a) branch circuit
   (b) disconnecting means
   (c) connection
   (d) none of these

5. Radio and television receiving antenna systems must have bonding or grounding electrode conductors that are _____.

   (a) copper or other corrosion-resistant conductive material
   (b) insulated, covered, or bare
   (c) securely fastened in place and protected where subject to physical damage
   (d) all of these

6. Branch-circuit conductors supplying a single continuous-duty motor shall have an ampacity not less than _____ rating.

   (a) 125 percent of the motor's nameplate current
   (b) 125 percent of the motor's full-load current rating as determined by 430.6(A)(1)
   (c) 125 percent of the motor's full locked-rotor
   (d) 80 percent of the motor's full-load current

7. Raceways and cables installed into the _____ of open bottom equipment shall not be required to be mechanically secured to the equipment.

   (a) bottom
   (b) sides
   (c) top
   (d) any of these

8. Article 645 does not apply unless an information technology equipment room contains ____.

   (a) a disconnecting means complying with 645.10
   (b) a separate heating/ventilating/air-conditioning (HVAC) system is provided
   (c) separation by fire resistance-rated walls, floors, and ceiling
   (d) all of these

9. When FMC is used where flexibility is necessary to minimize the transmission of vibration from equipment or to provide flexibility for equipment that requires movement after installation, ____ shall be installed.

   (a) an equipment grounding conductor
   (b) an expansion fitting
   (c) flexible nonmetallic connectors
   (d) none of these

10. The minimum clearance between an electric space-heating cable and an outlet box used for surface luminaires shall not be less than ____ in.

    (a) 6
    (b) 8
    (c) 14
    (d) 18

11. The ampacity adjustment factors in 310.15(B)(3)(a) shall be applied to a metal wireway only where the number of current-carrying conductors in any cross section of the wireway exceeds ____.

    (a) 30
    (b) 40
    (c) 50
    (d) 60

12. If the transfer switch for a portable generator switches the ____ conductor, then it is being used as a separately derived system and the portable generator shall be grounded in accordance with 250.30.

    (a) phase
    (b) equipment grounding
    (c) grounded
    (d) all of these

13. In one- and two-family dwellings where it is not practicable to achieve an overall maximum primary protector grounding conductor length of 20 ft or less for network-powered broadband communications systems, and a grounding means is not present, a separate ____ communications ground rod shall be driven and be bonded to the power grounding electrode system with a 6 AWG conductor.

    (a) 5-foot
    (b) 8-foot
    (c) 10-foot
    (d) 20-foot

14. Reinforcing bars for use as a concrete-encased electrode can be bonded together by the usual steel tie wires or other effective means.

    (a) True
    (b) False

15. Where installed to reduce electrical noise for electronic equipment, a metal raceway can terminate to a(n) ____ nonmetallic fitting(s) or spacer on the electronic equipment. The metal raceway shall be supplemented by an internal insulated equipment grounding conductor.

    (a) listed
    (b) labeled
    (c) identified
    (d) marked

16. An outdoor wire-strung antenna conductor of a receiving station with a 75 ft span using a hard-drawn copper conductor shall not be less than ____ AWG.

    (a) 17
    (b) 14
    (c) 12
    (d) 10

17. Where branch-circuit wiring in a dwelling unit is modified, replaced, or extended in any of the areas specified in 210.12(A), the branch circuit must be protected by a ____.

    (a) listed combination AFCI located at the origin of the branch circuit
    (b) listed outlet branch-circuit AFCI located at the first receptacle outlet of the existing branch circuit
    (c) GFCI circuit breaker or receptacle
    (d) a or b

18. Only electrical equipment and wiring associated with the operation of the information technology room is allowed to be installed in the room. This does include HVAC systems, communications systems, telephone, fire alarm systems, security systems, water detection systems, and other related protective equipment.

    (a) True
    (b) False

19. Access to electrical equipment shall not be denied by an accumulation of optical fiber cables that _____ removal of panels, including suspended-ceiling panels.

    (a) prevents
    (b) hinders
    (c) blocks
    (d) require

20. In assembly occupancies of fire-rated construction, nonmetallic raceways encased in not less than _____ in. of concrete shall be permitted.

    (a) 1
    (b) 2
    (c) 3
    (d) 4

21. Where livestock is housed, any portion of an underground equipment grounding conductor run to the building or structure shall be _____.

    (a) insulated
    (b) covered
    (c) either a or b
    (d) neither a nor b

22. Luminaires installed in Class I, Division 1 locations shall be protected from physical damage by a suitable _____.

    (a) warning label
    (b) pendant
    (c) guard or by location
    (d) all of these

23. A branch-circuit overcurrent protective device is capable of providing protection for _____.

    (a) service conductors
    (b) feeders
    (c) branch circuits
    (d) all of these

24. For ungrounded systems, noncurrent-carrying conductive materials enclosing electrical conductors or equipment shall be connected to the _____ in a manner that will limit the voltage imposed by lightning or unintentional contact with higher-voltage lines.

    (a) ground
    (b) earth
    (c) electrical supply source
    (d) none of these

25. Disconnecting means shall be provided to _____ each boat from its supply connection(s). The disconnecting means shall consist of a circuit breaker, switch, or both, and shall identify which receptacle it controls.

    (a) isolate
    (b) separate
    (c) guard
    (d) control

26. When HDPE conduit enters a box, fitting, or other enclosure, a(n) _____ shall be provided to protect the conductor from abrasion, unless the box design provides such protection.

    (a) bushing
    (b) adapter
    (c) a or b
    (d) reducing bushing

27. Any building or structure with a stand-alone PV system (not connected to a utility service source) must have a permanent _____ installed on the exterior of the building or structure at a readily visible location acceptable to the authority having jurisdiction. The _____ must indicate the location of the stand-alone PV system disconnecting means and that the structure contains a stand-alone electrical power system.

    (a) plaque
    (b) directory
    (c) a and b
    (d) a or b

28. Where batteries are used for _____ in auxiliary engines of emergency systems, the authority having jurisdiction shall require periodic maintenance.

    (a) starting
    (b) control or ignition
    (c) a and b
    (d) none of these

29. When separate equipment grounding conductors are provided in panelboards, a _____ shall be secured inside the cabinet.

    (a) grounded conductor
    (b) terminal lug
    (c) terminal bar
    (d) none of these

30. In Class III locations, receptacles and attachment plugs shall be of the grounding type, shall be designed so as to minimize the accumulation or the entry of _____, and shall prevent the escape of sparks or molten particles.

    (a) gases or vapors
    (b) particles of combustion
    (c) fibers/flyings
    (d) none of these

31. Type NM cables can be used for branch-circuit temporary installations without height limitation and without concealment.

    (a) True
    (b) False

32. Conductors for an appliance circuit supplying more than one appliance or appliance receptacle in an installation operating at less than 50V shall not be smaller than _____ AWG copper or equivalent.

    (a) 18
    (b) 14
    (c) 12
    (d) 10

33. Luminaires in Class III locations exposed to physical damage shall be protected by a(n) _____ guard.

    (a) plastic
    (b) metal
    (c) suitable
    (d) explosionproof

34. Wiring and equipment supplied from storage batteries must be in accordance with Chapters 1 through 4 of the *NEC* unless otherwise permitted by 480.5.

    (a) True
    (b) False

35. Where no statutory requirement exists, the authority having jurisdiction can be a property owner or his/her agent, such as an architect or engineer.

    (a) True
    (b) False

36. Article 551 covers combination electrical systems, generator installations, and _____, nominal, systems.

    (a) 120V
    (b) 120/208V
    (c) 120/240V
    (d) all of these

37. The _____ of a dc PV source circuit or output circuit is used to calculate the sum of the rated open-circuit voltage of the series-connected PV modules multiplied by the correction factor provided in Table 690.7.

    (a) minimum allowable ampacity of conductors
    (b) maximum allowable ampacity of conductors
    (c) minimum photovoltaic system voltage
    (d) maximum photovoltaic system voltage

38. A grounded _____-wire PV system must have one conductor grounded or be impedance grounded, and comply with 690.5.

    (a) 2
    (b) 3
    (c) 4
    (d) any of these

39. Which of the following wiring methods and enclosures that contain photovoltaic power source conductors must be marked "WARNING PHOTOVOLTAIC POWER SOURCE" by means of permanently affixed labels or other approved permanent marking?

    (a) Exposed raceways, cable trays, and other wiring methods.
    (b) The covers or enclosures of pull boxes and junction boxes.
    (c) Conduit bodies in which any of the available conduit openings are unused.
    (d) all of these

40. Branch circuits that supply signs _____.

    (a) are to be considered a continuous load for the purposes of calculations
    (b) must be rated 30A or less for neon tubing installations
    (c) must be rated not more than 20A for signs and outline lighting systems other than neon
    (d) all of these

41. Metal raceways shall be bonded to the metal pole with a(n) _____.

    (a) grounding electrode
    (b) grounded conductor
    (c) equipment grounding conductor
    (d) any of these

42. What is the minimum cover requirement for direct burial Type UF cable installed outdoors that supplies a 120V, 30A circuit?

    (a) 6 in.
    (b) 12 in.
    (c) 18 in.
    (d) 24 in.

43. Lighting systems operating at 30V or less can be concealed or extended through a building wall, floor or ceiling without regard to the wiring method used.

    (a) True
    (b) False

44. A _____ is an enclosed assembly that can include receptacles, circuit breakers, fused switches, fuses, watt-hour meter(s), panelboards and monitoring means approved for marine use.

    (a) marine power receptacle
    (b) marine outlet
    (c) marine power outlet
    (d) any of these

45. A disconnecting means is required within sight of the storage battery for all ungrounded battery system conductors operating at over _____ nominal.

    (a) 20V
    (b) 30V
    (c) 40V
    (d) 50V

46. The maximum number of conductors permitted in any surface nonmetallic raceway shall be _____.

    (a) no more than 30 percent of the inside diameter
    (b) no greater than the number for which it was designed
    (c) no more than 75 percent of the cross-sectional area
    (d) that which is permitted in Table 312.6(A)

47. The permitted conduit fill for five conductors is _____ percent.

    (a) 35
    (b) 40
    (c) 55
    (d) 60

48. When the calculated number of conductors or cables, all of the same size, installed in a conduit or in tubing includes a decimal, the next higher whole number shall be used when this decimal is _____ or larger.

    (a) 0.40
    (b) 0.60
    (c) 0.70
    (d) 0.80

49. For PV systems, a field-installable unit including a collection of modules mechanically fastened together and wired, is called a(n) _____.

    (a) panel
    (b) array
    (c) bank
    (d) gang

50. The _____ current for a hermetic refrigerant motor-compressor is the current resulting when the motor-compressor is operated at the rated load, rated voltage, and rated frequency of the equipment it serves.

    (a) full-load
    (b) nameplate rating
    (c) selection
    (d) rated-load

51. Receptacles of dc plugging boxes shall be rated at not _____ when used on a stage or set of a motion picture studio.

    (a) more than 30A
    (b) less than 20A
    (c) less than 30A
    (d) more than 20A

52. Luminaires can be installed in a commercial cooking hood if the luminaire is identified for use within a _____ cooking hood.

    (a) nonresidential
    (b) commercial
    (c) multifamily
    (d) all of these

53. Amplifiers, loudspeakers, and other equipment shall be located or protected so as to guard against environmental exposure or physical damage that might cause _____.

    (a) a fire
    (b) shock
    (c) personal hazard
    (d) all of these

54. Flexible cords and cables shall be protected by _____ where passing through holes in covers, outlet boxes, or similar enclosures.

    (a) bushings
    (b) fittings
    (c) a or b
    (d) none of these

55. Wet-niche luminaires installed in swimming pools shall be removable from the water for inspection, relamping, or other maintenance. The luminaire maintenance location shall be accessible _____.

    (a) while the pool is drained
    (b) without entering the pool water
    (c) during construction
    (d) all of these

56. The grounding conductor for an antenna mast or antenna discharge unit, if copper, shall not be smaller than 10 AWG.

    (a) True
    (b) False

57. The photovoltaic system voltage is the direct-current voltage of any PV source or PV output circuit.

    (a) True
    (b) False

58. A sign shall be placed at the service-entrance equipment indicating the _____ of on-site optional standby power sources.

    (a) type
    (b) location
    (c) manufacturer
    (d) a and b

59. In Class I locations, attachment plugs shall be of the type providing for _____ a flexible cord and shall be identified for the location.

    (a) sealing compound around
    (b) quick connection to
    (c) connection to the equipment grounding conductor of
    (d) none of these

60. In mobile/manufactured homes, portable appliances could be _____, if these appliances can be moved from one place to another in normal use.

    (a) refrigerators
    (b) range equipment
    (c) clothes washers
    (d) all of these

61. In Class II, Division 1 locations, switches, circuit breakers, motor controllers, and fuses, including pushbuttons, relays, and similar devices shall be provided with enclosures that are _____.

    (a) explosionproof
    (b) identified for the location
    (c) dusttight
    (d) weatherproof

62. Coaxial cables installed in buildings for CATV shall be listed except for the first 50 ft that enters a building in accordance with 820.48.

    (a) True
    (b) False

63. Where Type NM cable is run at angles with joists in unfinished basements and crawl spaces, it is permissible to secure cables not smaller than _____ conductors directly to the lower edges of the joist.

    (a) two, 6 AWG
    (b) three, 8 AWG
    (c) three, 10 AWG
    (d) a or b

64. For emergency systems, means for testing all emergency lighting and power systems during maximum anticipated load conditions shall be provided.

    (a) True
    (b) False

65. In marinas or boatyards, the *NEC* requires a(n) _____ disconnecting means, which allows individual boats to be isolated from their supply connection.

    (a) accessible
    (b) readily accessible
    (c) remote
    (d) any of these

66. A separate overload device used to protect continuous-duty motors rated more than 1 hp shall be selected to trip at no more than _____ percent of the motor nameplate full-load current rating if marked with a service factor of 1.15 or greater.

    (a) 110
    (b) 115
    (c) 120
    (d) 125

67. Boxes and conduit bodies, covers, extension rings, plaster rings, and the like shall be durably and legibly marked with the manufacturer's name or trademark.

    (a) True
    (b) False

68. All 15A and 20A, single-phase, 125V through 250V receptacles located within _____ ft of a fountain edge shall have GFCI protection.

    (a) 8
    (b) 10
    (c) 15
    (d) 20

69. Branch-circuit conductors for data processing equipment in information technology equipment rooms shall have an ampacity not less than _____ of the total connected load.

    (a) 80 percent
    (b) 100 percent
    (c) 125 percent
    (d) the sum

70. Interconnecting cables under raised floors that support information technology equipment shall be Type _____.

    (a) RF
    (b) Type UF
    (c) LS
    (d) DP

71. "Bonded" can be described as _____ to establish electrical continuity and conductivity.

    (a) isolated
    (b) guarded
    (c) connected
    (d) separated

72. In industrial establishments with restricted public access where only qualified persons will service the installation, MC-HL cable is allowed to be used in a Class I, Division 1 location if it _____, and terminated with fittings listed for the application. Such cable must comply with Part II of Article 330.

    (a) is listed for use in Class I, Zone 1, or Division 1 locations
    (b) has a gas/vaportight continuous corrugated metallic sheath, an overall jacket of suitable polymeric material
    (c) has a separate equipment grounding conductor(s) in accordance with 250.122
    (d) all of these

73. The connected load on lighting track is permitted to exceed the rating of the track under some conditions.

    (a) True
    (b) False

74. Conductors for nonpower-limited fire alarm circuits shall be _____.

    (a) solid copper
    (b) stranded copper
    (c) copper or aluminum
    (d) a or b

75. Class 2 and Class 3 cables listed as suitable for general-purpose use with the exception of risers, ducts, plenums, and other spaces used for environmental air, shall be Type(s) _____.

    (a) CL2P and CL3P
    (b) CL2R and CL3R
    (c) CL2 and CL3
    (d) PLTC

76. Cable _____ made and insulated by approved methods can be located within a cable tray provided they are accessible, and do not project above the side rails where the splices are subject to physical damage.

    (a) connections
    (b) jumpers
    (c) splices
    (d) conductors

77. Where an equipment grounding conductor is installed underground within an agricultural building, it shall be a(n) _____ conductor.

    (a) insulated or covered
    (b) copper
    (c) bare
    (d) any of these

78. The accessible portion of abandoned audio distribution cables shall be removed.

    (a) True
    (b) False

79. A run of RMC shall not contain more than the equivalent of _____ quarter bend(s) between pull points such as conduit bodies and boxes.

    (a) one
    (b) two
    (c) three
    (d) four

80. A GFCI shall be installed in the branch circuit supplying luminaires operating at more than the low-voltage contact limit so there is no shock hazard during _____.

    (a) construction
    (b) pool pump motor maintenance
    (c) relamping
    (d) overload conditions

81. The output of an ac module is considered an _____ output circuit as defined in 690.2.

    (a) inverter
    (b) module
    (c) PV
    (d) subarray

82. Branch circuits for pool-associated motors shall be installed in wiring methods including _____. Any wiring method employed shall include an insulated copper equipment grounding conductor sized in accordance with 250.122, but not smaller than 12 AWG.

    (a) PVC conduit
    (b) electrical metallic tubing where installed on or within buildings
    (c) flexible metal conduit
    (d) a or b

83. Article _____ covers the installation of portable wiring and equipment for carnivals, circuses, exhibitions, fairs, traveling attractions, and similar functions.

    (a) 518
    (b) 525
    (c) 590
    (d) all of these

84. Switches or circuit breakers shall not disconnect the grounded conductor of a circuit unless the switch or circuit breaker _____.

    (a) can be opened and closed by hand levers only
    (b) simultaneously disconnects all conductors of the circuit
    (c) opens the grounded conductor before it disconnects the ungrounded conductors
    (d) none of these

85. At least one lighting outlet containing a switch or controlled by a wall switch shall be installed in attic spaces containing ballasts for electric signs. At least one _____ shall be at the usual point of entry to these spaces. The lighting outlet shall be provided at or near the equipment requiring servicing.

    (a) receptacle
    (b) switch
    (c) point of control
    (d) luminaire

86. An encased or buried connection to a concrete-encased, driven, or buried grounding electrode shall be accessible.

    (a) True
    (b) False

87. _____ shall be installed so that the wiring contained in them can be rendered accessible without removing any part of the building or structure or, in underground circuits, without excavating sidewalks, paving, or earth.

    (a) Boxes
    (b) Conduit bodies
    (c) Handhole enclosures
    (d) all of these

88. The point of entrance of an optical fiber installation is the point _____ at which the optical fiber cable emerges from an external wall, from a concrete floor slab, from rigid metal conduit, or from intermediate metal conduit.

    (a) outside a building
    (b) within a building
    (c) on the building
    (d) none of these

89. Class 2 or Class 3 cables, installed in vertical runs penetrating more than one floor or installed in a shaft without being installed in a raceway, shall be Type _____.

    (a) CL2R
    (b) CL3R
    (c) CL2P
    (d) a or b

90. Direct-buried conductors or cables can be spliced or tapped without the use of splice boxes when the splice or tap is made in accordance with 110.14(B).

    (a) True
    (b) False

91. Generally speaking, conductors for lighting or power may occupy the same enclosure or raceway with conductors of power-limited fire alarm circuits.

    (a) True
    (b) False

92. The conductor insulation in Type MI cable shall be a highly compressed refractory mineral that provides proper _____ for all conductors.

    (a) covering
    (b) spacing
    (c) resistance
    (d) none of these

93. A multioutlet assembly can be installed in _____.

    (a) dry locations
    (b) wet locations
    (c) a and b
    (d) damp locations

94. Where GFCI protection for personnel is supplied by plug-and-cord-connection to the branch circuit or to the feeder for temporary wiring such as exhibition halls in assembly occupancies, the GFCI protection shall ____, whether assembled in the field or at the factory.

    (a) be listed as portable ground-fault circuit interrupter protection
    (b) provide a level of protection equivalent to a portable ground-fault circuit interrupter
    (c) must provide the same level of protection as ground-fault protection for equipment
    (d) a or b

95. Electric pipe organ circuits shall be arranged so that 26 AWG and 28 AWG conductors are protected from overcurrent by an overcurrent device rated not more than ____.

    (a) 2A
    (b) 4A
    (c) 6A
    (d) 8A

96. A feeder supplying fixed motor load(s) shall have a protective device with a rating or setting ____ branch-circuit short-circuit and ground-fault protective device for any motor in the group, plus the sum of the full-load currents of the other motors of the group.

    (a) not greater than the largest rating or setting of the
    (b) 125 percent of the largest rating of any
    (c) equal to the largest rating of any
    (d) none of these

97. EMT shall not be used where ____.

    (a) subject to severe physical damage
    (b) protected from corrosion only by enamel
    (c) used for the support of luminaires
    (d) any of these

98. Overcurrent devices for legally required standby systems shall be ____ with all supply-side overcurrent devices.

    (a) series rated
    (b) selectively coordinated
    (c) installed in parallel
    (d) any of these

99. Where PV source and output circuits operating at greater than ____ are installed in a(n) ____ location, the circuit conductors must be guarded or installed in a Chapter 3 wiring method.

    (a) 30V, accessible
    (b) 30V, readily accessible
    (c) 60V, accessible
    (d) 60V, readily accessible

100. Fountain equipment supplied by a flexible cord shall have all exposed noncurrent-carrying metal parts grounded by an insulated copper equipment grounding conductor that is an integral part of the cord.

    (a) True
    (b) False

Take Your Training to the next level

&

Save 25%
use discount code: B14PQ25